From
Members of Wes[illegible] [illegible]pter
Nov 17, 1976

The All New portal to good cooking

R.T

PUBLISHED BY MIDWEST DISTRICT VIII

Chicago Region
Des Moines Chapter-at-Large
Indianapolis Chapter-at-Large
Kansas City Chapter-at-Large
Lake County Region
Milwaukee Region
Northern Illinois Region
Omaha Chapter-at-Large
Peoria Chapter-at-Large
Quad Cities Chapter-at-Large
South Bend Chapter-at-Large
St. Louis Region
Twin Cities Region
West Suburban Region

WOMEN'S AMERICAN ORT

The Editor and Publisher wish to thank the many members of Women's American ORT who submitted recipes as well as those who so willingly served on the editing committee.

They further wish to express their most sincere appreciation to the Milton H. Kreines Co. for the invaluable assistance and advice in publishing this All New Portal to Good Cooking.

Edited by Joanne Will

Illustrated by Roy Moody

Introduction to ORT

ORT — Organization for Rehabilitation through Training —is a global program of vocational education dedicated to the building and rebuilding of human lives and human dignity.

For more than 92 years, ORT, the Vocational Training Agency of the Jewish People, has educated over 1,000,000 young people and adults in more than 70 modern skills. Responding to the technological demands of the 23 countries in which it operates, ORT has trained its students in such fields as computer programming, electrical engineering, industrial design, tele-communications, secretarial science and laboratory technology. New courses are constantly being added.

Women's American ORT, with a membership of more than 100,000, supports this worldwide program through its many activities and seeks ways of relating ORT's expertise toward the resolving of socio-economic problems in the United States. ORT is involved in teaching quality vocational education thereby helping man to help himself.

We dedicate this All New Portal to Good Cooking to the students, who, in passing through the PORTals of ORT schools learn the technical skills that open the doors of opportunity to become knowledgeable, productive and independent members of society.

CONTENTS

The All New Portal to Good Cooking is a blend of the traditional and the contemporary, and is filled with recipes from good cooks throughout the Midwest. The recipes and cooking secrets are shared in the spirit of friendship and dedication to an idea that has spread throughout the world.

As an introduction to this family cookbook, following are some recipe and cooking hints contributed by ORT cooks, both young and old.

RECIPE HINTS

Read each recipe carefully before beginning to cook.

Use standard measuring cups and spoons. All measurements are level unless otherwise stated.

Assemble ingredients before cooking to save preparation time.

Preheat oven for 10 to 20 minutes before baking, unless recipe states otherwise.

Do not substitute for key ingredients such as flour, sugar, liquid or leavening.

Seasonings usually can be altered to suit your family tastes.

BAKING TIPS

For cakes and baked goods, have all ingredients at room temperature before you begin to mix.

Separate eggs while cold, but for best volume, warm egg whites to room temperature before whipping. Whip egg whites first, then egg yolks to save washing beaters in between.

Use pan size as directed in recipe; if you change pan, adjust baking time and temperature as needed.

EGG & DAIRY HINTS

To hard-cook eggs, place in cold water and heat to boiling; cook in rolling boil for 20 minutes. Remove from heat immediately and fill and over-flow pot with cold running water. Crack egg shells and toss eggs back into pot. The shells will be easy to remove and the eggs will be white and shiny.

Stick butter and margarine can be used interchangeably in all recipes.

To get good volume when whipping cream, chill cream, beaters and bowl.

If a recipe calls for scalded milk, reconstituted dry milk may be substituted without scalding.

FLAVORING TRICKS

Add 1/8 teaspoon cinnamon and 1 teaspoon sugar to gefilte fish mixture for gourmet flavor.

Enhance the eye appeal of chicken or vegetable soups with a few drops of yellow food coloring.

As a general rule, use 1 teaspoon salt to season a pound of meat. If you oversalt a liquid such as soup, add a few slices of raw potatoes, simmer 5 minutes and remove.

VEGETABLE HINTS

To peel a tomato, put tomato on the end of a fork and hold it over burner until the skin blisters. Or scald in boiling water for a minute. Skin will peel off easily.

To saute onions, in shortening, butter, oil or chicken fat, cook over low heat until the onion is glazed and tender. This enhances flavor and makes the onions more digestible.

Tear rather than cut fresh greens for the salad bowl.

To cook frozen vegetables, use only enough water to cover bottom of pan. Add salt and heat to boiling. Add vegetable and heat to boiling again, lower heat, cover and cook for 2 to 4 minutes. Drain immediately and blanch with cold water. Season with salt, pepper, a teaspoon of sugar and butter. If preparing in advance, refrigerate, then reheat in oven, uncovered. Bring to table in casserole.

MEASUREMENTS AND EQUIVALENTS

3 teaspoons = 1 tablespoon
2 tablespoons = ⅛ cup
4 tablespoons = ¼ cup
5 tablespoons plus 1 teaspoon = ⅓ cup
8 tablespoons = ½ cup
12 tablespoons = ¾ cup
16 tablespoons = 1 cup

2 cups = 1 pint
4 cups = 1 quart
4 ounces = ¼ pound = ½ cup
8 ounces = ½ pound = 1 cup
16 ounces = 1 pound = 2 cups
1 fluid ounce = 2 tablespoons

Butter or margarine .... ¼ pound stick = ½ cup, 1 pound = 2 cups
Cheese, Cheddar .... ¼ pound = 1 cup grated or shredded
Cheese, cottage .... ½ pound = 1 cup
Cheese, cream .... 3-oz. package = 6 tablespoons
8-oz. package = 1 cup
Chocolate, unsweetened .... 1 square = 1 ounce
Cocoa .... 3 tablespoons cocoa plus 1 tablespoon fat = 1 ounce chocolate
Cornstarch .... 1 tablespoon = 2 tablespoons flour
Crackers .... 7 coarsely crumbled = 1 cup
Cream, whipping .... ½ pint = 2 cups whipped
Cream, sour .... ½ pint = 1 cup
Egg whites .... 8 to 10 = 1 cup
Egg yolks .... 12 to 14 = 1 cup
Flour, all-purpose .... 1 pound = 3½ to 4½ cups sifted
Flour, cake .... 1 pound = 4¾ cups sifted
Graham crackers .... 11 finely crumbled = 1 cup
Lemon juice .... 1 medium lemon = 3 tablespoons juice
Lemon rind .... 1 medium lemon = 1 tablespoon grated rind
Milk, evaporated .... 14½-oz. can = 1⅔ cups
Milk, condensed .... 15-oz. can = 1⅓ cups
Milk, sour .... 1 tablespoon vinegar plus milk to make 1 cup = 1 cup sour milk or buttermilk (let stand 5 minutes)
Nuts, chopped .... ¼ pound = 1 cup
Orange juice .... 1 medium orange = ⅓ cup juice
Orange rind .... 1 medium orange = 2 tablespoons grated rind
Sugar, brown .... 1 pound = 2¼ cups packed
Sugar, confectioners' .... 1 pound = 3 to 4 cups
Sugar, granulated .... 1 pound = 2¼ cups

FOOD FOR FIFTY

FOOD	SIZE SERVING	QUANTITY NEEDED
Beverages:		
Coffee	1 cup	1 to 1½ pounds
Cocoa	1 cup	½ pound
Fruit Punch	2 to 3 punch glasses	3½ gallons
Juice	½ cup	5—46-ounce cans
Tea	1 cup	⅓ pound
Cereal Products:		
Macaroni	½ cup	3 pounds
Noodles	½ cup	2½ pounds
Rice	½ cup	5 pounds
Spaghetti	½ to 1 cup	3 to 7 pounds
Dairy Products:		
Butter (36 pats/pound)	1 to 2 pats	1½ pounds
Cream (for dessert or beverage)	1 tablespoon	1 quart
Ice Cream, bulk	½ cup	2 gallons
Ice Cream, brick	1/6 of brick	9 bricks
Eggs, scrambling	1½ to 2 eggs	6¼ to 8⅓ dozen
Desserts:		
Cakes, 10-inch layer	1 piece	3 cakes
Cakes, plain sheet	1 piece	1 pan, 12x20
Bar Cookies	2 bars	2 pans, 15x10
Pies	1 wedge (1/6 or 1/7)	7 to 9 pies
Fish:		
Lobster, frozen or canned	⅓ cup for salad	18 to 20 pounds frozen 3 pounds canned
Shrimps, frozen	8 to 10 per cocktail	8 pounds frozen shelled
Tuna, canned	⅓ cup meat, about 4 servings/can	12 to 13 7-oz. cans

FOOD FOR FIFTY (Cont.)

FOOD	SIZE SERVING	QUANTITY NEEDED
Meats & Poultry:		
Beef, corned, sliced	3 servings/pound	17 pounds
Beef, for patties	4 ounces	13 pounds
Beef, rib roast (bone in)	½ pound	25 pounds
Lamb, roast leg	2 to 2½ servings/ pound	4 legs, about 6 pounds each
Beef, lamb, or veal stew meat, trimmed	4 servings/pound	12 to 14 pounds
Chicken, dressed for frying	¼ bird	13 fryers (38 to 40 pounds)
Chicken, a la king	⅓ to ½ cup	20 to 30 pounds
Turkey	6 ounces meat and bone	40 pounds
Salami	2 slices	3 pounds (36 to 50 slices/pound)
Relishes:		
Carrot sticks, 3-inch	2 to 3	2 to 2½ pounds
Celery Curls, 2½-inch	1	2 medium bunches
Olives, plain	1 to 2	4—9½-oz. bottles
Olives, stuffed	2 each	2—5¾-oz. bottles
Pickles, 3-inch	½ pickle	1½ pounds
Radishes	2 each	10 bunches
Salads:		
Cabbage or greens	½ cup	6¼ quarts
Potato Salad	½ to ⅔ cup	6½ to 8½ quarts
Combination Fruit	½ cup	6¼ quarts
Fish or Meat	⅔ cup	8 quarts
Gelatin	½ cup	6 quarts
Salad Dressings:		
French, Mayonnaise, or Sour Cream	2 tablespoons	2 quarts
Miscellaneous:		
Sugar, Loaf	1½ cubes	1½ pounds
Sugar, granulated	2 teaspoons	1 to 1½ pounds
Jam or Jelly	1 tablespoon	2 pounds
Mixed Nuts	1 tablespoon	2 pounds
Catsup	½ tablespoon	1—14-oz. bottle
Mustard	½ teaspoon	1—5-oz. bottle

AVOCADO-EGG SPREAD

- 1 ripe avocado, peeled and pitted
- 6 hard-cooked eggs
- 2 tablespoons mayonnaise
- 1 teaspoon pickle juice
- 1 white onion, minced
- Salt and pepper, to taste
- Red Caviar

Mash avocado and eggs. Add mayonnaise, pickle juice, onion and seasonings. Press mixture into an oiled mold; let stand several hours or overnight. Unmold on platter. Top with caviar. Serve with cocktail rye or crackers. Makes 6 servings.

Ruth Landsman, Chicago Region

BLENDER PATE

- 1/4 cup butter
- 1/4 cup chopped green onions and tops
- 1 cup sliced fresh mushrooms
- 1 pound chicken livers
- 1 4 3/4-oz. can chicken spread
- 1/4 cup Madeira
- 1 teaspoon salt
- Freshly ground pepper

Melt butter in a heavy skillet. Add green onion and cook until transparent. Add mushrooms and cook for 2 minutes; remove vegetables from pan. Add chicken livers and cook on low heat, turning as needed, until just cooked. Place livers, pan drippings and vegetables in blender. Add chicken spread, wine and seasonings. Switch blender on and off on medium speed, several times. Blend well, but stop while there is still some texture to the mixture. Turn mixture into a lightly oiled smooth mold, pressing down firmly, or place in a crock and seal with clarified butter (about 1/2 cup). Chill molded paté overnight before serving. Paté in crock with butter seal will keep refrigerated about a week.

Ruth Weissman, Lake County Region

CAVIAR-LOX MOLD

1 envelope (1 tablespoon) plain gelatin
¼ cup cold water
½ cup hot cream or milk
1 8-oz. package cream cheese
1 cup dairy sour cream
1 teaspoon worcestershire sauce
Dash of Tabasco sauce
2 tablespoons instant minced onion
1 teaspoon lemon juice
1 tablespoon parsley flakes
1 tablespoon horseradish
½ pound nova lox, chopped or diced
1 4-oz. jar red caviar

Soak gelatin in cold water; dissolve in hot cream. Let cool. Blend cream cheese with sour cream, worcestershire, Tabasco and onion; add gelatin. Stir in lemon juice, parsley, horseradish and lox. Carefully fold in caviar. Pour into a well oiled 4-cup mold. Chill for several hours. Unmold and serve with rye rounds or crackers. Makes 12 servings.

Judy Scheffres, Northern Illinois Region

CAVIAR MOLD

1 envelope (1 tablespoon) plain gelatin
2 tablespoons cold water
2 tablespoons lemon juice
1 cup mayonnaise
6 hard-cooked eggs, chopped
2 slices onion, grated
1 teaspoon worcestershire sauce
1 small jar black caviar

Soften gelatin in cold water and lemon juice; dissolve over hot water. Add to mayonnaise; mix with chopped egg, onion and worcestershire. Fold in caviar. Turn into a small oiled mold and refrigerate overnight. Makes 10 to 15 servings.

Joan R. Spaulder, Lake County Region

CHILI CHEESE LOGS

- 1 8-oz. package cream cheese
- 1 5-oz. jar pimento cheese spread
- 1 5-oz. jar smokey cheese spread
- 1/4 teaspoon salt
- 1 tablespoon worcestershire sauce
- Dash of Tabasco sauce
- 2 cloves of garlic, pressed
- 1/4 cup paprika
- 2 tablespoons chili powder

Cream the three kinds of cheese with salt, worcestershire, Tabasco and garlic. Chill mixture until firm. Mix paprika and chili powder; spread on a large piece of wax paper. Divide cheese into 2 or 3 equal portions and form each into a log about 1½ inches in diameter. Roll each loaf in paprika mixture until completely coated. Wrap firmly in wax paper and chill or freeze until needed. Serve with melba toast rounds or crackers. The logs will thaw in about an hour.

Ellen Kogen, Lake County Region

CRABMEAT DIP

- 1 7½-oz. can crabmeat, drained
- 2/3 cup dairy sour cream
- 2 teaspoons horseradish
- 1/2 teaspoon pepper
- 2 tablespoons Italian dressing mix (dry)
- Pumpernickel bread

Blend crabmeat, sour cream and seasonings. Chill several hours or overnight. Serve with pumpernickel. Makes 2 cups.

Judith Zwirn, West Suburban Region

TUNA-CHEESE MOLD

- 1 8-oz. package cream cheese
- 1 7-oz. can tuna, drained
- 1 medium onion, chopped
- 1/4 cup minced parsley
- 1/2 teaspoon Tabasco sauce
- 1/8 teaspoon pepper
- 1/2 teaspoon salt
- 1 4¾-oz. package chopped walnuts
- Whole walnuts (optional)

Blend all ingredients, reserving whole walnuts for garnish. Press into a fancy mold and chill. Unmold and garnish with nuts and additional parsley. Makes 8 to 10 servings.

Ellen Friend, Lake County Region

HERRING WITH APPLES

2 12-oz. jars herring in wine sauce drained of wine sauce and onions
1 Spanish onion, thinly sliced
2 large apples, pared and thinly sliced
Lemon juice
1 pint sour half-and-half

Mix herring thoroughly with onion. Add lemon juice to apples. Combine all ingredients. Refrigerate for at least 2 days, stirring twice. Serve with rye bread or crackers.

Sandra Becker, Lake County Region

STUFFED EDAM FOR A CROWD

1 Edam cheese, about 2 pounds
1 cup beer
1/4 cup softened butter
1 teaspoon Durkee's sauce
1/2 teaspoon celery salt
1 teaspoon caraway seeds (optional)

Slice a 1-inch round off the top of the whole Edam. Carefully scoop out cheese from slice and the ball, being careful not to break the red wax shell. Place the shell in the refrigerator. Let cheese soften at room temperature for 1 1/2 hours. Cube cheese; then mash in an electric mixer or blender. Add beer, butter, sauce and celery salt, blending well. Add caraway seeds and beat mixture by hand until well blended. Carefully stuff the shell with cheese, heaping it high. Wrap well with plastic wrap and refrigerate at least 2 to 3 days before serving. Serve with party rye bread or rye crackers.

Ruth Weissman, Lake County Region

HORSERADISH DIP

1/2 cup Miracle Whip salad dressing
1/2 cup dairy sour cream
4 to 6 teaspoons horseradish
1 teaspoon dry mustard
Salt to taste
Lemon juice to taste

Mix all ingredients; chill well. Serve with cucumber, celery or carrot slivers, cherry tomatoes and broccoli.

Arlene Baerson, West Suburban Region

HOT TOMATO SARDINES

- 2 14-oz. cans sardines in tomato sauce
- 1/4 cup sweet pickle relish
- 1/4 cup grated onion, optional
- 1/4 to 1/2 cup mayonnaise
- Grated Parmesan cheese, optional

Drain sardines and mash. Add pickle relish, onion and mayonnaise to moisten. Spread mixture in a small pie pan or ovenproof casserole. Sprinkle with cheese if you wish. Bake at 350° for 30 minutes. Serve hot with crackers.

Natalie Sklansky, Chicago Region

HOT LOBSTER DIP

- 1 8-oz. package cream cheese
- 1/4 cup mayonnaise
- 1 clove garlic, crushed
- 1 teaspoon grated onion
- 1 teaspoon prepared mustard
- 1 teaspoon sugar
- Dash of seasoned salt
- 1 5-oz. can lobster, drained and flaked
- 3 tablespoons cooking sauterne wine

Melt cream cheese in a heavy saucepan over low heat, stirring constantly. Blend in mayonnaise, garlic, onion, mustard, sugar and salt. Stir in lobster and wine; heat through, stirring. Serve in fondue pot or chafing dish with melba toast or crackers. Makes 1 3/4 cups dip.

Marilyn Hurwitz, Chicago Region

HOT SEAFOOD-CHEESE DIP

- 2 pounds Velveeta cheese, grated
- 1/2 cup dairy sour cream
- 1 1/2 cups mayonnaise
- 3/4 cup chives, chopped
- 3 7 1/2-oz. cans crabmeat (or shrimp)

Melt cheese with sour cream and mayonnaise in top of double boiler. Add chives and seafood. Serve in chafing dish with melba toast rounds or crusty bread cubes.

Adele Levin, West Suburban Region

LOX AND CREAM CHEESE MOLD

- ½ pound lox, chopped or diced
- 2 8-oz. packages cream cheese
- 1 cucumber, chopped
- 1 bunch green onions, minced

Combine all ingredients; blend well. Press into a fish shaped mold. Chill until firm. Unmold and serve with toasted cocktail bagels. Makes 8 servings.

Mrs. Selwyn Schwartz, West Suburban Region

MAYFAIR VEGETABLE DIP

- 1 clove garlic
- 1 rib celery
- ½ onion
- 1 2-oz. can flat anchovies
- 3 eggs
- ½ teaspoon ground black pepper
- 1 teaspoon monosodium glutamate
- ½ teaspoon sugar
- ½ teaspoon curry powder
- 2 teaspoons prepared mustard
- 1 tablespoon lemon juice
- 2 cups salad oil

Place all ingredients except oil in blender; blend for 10 seconds. Add oil a small amount at a time; blend. Chill well. Serve as salad dressing or as a dip for raw vegetables. Makes 1 quart.

Roz Levin, St. Louis Region

MEXICAN CHEESE AND CHILI DIP

- ¼ cup onion, chopped
- ½ green pepper, chopped
- 3 tablespoons butter
- 1 16-oz. can tomatoes, well drained
- 1 4-oz. can Old El Paso red and green peppers, cut up
- ½ teaspoon chili powder
- 1 pound Velveeta cheese, cut up
- 1 4-oz. can button mushrooms
- Chopped green olives
- Carrot and celery sticks
- Cauliflowerets

Saute onion and green pepper in butter for 5 minutes. Add tomatoes, peppers, chili, cheese, mushroom and olives. Heat thoroughly, blending well. Serve in chafing dish with crisp vegetable dippers.

Norma Glass, Lake County Region

SESAME CHEESE SPREAD

- 1 8-oz. package cream cheese
- Sesame seeds

Cover entire cake of cheese with sesame seeds. Place in pie pan or on sizzle plate. Bake at 375° for 30 minutes, or until golden brown. Remove with spatula to serving plate. Surround with crackers and serve hot.

Helen Meyerson, Omaha Chapter-at-Large

SPINACH DIP

- 1 10-oz. package frozen chopped spinach
- ½ cup chopped parsley
- ½ cup chopped green onions and tops
- ½ teaspoon salt
- ½ teaspoon pepper
- 2 cups mayonnaise

Thaw spinach; drain thoroughly (several hours). Mix with remaining ingredients; chill to blend flavors. Serve as a dip with potato chips. Makes 12 servings.

Phyllis Frankel, Chicago Region

SHRIMP BALL OR MOLD

- 1 8-oz. package cream cheese
- 1 tablespoon prepared mustard
- 1 tablespoon grated onion
- 1 tablespoon lemon juice
- Salt and pepper, to taste
- Pinch cayenne pepper
- 3 4½-oz. cans shrimp, drained and chopped

Blend all ingredients; shape into a ball or press into a small mold. Refrigerate for several hours, or until ready to serve.

Edith Dratler, Lake County Region

ANTIPASTO I

- 3 7-oz. cans tuna, drained
- 1 14-oz. can artichoke hearts, drained
- 1 5¾-oz. can pitted black olives, drained
- 1 4-oz. jar button mushrooms, drained
- 1 small cauliflower, cut up
- 1 dill pickle, diced
- 1 12-oz. bottle chili sauce
- Worcestershire sauce to taste
- Steak sauce to taste

Combine all ingredients in a large bowl; chill before serving. Makes 8 to 10 servings.

Ann Adasheh, Milwaukee Region

ANTIPASTO II

- 2 12-oz. bottles chili sauce
- 2 14-oz. bottles catsup
- 1 tablespoon worcestershire sauce
- Juice of 1 lemon
- Horseradish to taste
- Vinegar
- 4 7-oz. cans tuna, broken into small chunks
- 1 small jar miniature sweet gherkins, drained
- 1 4½-oz. jar pickled cocktail onions, drained
- 1 4-oz. can button mushrooms, drained
- 1 small jar pickled cauliflower, drained
- 1 4½-oz. jar stuffed olives, drained
- 3 medium carrots, sliced
- 4 ribs celery, diced

Combine chili sauce, catsup, worcestershire, lemon juice and horseradish. Rinse catsup and chili sauce bottles with a little vinegar; add to mixture. Mix remaining ingredients in a large bowl; add chili sauce blend and toss well. Refrigerate. Will keep for about a week.

Masia Balsam, Lake County Region

QUICK CHEESE FONDUE

- 1 10¾-oz. can Cheddar cheese soup
- 1 10¾-oz. can tomato soup
- 1 cup shredded Swiss Cheese
- 1 loaf Italian or French bread, cut in cubes

Mix soups in fondue pot; add cheese gradually, cooking and stirring until mixture is hot and cheese is melted. Dip bread cubes in fondue. Makes 4 to 6 appetizer servings.

Lillian Neimark, Northern Illinois Region

PIZZA APPETIZER FONDUE

- 1 29-oz. jar meatless spaghetti sauce
- 1 8-oz. package Mozzarella cheese, shredded
- ¼ cup grated Parmesan cheese
- 2 teaspoons oregano
- 1 teaspoon instant minced onion
- ¼ teaspoon garlic salt
- 1 long loaf Italian bread, cut in 1-inch cubes

In fondue pot, combine all ingredients except bread cubes. Heat over low heat on range, stirring frequently, until cheese is melted and sauce is hot. Place fondue pot on stand over low heat. Serve with bread cubes for dipping, providing fondue forks for each guest. Makes 12 servings.

Pauline Flower, Northern Illinois Region

PUMPERNICKEL FONDUE DIP

- 2 pound round loaf of pumpernickel
- 1 16-oz. jar Cheez Whiz
- ¼ cup beer

Slice top off of bread. Cut out inside of loaf leaving a bread shell for serving. Cut bread into cubes. In saucepan mix cheese spread and beer until cheese melts and mixture is hot. Pour into bread server. Serve with bread cubes for dipping.

Rosalie Emanuel, Lake County Region

SWISS-CHEDDAR FONDUE

1 clove garlic, halved
2 packages white sauce mix (or sour cream sauce mix)
1 cup half-and-half
½ cup water
2 teaspoons mustard
2 cups shredded Swiss cheese (½ pound)
2¾ cups shredded Cheddar cheese
½ cup dry white wine
French bread, cubed
Apple wedges

Rub fondue pot with garlic; discard. Blend sauce mix, half-and-half and water in pot over moderately low heat. Blend in mustard and cheese, stirring until melted and blended. Add enough wine to make good dipping consistency. Serve with french bread (dry) and apple. Mixture can be frozen and reheated. Makes 8 servings.

Michele Gutter, South Bend Chapter-at-Large

APPETIZER HAMBURGERS

½ pound ground beef
1 teaspoon prepared mustard
1 teaspoon horseradish
1 teaspoon worcestershire sauce
¼ cup chili sauce
4 drops Tabasco sauce
2 teaspoons onion juice or grated onion
½ teaspoon monosodium glutamate
½ teaspoon salt
½ teaspoon pepper
1 loaf cocktail rye bread
Parmesan cheese

Mix ground beef with remaining ingredients except rye bread and cheese. Spread on rye bread; top with parmesan cheese. Broil until beef is cooked and cheese melts. Mixture can be prepared in advance and refrigerated for 24 hours.

Reggie Waxberg, Chicago Region

ARTICHOKE SURPRISE

24 bread rounds
1 14-oz. can artichokes
1 cup mayonnaise
1 cup grated Parmesan cheese
Paprika

Toast bread rounds on one side. Drain artichokes and quarter. Place an artichoke on each bread round, untoasted side up. Mix mayonnaise and cheese. Cover artichoke with a dab of mixture; sprinkle with paprika. Broil for about 1 minute, until puffed and delicately browned. Appetizers may be prepared in advance and frozen. Makes 24.

Sari Wolf, Lake County Region

CHAFING DISH STEAK BITES

Seasoned meat tenderizer
1 3 to 4-lb. round steak, cut 2 inches thick
1 cup red wine or beer
1 clove garlic, crushed
½ cup butter, melted
1 tablespoon dry mustard
½ teaspoon garlic salt
1 teaspoon worcestershire sauce
Pepper
Tabasco sauce

Sprinkle tenderizer on meat according to directions. Place steak in a shallow pan; add wine or beer and garlic. Marinate in refrigerator for 1 hour, turning once. Combine remaining ingredients in small saucepan; heat to blend flavors. Broil steak 3 to 4 inches from heat for about 18 to 20 minutes, turning once. Steak will be medium rare. Carve steak into bite-size thin strips; heap into chafing dish. Pour butter sauce over all. Serve with picks or on party rye slices. Makes 12 to 16 servings.

Jill Kneeter, Des Moines Chapter-at-Large

MUSHROOM PUFFS

1 pound large fresh mushrooms
1/4 cup seasoned croutons
Pinch of salt
1/8 teaspoon pepper
Pinch of garlic powder
2 eggs, slightly beaten
1/2 cup grated Romano or Parmesan cheese
Melted butter

Soak mushrooms in salted water for about 15 minutes. Rinse well in cold water and drain. Carefully break off stems and chop fine. Mix chopped mushrooms with remaining ingredients except butter. Using teaspoon, round mixture into mushroom caps. Drizzle with butter. Broil until browned and puffed, about 3 minutes.

Emma Oesterreicher, Chicago Region

CURRIED SHRIMP CUPS

Pastry:
1/2 cup butter (1 stick)
1/2 cup cream cheese
1 cup plus 2 tablespoons sifted all-purpose flour
1/2 teaspoon baking powder
1/4 teaspoon salt

Filling:
1 8-oz. package cream cheese
2 tablespoons chopped chutney with liquid
1 4 1/2-oz. can shrimps, drained and chopped
Curry powder to taste

Cream butter and cream cheese; blend in flour sifted with baking powder and salt. Divide dough and shape into 1-inch balls. Press into 1 1/2-inch diameter muffin cups covering bottom and up sides. Bake at 350° until golden brown, about 20 to 30 minutes. Fill cups with mixture of cream cheese, chutney, shrimp and curry. Serve hot or cold. Makes about 24 appetizers.

Mrs. Bernard Rubin, Chicago Region

CRABMEAT TOASTIES

- ½ cup butter (1 stick)
- 1 5-oz. jar Old English Sharp Cheese Spread
- 1 7½-oz. can crabmeat, drained and flaked
- 6 English muffins, split and quartered

Bring butter and cheese to room temperature, blend well. Add crabmeat, mixing well. Spread on 12 muffin rounds; arrange on cookie sheet and broil until golden and bubbly, about 3 minutes. Makes 48 appetizers.

Francine Lowtwait, Northern Illinois Region

BAKED CLAMS

- 2 tablespoons minced onion
- 2 cloves garlic, minced
- 1 teaspoon oregano
- 2 tablespoons chopped parsley
- ¼ cup olive oil
- 1 cup bread crumbs
- 2 8-oz. cans minced clams
- 1 teaspoon salt

Saute onions, garlic, oregano and parsley in olive oil. Add bread crumbs and clams plus liquid. Add salt; mix well. Turn into 4 to 6 individual shells or a greased baking dish. Bake at 350° 30 minutes, for individual shells, 45 minutes for casserole. Makes 4 to 6 servings.

Mrs. Harvey A. Schwartz, West Suburban Region

CHICKEN WINGS, SHANGHAI

- 2 pounds chicken wings
- ⅓ cup soy sauce
- 2 tablespoons sugar
- 1 tablespoon dry sherry
- 2 slices fresh ginger root
- ⅓ cup water

Wash chicken wings and place in large saucepan or dutch oven with remaining ingredients. Heat to boiling; lower heat and simmer, covered, for 20 minutes. Stir occasionally. Uncover and cook for 15 minutes, basting with liquid until only ½ cup liquid remains. For dark even color, baste frequently with liquid and stir often. Serve hot or cold. Can be frozen.

Joan Dicker, West Suburban Region

CHINESE EGG ROLLS

- 2 cups chopped cabbage (medium fine)
- ⅔ cup chopped celery (medium fine)
- ⅓ cup boiling water
- ½ pound ground beef
- ½ cup minced green onions and tops
- 1 5-oz. can water chestnuts, drained and sliced
- 1 16-oz. can bean sprouts, drained
- 1 tablespoon sugar
- 1 teaspoon salt
- 1 4½-oz. can shrimps, drained and cut up
- 1 tablespoon peanut butter
- ⅛ teaspoon black pepper
- 1 teaspoon monosodium glutamate
- 1 pound egg roll skins
- 1 egg, beaten
- Oil for frying

Cook cabbage and celery in boiling water for 4 to 5 minutes; stir occasionally. Drain well. Brown ground beef; drain well. Mix vegetables and beef with remaining ingredients except egg roll skins, egg and oil. Cut off corners of skins; brush edges with beaten egg. Place a large tablespoon of filling on each skin. Fold in sides of skin and roll. Fry in deep fat heated to about 375° until egg rolls are golden brown. Makes 10 to 12 egg rolls.

Merle Salzman, Northern Illinois Region

CRAB BITE DELIGHT

- 1 7½-oz. can crabmeat, drained and flaked
- 2 tablespoons mayonnaise
- 3 tablespoons steak sauce
- 3 tablespoons minced onion
- ½ cup grated sharp Cheddar cheese
- Salt and pepper, to taste
- 24 toasted bread rounds

Blend crabmeat with remaining ingredients except bread; mix well. Spread on toasted bread rounds. Arrange on cookie sheet and bake at 400° for 8 to 10 minutes, or until heated through. Makes 24 appetizers.

Michele Gutter, South Bend Chapter-at-Large

FRENCH FRIED MUSHROOMS

- 3 pints fresh mushrooms
- 1 cup flour
- ½ cup milk
- 2 eggs
- 2 tablespoons oil
- ½ teaspoon salt
- Fat for frying

Wash and dry mushrooms. Mix flour with milk, eggs, oil and salt. Refrigerate for about 30 minutes. Dip mushrooms into batter and fry in deep fat heated to 350° for 3 minutes. Drain and serve plain or with cocktail sauce. May be reheated at 375° for 10 minutes. Makes 12 servings.

Mrs. Irving H. Levy, Lake County Region

HOT CRABMEAT APPETIZER

- 1 8-oz. package cream cheese
- 1 7½-oz. can crabmeat, drained and flaked
- 1 tablespoon milk
- ½ teaspoon mustard
- 2 tablespoons minced onion
- Monosodium glutamate
- Salt and pepper, to taste
- ⅓ cup sliced almonds

Combine all ingredients except almonds. Turn into a small casserole or souffle dish. Top with almonds. Bake at 350° for 35 to 45 minutes. Makes 8 servings.

Anita Ruttenberg, Chicago Region

HOT DOG APPETIZERS

- 1 10-oz. jar currant jelly
- 1 12-oz. bottle chili sauce
- Juice of 1 lemon (about 2 tablespoons)
- 3 tablespoons brown sugar
- 2 pounds hot dogs

Melt jelly with chili sauce, lemon juice and brown sugar. Parboil hot dogs; cut into 1-inch lengths. Add hot dogs to sauce and cook 10 minutes. Chill in sauce overnight if you wish. Reheat for about 20 minutes before serving. Makes 16 servings.

Barbara Korman, Lake County Region

PARMESAN RYE PUFFS

- 1 16-oz. jar mayonnaise
- 1 2½-oz. jar shredded Parmesan cheese
- ½ to 1 teaspoon instant minced onion
- 1 large package cocktail rye bread

In bowl, blend mayonnaise, cheese and onion; spread on bread. Arrange on cookie sheet and heat under the broiler until lightly browned and bubbly, about 2 minutes. Makes 8 to 10 servings.

Vivian Drexler, Northern Illinois Region

PIZZA APPETIZERS I

- 3 hard-cooked eggs
- 1 small onion
- 1 4½-oz. can chopped black or green olives
- 1 pound grated Cheddar cheese
- 1 6-oz. can tomato paste
- ½ cup oil
- 20 miniature bagels, split

Chop eggs and onion; add olives, grated cheese, tomato paste and oil. Spread mixture on bagel halves. Broil until lightly browned and bubbly. Makes 40 appetizers.

Pauline Flower, Northern Illinois Region

PIZZA APPETIZERS II

- ½ pound Cheddar cheese
- ½ pound Swiss cheese
- 1 4-oz. jar pimentos, drained
- ¼ green pepper
- 1 medium onion
- 4 strips raw beef fry
- ¼ cup soft margarine
- ¼ cup mayonnaise
- Cocktail rye
- Oregano
- Basil
- Garlic salt

Grind cheese with pimento, green pepper, onion and beef fry. Blend in margarine and mayonnaise. Spread mixture on rye bread; sprinkle with seasonings. Arrange on cookie sheet and bake at 350° for 10 to 15 minutes. Makes about 60 appetizers.

Posi Tucker, South Bend Chapter-at-Large

SHERRIED MUSHROOMS

12 large mushroom caps
Lemon juice
¼ cup butter
1 clove garlic, minced
2 tablespoons grated Gruyere or Parmesan cheese
6 tablespoons soft fresh bread crumbs
¼ teaspoon grated nutmeg
2 tablespoons minced parsley
1 tablespoon minced chives
Salt and freshly ground pepper
¼ cup dry sherry

Remove stems from mushrooms; chop fine and sprinkle caps with lemon juice. Melt 2 tablespoons butter in a small saucepan; add chopped mushrooms and cook until soft. Add garlic. Stir in remaining ingredients except sherry. Stuff mushroom caps with mixture and arrange in a buttered baking dish. Sprinkle with sherry and dot with remaining 2 tablespoons butter. Bake at 350° for 15 minutes.

Gale Levinson, Lake County Region

SWEET-SOUR MEATBALLS I

2 pounds ground beef
1 small onion, grated
½ teaspoon garlic salt
½ teaspoon pepper
1 teaspoon salt
5 slices dry bread, soaked in water and squeezed dry

Sauce:
1 15-oz. can tomatoes
½ cup brown sugar
¼ cup vinegar
½ teaspoon salt
½ small onion, grated
8 to 10 gingersnaps, crumbled

Combine all ingredients for meatballs; shape into balls the size of walnuts. Bake on jelly roll pan at 450° until browned on all sides, about 5 to 10 minutes. In saucepan, combine remaining ingredients for sauce. Cook and stir until gingersnaps are dissolved. Add meat balls; heat through and serve in chafing dish. Makes 4 dozen.

Marion Sallerson, Twin Cities Region

SWEET-SOUR MEATBALLS II

- 1 pound ground beef chuck
- Seasoning to taste
- 1 10-oz. jar grape jelly
- 1 12-oz. bottle chili sauce

Season ground beef and shape into miniature meat balls, using a heaping tablespoon for each. In deep saucepan, combine jelly and chili sauce; blend well and simmer for 30 minutes. Add meat balls and cook on low heat for 30 minutes. Remove from heat; cool. Place mixture in bowl in refrigerator overnight. Remove fat. Reheat and serve in fondue pot or chafing dish. Makes 3 dozen.

Mrs. Jules Deutsch, Northern Illinois Region

CHEDDAR QUICHE

- 1 frozen pie crust
- 3 to 4 medium onions, chopped
- ¼ cup butter
- 3 eggs
- 1 6-oz. can evaporated milk
- ½ teaspoon worcestershire sauce
- ¼ teaspoon Tabasco sauce
- Shredded Cheddar cheese, about 1 cup

Bake pie crust according to directions. Cook onion in butter until golden. Beat eggs; add milk and seasonings. Blend in onions. Sprinkle cheese on bottom of pie crust. Top with egg mixture. Bake at 450° for 10 minutes, then at 325° for 30 minutes. Makes 8 servings.

Judith Zwirn, West Suburban Region

MUSHROOM QUICHE

- 1 cup sliced fresh mushrooms
- 1 cup sliced onion
- ¼ cup butter
- 1 9-inch pie shell, unbaked
- ½ cup grated Swiss cheese
- 1 tablespoon flour
- 3 eggs
- ¾ cup half and half cream
- 1 teaspoon salt
- ⅛ teaspoon pepper

Saute onions and mushrooms in butter for 5 minutes; spread in pie shell. Toss cheese with flour; sprinkle over mushrooms and onions. Beat eggs with remaining ingredients. Pour into pie shell. Bake at 375° for 40 minutes. Can be frozen. Makes 8 servings.

Mrs. Z. Buchsbaum, Northern Illinois Region

SEAFOOD QUICHE

- 1 6-oz. package crabmeat, thawed and drained
- 1½ cups chopped cooked shrimp
- 1 8-oz. package Swiss cheese, grated
- ½ cup chopped celery
- ½ cup chopped green onions
- 2 frozen 9-inch pie shells
- 1 cup mayonnaise
- 2 tablespoons flour
- 1 cup dry white wine or Sherry
- 4 eggs, beaten

Mix crab, shrimp, cheese, celery and onions. Divide between two unbaked pie shells. Combine remaining ingredients and pour over seafood mixture. Bake at 350° for 35 to 40 minutes, or until knife inserted near center comes out clean. Cool. Cover with plastic wrap and refrigerate. Reheat at 300° for 15 to 20 minutes. Can be frozen; if prepared for freezing, do not bake first. Makes 8 to 12 servings.

Ellen Kogen, Lake County Region

FRENCH ONION PIE

- Pastry for 9-inch pie
- 1 3½-oz. can french fried onions
- 4 eggs
- 2 cups milk
- ½ cup (2 oz.) shredded sharp process American cheese
- ½ teaspoon salt
- Dash of cayenne
- 1 cup (4 oz.) shredded sharp process American cheese

Line 9-inch pie pan with pastry; flute edges. Bake at 450° for 7 to 8 minutes, or until golden brown. Reduce oven temperature to 325°. While pastry is still warm, fill bottom with 1½ cups onions; reserve remaining ½ cup for garnish. Beat eggs slightly; add milk, ½ cup cheese, salt and cayenne. Pour over onions in pastry shell. Sprinkle with 1 cup cheese. Bake at 325° for 45 minutes. Sprinkle reserved onions around edge of pie. Bake 5 to 10 minutes longer, or until custard tests done. Let stand 10 minutes before serving. Great as a beef fondue accompaniment. Makes 8 servings.

Millicent Pine, Northern Illinois Region

BLENDER-MADE BROCCOLI SOUP

- 1 10-oz. package frozen chopped broccoli, cooked and drained
- 1 medium onion, chopped
- 1 teaspoon nutmeg
- 1 cup chicken broth
- 1 10½-oz. can condensed cream of mushroom soup
- 1 cup sour cream
- 2 teaspoons butter

In blender, combine broccoli, onion, nutmeg and chicken broth; blend until smooth. Pour into 1½-quart saucepan; cook for 6 minutes. Return to blender; add remaining ingredients; blend until smooth. Return to saucepan; reheat and serve. Makes 6 to 8 servings.

Eileen Kiess, Des Moines Chapter-at-Large

BLENDER COCONUT-CURRY SOUP

- 1⅓ cups flaked coconut
- 1⅓ cups milk
- 1 tablespoon cornstarch
- ½ teaspoon curry
- ⅛ teaspoon salt
- 1½ cups chicken broth
- Dairy sour cream
- Toasted coconut

Whirl coconut and milk in blender. Strain mixture, reserving milk and pressing as much milk as possible through strainer. Discard coconut. In saucepan, blend cornstarch, curry and salt. Gradually stir in coconut milk and broth. Cook, stirring, until mixture comes to a boil. Serve hot or cold, with sour cream and coconut garnish. Makes 4 servings.

Sandy Rosen, Northern Illinois Region

CABBAGE SOUP WITH MEAT BALLS

Meat Balls:

3 pounds ground beef
1 envelope dried onion soup mix
1 egg, slightly beaten
Worcestershire sauce, to taste

Soup:

2 11-oz. cans tomato bisque
2 soup cans water
1 28-oz. can whole tomatoes
1/4 cup raisins
Dash of dark ginger
8 grains sour salt
2/3 cup brown sugar
1 large head cabbage, shredded

For meat balls, blend ground beef with onion soup mix, egg and worcestershire; refrigerate until chilled; shape into balls. For soup, mix remaining ingredients in large saucepot; simmer for 2½ hours. Add meat balls and cook 1½ hours longer. Makes 8 to 10 servings.

Ellen Friend, Lake County Region

CLAM VICHYSSOISE

1 10½-oz. can concentrated New England clam chowder
1 teaspoon minced fresh or frozen dill
1 cup chicken broth (canned or made with chicken stock base)
1/2 cup sour cream

In blender, combine chowder, chicken broth and dill; blend until pureed. Chill thoroughly. Just before serving, stir in sour cream. Makes 4 servings.

Beatrice Rapkin, Milwaukee Region

CREAM OF FRESH MUSHROOM SOUP

1 pound fresh mushrooms, finely chopped
1/4 pound butter (1 stick)
1/4 cup flour
2 quarts milk, scalded
Salt and pepper, to taste

In skillet, saute mushrooms in butter; remove from heat and stir in flour. Add mushrooms to scalded milk and cook, stirring until thickened and mixture comes to a boil. Add seasonings to taste. Makes 8 servings.

EASY BEET BORSHT

1 1-lb. can shoestring beets
2 cans water
½ cup sugar
½ cup bottled lemon juice
2 teaspoons salt
Sour cream
Cucumber slices, optional

In 2-quart saucepan, combine beets, water, sugar, lemon juice and salt; heat to boiling. Lower heat and simmer for about 2 minutes. Chill thoroughly. When ready to serve, top with sour cream and cucumber slices. Makes 4 to 6 servings.

Florence M. Mayron, Chicago Region

FRENCH ONION SOUP WITH SHERRY

4 large Spanish onions, thinly sliced
¼ cup butter
4 10½-oz. cans condensed beef broth
½ cup dry Sherry
2 teaspoons worcestershire sauce
Dash pepper
6 slices French bread, cut 1-inch thick
¾ cup grated Parmesan cheese
6 slices gruyere or Swiss cheese

In large saucepan or dutch oven, cook onion in butter until tender but not brown, about 20 minutes. Add broth, Sherry, worcestershire and pepper. Heat to boiling. Pour into 6 individual casseroles or heatproof bowls or a large oven crock Float a slice of bread on each serving. Sprinkle generously with Parmesan, then top each with a slice of cheese. Bake at 375° for 15 minutes, or broil for about 5 minutes, until cheese melts and is bubbly. The dish can be prepared in advance, except for cheese topping. Makes 6 hearty servings.

Judith Fischer, West Suburban Region

GAZPACHO

2 cups tomato puree
1 onion, chopped
1 green pepper, chopped
1 cucumber, chopped
2 cups tomato juice
½ cup olive oil
3 tablespoons vinegar
1 clove garlic, minced
1 teaspoon salt
¼ teaspoon cumin (optional)

Combine all ingredients and refrigerate for at least 2 hours. If you wish, serve with additional chopped vegetables (onion, pepper, cucumber). Makes 8 to 10 servings.

Gert Kaufman, Northern Illinois Region

INSTANT ICY SPINACH BORSHT

1 1-lb. can spinach
Juice of 1 lemon
1 spinach can ice water
Sugar or artificial sweetener, to taste
Sour cream
Chopped green onion

Break up spinach and blend with vegetable liquid, by beating slightly with a fork. Add lemon juice, ice water and sugar to taste. Serve in glass sherbets or cups, garnishing with sour cream and green onion. Makes 4 to 6 servings.

Helen Eisenberg, Lake County Region

MUSHROOM-BARLEY SOUP

2 pounds beef chuck and bones or beef shanks
6 quarts water
2 onions, diced
2 carrots, diced
1½ cups celery, diced
Few sprigs parsley
1 1-lb. can tomatoes
1 pound fresh mushrooms, sliced
1½ cups pearl barley
2 tablespoons sugar
3 to 4 tablespoons salt
1 teaspoon monosodium glutamate

Place meat and bones and water in large saucepot; heat to boiling. Add remaining ingredients, adjusting seasonings to taste. Cover and simmer for about 2½ hours.

Florence M. Mayron, Chicago Region

SEAFOOD TOMATO CHOWDER

- 2 cups water
- 1 28-oz. can tomatoes, cut up
- 1 16-oz. package frozen halibut or turbot fillets
- 1 16-oz. package frozen hash brown potatoes (loose pack)
- 1 10-oz. package frozen peas and carrots
- 1 7-oz. package frozen shrimps (optional)
- 1 tablespoon instant minced onion
- 2 teaspoons parsley flakes
- 1 teaspoon marjoram
- 1½ teaspoons salt

In dutch oven, combine water and undrained tomatoes. Heat to boiling; add remaining ingredients (still frozen). Cover pan; place in oven at 350° and cook for 2 hours, stirring occasionally. Makes 6 to 8 servings.

June Minkus, Lake County Region

MEATLESS VEGETABLE SOUP

- ¼ cup green split peas
- ¼ cup yellow split peas
- ¼ cup barley
- ¼ cup northern beans
- ½ pound fresh mushrooms, coarsely chopped
- 1 cup chopped celery
- ½ cup diced carrots
- Salt and pepper to taste
- ¼ cup butter
- 1 cup tomato juice
- 3 quarts water
- 1 cup milk

In large soup pot, combine all ingredients except milk. Cook on medium low heat for 3 hours, or until mixture is thick. Add 1 cup milk; heat through and serve hot. Makes 10 to 12 servings.

Betty Grossman, Northern Illinois Region

VICHYSSOISE

- 3 leeks
- ¼ cup butter
- 1 cup chopped celery
- 4 medium potatoes, pared and thinly sliced
- ½ cup minced parsley
- 3 cups chicken broth
- 1½ teaspoons salt
- ¼ teaspoon pepper
- 2 cups heavy cream
- Chopped chives

Wash leeks thoroughly; trim off roots and most of tops. Cut into thin slices. In large saucepan, cook leeks in butter for 10 minutes. Add celery, potatoes, parsley, broth and seasonings. Cover and simmer on low heat for 30 minutes. Put in blender container; blend on high speed for 30 seconds. Cool and chill thoroughly. Just before serving, add cream. Garnish with chives and serve in soup bowls surrounded by crushed ice. Makes 6 to 8 servings.

Marcia Levy, Lake County Region

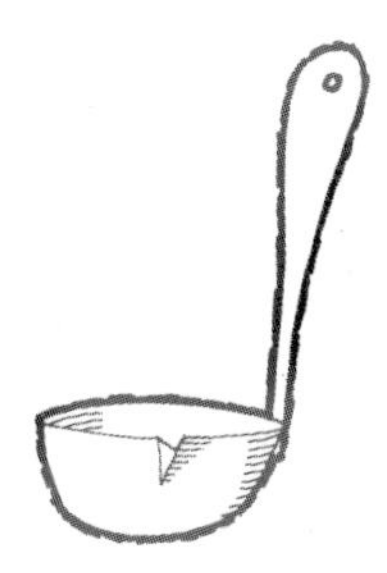

WATERMELON SOUP

- 5 to 6 pounds watermelon
- 1 12-oz. can apricot nectar
- ⅓ cup lime juice
- 2 to 4 tablespoons honey

Line a large sieve with cheesecloth. Cut melon into pieces and discard seeds. At high speed of electric blender, liquify about 2 cups of watermelon pieces at a time; pour into sieve. Repeat until you have 4 cups watermelon juice. Pour juice into a large bowl. Add apricot nectar, lime juice and honey to taste. Stir until honey is dissolved. Chill at least 2 hours before serving with lime slice garnish. Makes 8 servings.

Sandy Rosen, Northern Illinois Region

BREADS

BANANA NUT BREAD

- ½ cup butter (1 stick)
- ¾ cup sugar
- 2 eggs
- 1½ cups flour
- 1 teaspoon baking soda
- 1 teaspoon salt
- 3 medium bananas, mashed
- 3 tablespoons dairy sour cream
- ½ cup nuts

Cream butter and sugar until light and fluffy. Add eggs and beat well. Add sifted dry ingredients, mashed banana and sour cream. Beat well. Fold in nuts. Pour into a well-greased 9x5x3-inch loaf pan. Let stand ½ hour. Bake at 325° for 1 hour. Makes 1 loaf.

Arlene Baerson, West Suburban Region

BLUEBERRY MUFFINS

- 2 cups flour
- 2 teaspoons baking powder
- ¼ teaspoon salt
- ½ cup vegetable shortening
- 1 cup sugar
- 1 egg
- ½ cup milk
- 3 cups fresh or frozen blueberries
- Sugar

Sift together flour, baking powder and salt. Reserve ½ cup of flour mixture to sprinkle over blueberries. Cream shortening and sugar together; add egg and mix well. Add dry ingredients alternately with milk. Sprinkle the ½ cup reserved flour over the blueberries; then mix berries carefully into batter. Spoon into paper-lined muffin tins. Sprinkle generously with sugar. Bake at 400° for 20 to 25 minutes, until lightly browned. Makes 16 to 18 muffins.

Emma Oesterreicher, Chicago Region

BUTTERHORNS

2 cups sifted flour
1 cup butter (2 sticks)
1 egg yolk
3/4 cup sour cream

Filling:
3/4 cup sugar
1 teaspoon cinnamon
3/4 cup chopped nuts

Measure flour into bowl. Cut butter into flour with pastry blender or knife. Then add egg yolk and sour cream and mix well. When blended, shape into ball. Sprinkle with flour. Wrap well in waxed paper and chill in refrigerator for several hours or overnight. Prepare filling by mixing together sugar, cinnamon and nuts. Sprinkle board lightly with flour. Remove dough from refrigerator. Divide into three parts. Roll out one part at a time on board making large circle about 1/8-inch thick. Sprinkle with filling. Cut into 12 wedge-shaped sections. Roll up each wedge, starting at the widest portion. Place on a lightly-greased baking sheet and bake at 375° for 25 to 30 minutes. These may also be used as strudel with apricot preserve and coconut filling. Makes 3 dozen.

Rosalie S. Albin, Lake County Region

CHERRY COFFEE CAKE

1 cup butter (2 sticks)
1 cup sugar
2 beaten eggs
1 teaspoon vanilla
3 cups sifted cake flour
1 teaspoon baking powder
1 teaspoon baking soda
1 cup sour cream
1 1 lb. 4 oz. can cherry pie filling (or blueberry filling)

Topping:
1/4 cup cake flour
1 tablespoon soft butter
1/4 cup sugar

Cream together butter and sugar. Beat in eggs and vanilla. Sift dry ingredients and add alternately with sour cream to butter mixture. Beat well. Spread half of batter in greased and floured 13x9-inch pan. Pour pie filling over batter. Carefully spread remainder of batter over pie filling. Mix together topping ingredients until crumbly. Sprinkle over batter. Bake at 375° for 40 to 50 minutes. Makes 15 servings.

Lylus Brash, Chicago Region

CHERRY-PECAN BREAD

3 cups biscuit mix
¼ cup sugar
1 teaspoon nutmeg
½ teaspoon salt
1 1 lb. 4 oz. can cherry pie filling
⅓ cup milk
¼ cup butter, melted (½ stick)
1 beaten egg
1 tablespoon vanilla
1 cup chopped pecans

Combine biscuit mix, sugar, nutmeg and salt. Stir in pie filling, milk, butter, egg and vanilla. Mix until well blended. Fold in chopped pecans. Pour into well-greased 9 x 5 x 3-inch loaf pan. Bake at 350° 1¼ hours. Let cool in pan. Makes 1 loaf.

Susan Kaplan, Northern Illinois Region

DARK DATE NUT BREAD

½ cup boiling water
½ cup mixed light and dark raisins
½ cup chopped dates
1½ tablespoons butter
¾ teaspoon baking soda
¾ cup plus 2 tablespoons flour
½ cup sugar
¼ teaspoon salt
1 egg
½ teaspoon vanilla
¼ cup chopped nuts

Pour boiling water over raisins, dates, butter and soda. Let stand. Mix together flour, sugar and salt. Add to fruit mixture with egg, vanilla and chopped nuts. Blend all ingredients well and pour into a greased and floured 1-lb. coffee can. Bake at 350° for 60 to 70 minutes. Makes 1 round loaf.

Fay Nicholas, Northern Illinois Region

COTTAGE CHEESE MUFFINS

12 ounces dry cottage cheese
3 tablespoons sugar
½ cup melted butter (1 stick)
2 eggs
Pinch salt
1 cup flour
2 teaspoons baking powder

Combine in order in mixing bowl. Spoon into greased muffin tins. Bake at 400° 20 minutes. Serve with sour cream and fresh strawberries. Makes 10.

Laura Annes, Lake County Region

FAST CHERRY SPONGE BREAD

- 3 eggs, separated
- Pinch of salt
- ½ cup sugar
- ½ teaspoon lemon peel
- ½ teaspoon vanilla
- 2 teaspoons lemon juice
- ½ cup flour
- 1 cup drained canned pitted cherries

Beat egg whites with salt until foamy. Add sugar slowly and beat until whites are very stiff. Blend egg yolks with lemon peel, vanilla and lemon juice. Pour ¼ of the whites into yolk mixture, mix, then reverse and pour yolk mixture into whites. Sprinkle with flour, and fold gently, but well. Grease the bottom of a 9-inch layer cake pan. Pour batter into pan, top with cherries and bake at 350° for 35 to 40 minutes. Cool in pan. Makes 8 to 10 servings.

Erika Brodsky, Lake County Region

FRUIT BREAD

- ½ cup butter (1 stick)
- 1 cup sugar
- 2 eggs
- 2 cups flour
- 1 teaspoon baking soda
- 1 cup mashed ripe banana
- ¼ cup chopped maraschino cherries
- ¼ cup semi-sweet chocolate pieces
- ¼ cup chopped nuts
- Confectioners' sugar icing, if desired

Cream butter and sugar. Add eggs and beat well. Sift flour and baking soda and add alternately with banana to egg mixture. Mix in cherries, chocolate and nuts. Pour into greased 4½ x 9-inch loaf pan and bake at 350° for 1 hour. While still warm, drizzle with icing. (The addition of the chocolate pieces, though unusual in bread, enhances this recipe.) Can be frozen. Makes 1 loaf.

Florence Purnell, Des Moines Chapter

NORWEGIAN COFFEE CAKE

- 2 cups sifted flour
- 2 cups firmly packed brown sugar
- ½ cup soft butter (1 stick)
- 1 egg
- ½ teaspoon salt
- 1 teaspoon baking soda
- 1 cup buttermilk
- ½ cup raisins
- ½ cup chopped nuts

Mix together flour and brown sugar. Cut in butter with a pastry blender. Reserve ½ cup for topping. Add egg, salt, soda and buttermilk and mix well. Stir in raisins and nuts. Pour into a greased 9-inch square or 9x5x3-inch loaf pan. Sprinkle with topping. Bake at 350° for 30 minutes, longer for loaf. Serve warm. Makes 12 servings.

Bina Levin, Northern Illinois Region

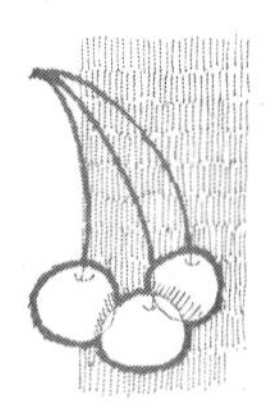

PUMPKIN BREAD

- 3 ⅓ cups flour
- 2 teaspoons baking soda
- 1½ teaspoons salt
- 1 teaspoon cinnamon
- 1 teaspoon nutmeg
- 3 cups sugar
- 1 cup vegetable oil
- 4 eggs
- ⅔ cup water
- 2 cups (1 lb. can) pumpkin
- 2 cups chopped pecans

Sift dry ingredients, including sugar, into mixing bowl. Make a well and add all remaining ingredients except nuts. Blend thoroughly; then stir in nuts. Pour into three greased and floured 8½x4½x2½-inch loaf pans. Bake at 350° about 1 hour. Cool slightly in pans before turning out on rack to finish cooling. Can be frozen. May also be baked in two 9x5x3-inch loaf pans. Makes 2 or 3 loaves.

Toby Newman, Northern Illinois Region

ONION-RYE BREAD

- 2 cups milk
- 1/4 cup sugar
- 4 teaspoons salt
- 1/4 cup vegetable oil
- 2 packages active dry yeast
- 1 cup warm water
- 6 cups flour
- 3 tablespoons caraway seeds
- 1 cup chopped onions
- 2 1/2 cups rye flour
- Corn meal
- Cream
- Coarse salt

Scald milk; add sugar, salt and oil. Cool to lukewarm. Soften yeast in water and add to milk. Blend in 6 cups flour, mixing well. Add caraway seeds, onions and 2 cups of rye flour. Sprinkle remaining rye flour on board and knead until smooth. Put into greased bowl, cover and allow to rise in warm place until doubled in size. Punch down and fold dough from edges to center. Cover and let rise again until doubled. Divide into 3 loaves. Put into greased pans sprinkled with corn meal. Brush tops with cream and sprinkle with coarse salt. Cover with towel and allow to rise until double in size. Bake at 350° for 45 to 60 minutes. Makes 3 loaves.

Gert Kaufman, Northern Illinois Region

RHUBERRY COFFEE CAKE

- 1 cup flour
- 1 teaspoon baking powder
- 1/4 teaspoon salt
- 2 tablespoons sugar
- 1/4 cup butter (1/2 stick)
- 1 tablespoon milk
- 1 egg
- 3 cups cut-up rhubarb
- 1/2 package (1 1/2 oz.) strawberry-flavored gelatin

Topping:

- 1/2 cup flour
- 1/2 teaspoon cinnamon
- 1/2 cup sugar
- 1/4 cup butter (1/2 stick)

Mix together flour, baking powder, salt and sugar. Cut in butter. Blend in milk and egg. Press mixture into a well-greased 8-inch square pan. Cover with rhubarb. Sprinkle gelatin evenly on top. Blend together topping ingredients and sprinkle over all. Bake at 375° for 40 minutes. Makes 9 servings.

Phyllis Galst, Milwaukee Region

ALEX'S BAGELS

- 3 packages active dry yeast
- 3/4 cup lukewarm water
- 2 eggs
- 2 tablespoons salt
- 3½ tablespoons sugar
- 6 tablespoons vegetable oil
- 7 heaping cups flour

Dissolve yeast in water. In a small bowl, beat eggs. Add salt, sugar, oil and yeast. Measure flour into a large mixing bowl. Blend in egg mixture. Use enough additional water to make a stiff dough. Knead well until smooth and elastic. Divide dough into 4 parts. Roll each into the shape of a pencil. Pinch off pieces of dough and shape like doughnuts. Let rise in warm place. Boil water in large pot. Put bagels in boiling water. When bagel rises to top of pot, remove to baking sheet and bake at 375° for 30 minutes or until brown.

Madlyn Spark, Lake County Region

APRICOT PASTRIES

Filling:

- 2 cups dried apricots
- 2 cups water

Pastry:

- 3 cups sifted flour
- 1 tablespoon sugar
- ½ teaspoon salt
- 1 cup shortening
- ½ cup milk
- 1 package active dry yeast
- 1 slightly beaten egg
- ½ teaspoon vanilla
- Confectioners' sugar

Simmer apricots in water until tender. Cool and set aside. Sift together flour, sugar and salt. Cut in shortening until mixture resembles coarse crumbs. Scald milk, cool to lukewarm, add the dry yeast and let soften. Add slightly beaten egg and vanilla. Blend yeast mixture with flour mixture until thoroughly combined. Divide dough in 4 parts. On a surface well dusted with confectioners' sugar, roll one part at a time to 10-inch squares. Cut each in sixteen 2½-inch squares; place a heaping teaspoon of apricots in the center of each. Pinch two opposite corners together. Place 2 inches apart on a greased cookie sheet. Let stand 10 minutes. Bake at 350° 10 to 12 minutes. Remove immediately from pan; roll in confectioners' sugar. Cool on rack. These freeze well. Makes about 5 dozen.

Florence M. Mayron, Chicago Region

BRAIDED ONION LOAF

1 package active dry yeast
1/4 cup warm water
4 cups flour
1/4 cup sugar
1 1/2 teaspoons salt
1/2 cup hot water
1/2 cup milk
1/4 cup butter, softened
1 egg

Filling:
1/4 cup butter, melted
1 cup finely chopped onion or
1/4 cup instant minced onion
1 tablespoon grated Parmesan cheese
1 tablespoon poppy or sesame seeds
1 teaspoon garlic salt
1 teaspoon paprika

In large mixing bowl, dissolve yeast in warm water. Add 2 cups flour, sugar, salt, water, milk, butter and egg. Blend at low speed until moistened; beat 2 minutes at medium speed. By hand, stir in remaining flour to form a soft dough. Cover; let rise in warm place until light and doubled in size, 45 to 60 minutes. Stir down dough. Toss on floured surface until no longer sticky. Roll out to an 18 x 12-inch rectangle. Mix together filling ingredients and spread on dough. Cut lengthwise into three 18 x 4-inch strips. Starting with the 18-inch side, roll up each strip; seal edges and ends. On greased cooky sheet, braid together the three rolls. Cover and let rise again in warm place until doubled in size, 45 to 60 minutes. Bake at 350° for 30 to 35 minutes, until golden brown. Serve warm or cool. To make 2 small loaves instead of 1 large loaf, cut the three filled rolls in half before braiding. Braid each set of rolls separately on greased cooky sheet and bake as directed. May be prepared in advance and frozen. Makes 1 large or 2 small loaves. Serves 20 to 24 people.

Carol Linch, Lake County Region

CHEESE COFFEE CAKE

- 1 1-oz. cake fresh yeast
- 1/4 cup scalded cream, slightly cooled
- 1 tablespoon sugar
- 1 cup butter (2 sticks)
- 2 1/2 cups sifted flour
- 1/2 teaspoon salt
- 4 egg yolks, slightly beaten

Filling:

- 2 8-oz. packages cream cheese
- 1 egg, separated
- 1 cup sugar
- 1 teaspoon vanilla
- 1/2 cup chopped walnuts
- Confectioners' sugar

Dissolve yeast in cream and add sugar. Cut butter into flour and salt same as for pie crust. Add egg yolks and yeast mixture, blending thoroughly. Divide dough into two parts. Roll each piece to fit a 13 x 9-inch pan. Place one piece in bottom of pan. Prepare filling by beating cream cheese with egg yolk, sugar and vanilla until light and fluffy. Spread over dough. Place second piece of dough on cheese. Brush top with slightly beaten egg white. Sprinkle nuts over all. Cover and let rise for 2 hours. Bake at 350° for 30 minutes. When cool, sprinkle generously with confectioners' sugar. This coffee cake freezes well and can be prepared in advance. Makes 15-20 servings.

Vivian Stolman, Northern Illinois Region

YEAST CRESCENTS

- 2 1/2 cups flour
- 2 eggs
- 1 package active dry yeast
- 1/4 cup warm water
- 1 cup butter, melted and cooled (2 sticks)
- Cinnamon sugar mixture

Mix 2 cups flour with eggs. Dissolve yeast in warm water; then add to egg-flour mixture. Add remaining 1/2 cup flour. Blend in butter. Refrigerate 1 hour. Divide dough into 4 parts. Put mixture of cinnamon and sugar on waxed paper. Pull out dough to form a circle. Sprinkle more cinnamon and sugar on top. Cut circle into 8 pie-shaped wedges. Roll up into crescents, beginning at wide end. Bake on ungreased cooky sheet at 350° for 20 minutes. Makes 32 crescents.

Phyllis Frankel, Chicago Region

CHOCOLATE GOOD COFFEE CAKE

- ¾ cup milk
- ½ cup butter (1 stick)
- ⅓ cup sugar
- 1 teaspoon salt
- 2 packages active dry yeast
- ¼ cup warm water
- 2 beaten eggs
- 3½ cups sifted flour
- ½ cup semi-sweet chocolate pieces

Topping:

- ½ cup sifted flour
- ⅓ cup sugar
- ½ cup chopped nuts
- ½ cup semi-sweet chocolate pieces
- ¼ cup butter (½ stick)
- 1½ teaspoons cinnamon

Scald milk. Stir in butter, sugar and salt. Cool to lukewarm. Sprinkle yeast into warm water in large bowl of mixer. Stir to dissolve. Add milk mixture, eggs and 2½ cups flour. Beat at medium speed until smooth. With spoon, blend in 1 cup flour and chocolate pieces. Turn into well-greased 10-inch tube pan. To prepare topping, rub together with fingers all ingredients until crumbly. Sprinkle over coffee cake. Cover; let rise in warm place, free from draft until double in bulk, about 1 hour. Bake at 400° for 35 minutes. Turn out of pan immediately; let cool on wire rack. Makes 16 servings.

Miriam Witt, Chicago Region

DILL CASSEROLE BREAD

- 1 package active dry yeast
- ¼ cup warm water
- 1 cup creamed cottage cheese
- 2 tablespoons sugar
- 1 tablespoon instant minced onion
- 1 tablespoon butter
- 2 teaspoons dill weed or seeds
- ¼ teaspoon baking soda
- 1 teaspoon salt
- 1 egg, unbeaten
- 2¼ cups flour
- Coarse salt

Soften yeast in warm water. Heat cottage cheese to lukewarm. Combine in mixing bowl cottage cheese, sugar, onion, butter, dill, soda, salt, egg and softened yeast. Add flour gradually, beating after each addition. Let rise in warm place until doubled. Stir down dough. Turn into a greased 8-inch round 2-quart casserole. Let rise. Sprinkle coarse salt on top. Bake at 350° about 50 to 60 minutes. Makes 1 round loaf.

Mrs. Marvin Topper, Milwaukee Region

KUGELHOPF

- 2 packages active dry yeast
- ¼ cup warm water
- ½ cup butter (1 stick)
- ½ cup sugar
- 2 egg yolks
- 2 eggs
- Grated rind of 1 lemon
- 3 cups flour
- ½ teaspoon salt
- ½ cup scalded milk
- ½ cup raisins
- 1 teaspoon butter for greasing pans
- 2 tablespoons confectioners' sugar

Sprinkle yeast over water in a 1-qt. pan and set aside until it bubbles. Place butter and sugar in bowl of electric mixer and beat at low speed for 3 minutes. Add egg yolks, eggs, lemon rind, flour, salt and milk alternately. Add raisins. Add yeast mixture and beat in by hand with heavy spatula. Remove dough to a floured working area. Knead 1 minute. If too sticky, add ¼ cup more flour. Place dough in a 3-qt. Kugelhopf mold greased with butter (or two greased 9-inch tube pans.) Let rise until it reaches the top (about 45 minutes). Bake at 375° for 25 minutes. Test for doneness with a cake tester. Remove Kugelhopf immediately from mold, turning out on a cooling rack. Sprinkle generously with confectioners' sugar. This bread freezes well. Makes 1 Kugelhopf or 2 9-inch loaves.

Claire Palmer, Lake County Region

RAISIN BREAD

- 2 cups golden raisins
- 2 cups water
- ¼ cup butter or margarine
- 2 eggs
- 2 cups sugar
- 4 cups sifted flour
- 2 teaspoons baking soda

Place raisins in water and bring to a boil. Let cool. Beat together butter, eggs and sugar until smooth and creamy. Mix sifted flour and soda together. Add to creamed mixture alternately with raisins and water. Grease and flour 2 9x5x3-inch loaf pans. Pour batter evenly in both and bake at 350° 65 to 70 minutes. Freezes well. Serve with cream cheese. Makes 2 loaves.

Florence M. Mayron, Chicago Region

BABY CHALLAHS

1 package active dry yeast
¼ cup lukewarm water
1 teaspoon sugar
½ cup sugar
1½ teaspoons salt
½ cup butter (1 stick)
1 egg, beaten
½ cup instant or mashed potatoes
½ cup lukewarm water
1 cup scalded milk
5 to 6 cups flour

Topping, if desired:
1 egg
1 teaspoon water
1 teaspoon honey

Dissolve yeast in water with 1 teaspoon sugar. Allow to stand about 5 minutes, until mixture bubbles. Combine in mixing bowl sugar, salt, butter, egg, potatoes and water and mix well. Pour in scalded milk. Add yeast mixture to **cooled** ingredients. Add 2 to 3 cups flour. Beat well. Cover and let rise about 1 hour until bubbly. Punch down with spoon. Add remaining flour. Let rise again until bubbly. Punch down again. Knead dough approximately 5 minutes. Divide into 4 pieces and shape into logs; braid, if desired. Put into greased 2¼x7½-inch loaf pans. Let rise until doubled in size. If desired, gently brush with beaten egg topping, made by combining egg with water and honey. Bake at 350° for 1 hour. Can be frozen. Makes 4 small loaves.

Mrs. Howard Adler, Northern Illinois Region

STEAK DIANE

1 sirloin steak, 2 to 3 pounds
Salt
Pepper
Dry mustard
Butter
Worcestershire sauce
2 tablespoons parsley or chives
Lemon juice
2 tablespoons red wine

Slice meat in 1 to 2 inch slices and season with salt, pepper and dry mustard. Pound with mallet. Melt butter in fry pan over high heat. Sprinkle with worcestershire sauce and brown. Then lay steak in pan and brown for 2 minutes. Sprinkle parsley and lemon juice on top; add wine and light with match. When serving, pour sauce over steak. Makes 6 to 8 servings.

Elaine Achler, Northern Illinois Region

STEAK IN WINE SAUCE

2 pounds beef, cut into thin strips and seasoned
Butter
1 large onion, chopped
1 pound mushrooms, sliced
1 cup dry wine
1 cup catsup

Saute meat in butter with a little oil. Saute mushrooms and onions. Combine with remaining ingredients and simmer 1 hour. Thicken with cornstarch if you wish. Serve over noodles or rice. Makes 4 to 6 servings.

Theresa Weisberg, Chicago Region

BEEF BORDELAISE

- 5 to 6-lb. rib or rib eye roast
- 2 cups sliced onions
- ½ cup shallots or green onions, sliced
- 2 cloves garlic, minced
- 1 bay leaf
- ½ teaspoon thyme
- 1 teaspoon peppercorns
- 4 or 5 sprigs parsley
- 1 teaspoon salt
- 2 cups dry red wine
- 5 tablespoons melted margarine
- 2 10½ oz. cans beef broth
- 1 tablespoon flour

Place meat in roasting pan large enough to hold both meat and vegetables. Combine vegetables, herbs, salt and wine, pour over meat. Cover. Refrigerate 8-12 hours, turning occasionally. Heat oven to 475°. Remove meat from marinade, pat dry. Strain marinade, reserve liquid and vegetables. Place meat on rack in shallow roasting pan. Roast 30 minutes, basting once or twice with 4 tablespoons margarine. Reduce heat to 400°. Add reserved vegetables to pan. Roast 40-45 minutes. Estimate total roasting time at 12 minutes per lb. for rare. Baste occasionally with pan drippings. Let stand 15-20 minutes before carving. Heat pan drippings to boiling, cook 1 minute. Discard fat from pan. Add marinade. Bring to boiling, cook down until only a few tablespoons are left. Add broth. Blend margarine and flour and add to pan. Cook, stirring constantly, until sauce is thick and smooth. Strain. Makes 8 to 10 servings.

Doris Charak, Lake County Region

BRAISED BEEF

- 1 4-lb. top of the round
- 1 tablespoon salt
- 1 teaspoon pepper
- ¼ cup salad oil
- 2 cups red Burgundy wine
- 1 cup beef consomme
- ½ cup diced onion
- Dash of thyme
- Dash of nutmeg
- 1 tablespoon brown sugar
- 2 cloves garlic, minced
- 2 tablespoons peppercorns
- ¼ cup chopped parsley

Rub meat with salt and pepper. Heat oil and add meat. Brown on all sides. Add rest of ingredients except parsley and roast in a 350° oven basting frequently for about 2 hours or until desired doneness. Remove meat to serving platter. Add 2 tablespoons fresh peppercorns to gravy. Simmer for 10 minutes. Pour over meat and sprinkle with chopped parsley. Slice and serve with sauce. Makes 6 to 8 servings.

Amy Driss, Chicago Region

4 HOUR BEEF STEW

- 2 pounds beef stew meat
- 6 carrots, sliced
- 4 potatoes, cut up
- 4 ribs celery, cut up
- 2 onions, diced
- 1 tablespoon salt
- 1 tablespoon sugar
- 2 tablespoons quick cooking tapioca
- ¾ cup tomato juice

Place in casserole and cook, covered in a 250° oven for 4 hours. Makes 6 servings.

Eileen Kiess, Des Moines Chapter-at-Large

MOCK BEEF WELLINGTON

- 1 4 to 6-lb. beef tenderloin
- Salt, pepper, garlic
- 2 packages refrigerated biscuit dough
- 2 egg yolks
- 2 tablespoons water
- Bearnaise sauce:
- 1 clove garlic, mashed
- Salt and pepper
- 1 10½-oz. can cream of chicken soup
- ¼ cup melted butter
- 3 teaspoons lemon juice
- 3 teaspoons tarragon vinegar
- ¼ cup dry white wine
- 3 tablespoons chopped green onion
- ¼ cup minced parsley

Season beef early in day with salt, pepper and cut clove of garlic. Roast at 400° for 25 minutes. Set aside to cool. Divide biscuits in half and spread over roast until it is completely covered. Pinch edges together. Beat egg yolks with water; brush over dough. Bake at 425° for 30-35 minutes for rare beef, or until the dough is golden brown. Wrap in dough in advance if desired, but bring to room temperature before baking the second time. Serve with bearnaise sauce prepared by combining all ingredients and heating. Makes 6 to 8 servings.

Judith Zwirn, West Suburban Region

MINUTE STEAKS PARMESAN

- 4 to 6 beef cube steaks, about 4 ounces each
- 1 egg
- 1 tablespoon water
- Dash pepper
- 1/4 cup finely crushed saltine crackers (6 to 7)
- 1/4 cup grated Parmesan cheese
- 1/4 cup cooking oil
- 1 8-ounce can pizza sauce

Beat together egg, water and pepper. Combine crumbs and half of the cheese. Dip steaks into egg mixture, then into crumbs. In skillet, brown steaks in hot oil. Drain on paper toweling. Arrange steaks in 10x6x1½-inch baking dish; cover with pizza sauce and sprinkle with remaining cheese. Bake at 325° for 20 minutes. Makes 4 to 6 servings.

Rochelle Kroot, Indianapolis Chapter-at-Large

FRENCH SKILLET BEEF

- 4 cups diced cooked roast beef
- 2 onions, diced
- 2 potatoes, diced
- 2 medium green peppers, diced
- 1/4 cup butter
- 2 cloves garlic
- Leftover gravy
- 1 cup burgundy wine
- Salt

Dice beef, onions, potatoes and green peppers into fairly small pieces. Melt butter in large skillet and lightly brown cut up garlic. Add meat and vegetables, gravy and mix well. Salt lightly and pour in wine. Cover and simmer for 45 minutes. Serve with french bread. Makes 4 to 6 servings.

Judy Scheffres, Northern Illinois Region

STEAK ROAST

- 1 sirloin steak, 4 inches thick, or 1 whole tenderloin
- 2 10½-oz. cans onion soup
- 4 tablespoons catsup
- 4 tablespoons worcestershire sauce
- 4 tablespoons Sherry wine
- ½ pound fresh mushrooms

Broil meat on one side. Turn over and place in baking pan. Mix remaining ingredients and pour over meat. Bake at 350° until desired doneness, about 2 hours. Makes 8 to 10 servings.

Phyllis Silver, Northern Illinois Region

BEEF PARMEGIANA

- 1½ pounds round steak (½-inch thick)
- ½ cup grated Parmesan cheese
- ¼ cup bread crumbs
- 1 egg, beaten
- ¼ cup oil
- 1 onion, chopped
- 1 6-oz. can tomato paste
- 1 cup hot water
- 1 cup beef broth
- ½ teaspoon pepper
- 1 teaspoon sugar
- Salt to taste
- ½ teaspoon marjoram
- Mozzarella cheese

Combine Parmesan cheese and bread crumbs. Dip meat first into egg, then into crumbs. Brown in oil and put in oblong baking dish. In same skillet, saute onion, then add tomato paste, water, broth, pepper, sugar, salt and marjoram. Boil 5 minutes. Then pour over meat, cover and bake 1 hour, or until meat is tender. Uncover, top with cheese and bake until cheese melts. Makes 4 to 6 servings.

Judy Mazor, Northern Illinois Region

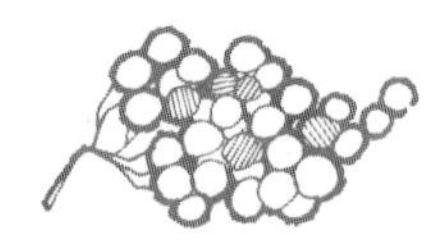

ROUND STEAK WITH WINE SAUCE

- 2 pounds top round steak, 1-inch thick
- ½ cup burgundy or other dry red wine
- ¼ teaspoon garlic powder
- Dash of oregano
- ½ cup chopped onion
- 2 tablespoons butter
- 1 10¾-oz. can condensed tomato soup
- 2 tablespoons brown sugar

Score meat. Combine wine, garlic powder and oregano. Pour over meat and marinate for 4 hours. Turn meat occasionally. In saucepan, cook onion in butter until tender. Add soup, brown sugar and the drained marinate. Heat, stirring occasionally. Place steak on broiler pan 3 inches from heat and brush with sauce. Broil 10 minutes on each side, basting with remaining sauce until desired doneness. Makes 6 to 8 servings.

Myra Weis, Chicago Region

BEEF AND MUSHROOMS

- 2 tablespoons flour
- 2 teaspoons salt
- 2 pounds lean chuck or book steak, cut into strips about 2 inches long
- 4 tablespoons margarine
- 1 clove garlic, minced
- 1 medium onion, sliced
- 1 8-oz. can tomato sauce
- 1 bouillon cube dissolved in 6 oz. of hot water (if using Kosher bouillon cube, use only ½ cube)
- 5 drops Tabasco sauce
- 1 pound fresh mushrooms, sliced
- 1 cup raw rice (equivalent to 3 cups cooked)

Combine flour and salt in paper bag. Add meat and shake well. Set aside. Cook onion and garlic until glazed (do not brown). Remove from skillet. Add meat and brown well, stirring until done. Add onions, tomato sauce, bouillon and Tabasco. Cover and simmer until meat is tender. Add sliced mushrooms and cook about 10 minutes longer. Serve with rice. Makes 6 to 8 servings.

Gert Lederman, Lake County Region

FLANK STEAK WITH SPAGHETTI

- 2 medium onions, sliced
- 1 green pepper, sliced
- 1 clove garlic, minced
- 3 tablespoons oil
- 2 8-oz. cans tomato sauce
- ¼ cup hickory flavored catsup
- ¼ teaspoon pepper
- 1 bay leaf
- ¼ teaspoon oregano
- ¼ teaspoon basil
- 1 8-oz. package spaghetti
- 1 flank steak
- Instant unseasoned meat tenderizer
- ½ teaspoon salt

Cook onions, green pepper and garlic in oil until tender. Stir in tomato sauce, catsup, pepper and bay leaf. Cover and simmer for 30 minutes. During last 10 minutes add basil and oregano. Cook spaghetti. Tenderize meat and broil 3 to 5 minutes on each side. Slice steak diagonally. Drain spaghetti and arrange on platter with meat slices on top. Garnish with sauce.

Carol Linch, Lake County Region

BARBECUED SIRLOIN STEAK

- **1 sirloin steak, 3 inches thick**
- **Salt**
- **Pepper**
- **Garlic salt**
- **½ bottle catsup (14 oz.)**
- **3 tablespoons worcestershire sauce**
- **1 large bermuda onion**
- **1 pound fresh mushrooms**
- **½ cup butter (1 stick)**
- **Lemon juice to taste**

Brown steak under broiler on one side. Turn and season with salt, pepper and garlic salt. Mix remaining ingredients. Spread on raw side and bake uncovered at 350° for 1¾ hours. Baste occasionally. Makes 6 to 8 servings.

Louise Stein, Chicago Region

PEPPER STEAK

- **3 pounds tenderloin steak, sliced thin and cut into 2-inch squares**
- **¼ cup butter**
- **Salt, garlic salt and pepper**
- **1 teaspoon oregano**
- **1 pound fresh mushrooms**
- **3 green peppers, cut into 1-inch squares**
- **3 tomatoes, quartered**
- **¼ cup tomato paste**
- **¼ cup Sherry wine**

Brown meat in 2 tablespoons butter. Add seasonings and cook until tender, about 15 minutes. Saute mushrooms and green pepper in remaining butter for 5 minutes; add to the meat mixture along with the tomatoes and tomato paste. Heat thoroughly. Add Sherry and serve at once. Makes 8 servings.

Mrs. Victor Wexler, Milwaukee Region

SWEET 'N SOUR SWISS STEAK

- **4 pounds round steak**
- **Flour**
- **2 medium onions, chopped**
- **2 cloves garlic, minced**
- **1 large green pepper, diced**
- **1 pound fresh mushrooms**
- **1 1-lb. can tomatoes**
- **½ cup vinegar**
- **Sugar**

Season and flour meat; pound on both sides. In skillet, brown onion and cut up garlic lightly in small amount shortening. Add meat and brown on both sides. In roasting pan mix diced green pepper and mushrooms with tomatoes and vinegar. Add sugar, salt and pepper to taste. Cover and bake in a skillet or roasting pan at 350° for 3½ hours. Makes 4 servings.

Judy Scheffries, Northern Illinois Region

BEEF STROGANOFF

- 4 tablespoons flour
- 4 teaspoons salt
- 3 pounds sirloin, cut into strips
- ½ cup butter (1 stick)
- 2 medium onions, chopped
- ¾ teaspoon garlic powder
- 2 10½-oz. cans condensed mushroom soup
- 1 cup bouillon
- ½ teaspoon Tabasco sauce
- 2 pounds fresh mushrooms, sliced
- 1 cup dairy sour cream, if desired

Combine flour and salt; sprinkle over meat. Melt butter in skillet; add onion and garlic powder. Cook until onion is tender, but not brown. Remove from skillet; add meat and brown well. Stir in soup, bouillon, Tabasco and onion. Cover. Simmer 30 minutes, or until meat is tender. Add mushrooms; cook 10 minutes. And sour cream, if desired. Serve with noodles or rice. Makes 12 servings.

Bobbi Katz, West Suburban Region

STEAK A LA CHICKEN LIVERS

- 4 oz. (½ cup) chicken livers, sliced
- 2 tablespoons butter
- ¼ cup chopped green onions
- 1 cup sliced fresh mushrooms
- ½ cup dry white wine
- ¼ teaspoon salt
- Pepper
- 2½ pounds beef sirloin steak, cut 1½ inches thick

In small skillet, quickly cook chicken livers in butter; remove from pan. In same skillet, cook onion until almost tender, add mushrooms and cook 1 to 2 minutes. Return liver to skillet. Stir in wine, salt and pepper, heat through, do not boil. Broil or grill steak about 7 minutes on each side for medium rare. Serve sauce over steak. Makes 4 servings.

Lee Bateman, Lake County Region

HUNGARIAN BEEF SHORT RIBS

- 4 pounds beef short ribs
- 2 medium onions, sliced
- 1 15-oz. can tomato sauce
- 1 cup water
- ¼ cup brown sugar
- ¼ cup vinegar
- 1 teaspoon salt
- 1 teaspoon dry mustard
- 1 teaspoon worcestershire sauce

Brown meat in its own fat; add onions and brown. Drain off fat. Blend together tomato sauce, water, brown sugar, vinegar, salt, dry mustard and worcestershire; pour over meat. Cover and simmer to 2½ hours or until meat is tender. Serve over cooked noodles. Can be prepared in advance. Freezes well. Makes 6 to 8 servings.

Michele Gutter, South Bend Chapter-at-Large

PICNIC MEAT, MUSHROOM BASKET

- 1 pound round Italian bread, or 1 pound round rye bread
- 2 pounds ground chuck
- 4 eggs, beaten
- 1 teaspoon salt
- ¼ teaspoon pepper
- ½ cup oatmeal
- 1 cup milk

Filling:

- 1 lb. fresh mushrooms, sliced
- 3 teaspoons dehydrated onions
- 4 tablespoons butter
- ¼ cup sherry
- 2 tablespoons instant blending flour
- ¼ teaspoon salt
- ⅛ teaspoon pepper

Cut slice off top of bread. Scoop out inside and leave about ¼-inch shell. Brush inside of bread with melted butter and toast in oven. Mix meat, seasonings, eggs, oatmeal and milk. Steam mushrooms in butter with dehydrated onions. Add sherry and thicken with flour, salt and pepper. Place half of meat mixture in bread basket. Cover with mushroom mixture, then with meat. Dot with butter. Bake at 350° for about 2 hours. To take to picnic, wrap in foil and newspaper. Will stay hot for hours. Slice in wedges. Makes 6 to 8 servings.

Madlyn Spark, Lake County Region

GRILLED STEAK AU POIVRE

- 1 sirloin steak, about 2 inches thick, 4 lbs.
- 2 tablespoons cracked pepper
- Salt

The success of this depends upon the cracked pepper, ground pepper is not effective. Using your fingers and heel of hand, press half of pepper into both sides of steak and let stand at room temperature for 1 hour. Grill about 5 inches from hot coals, about 8-10 minutes on each side for medium rare. Sprinkle with salt. HINT: To crack pepper, put peppercorns into paper or plastic bag and crush with a rolling pin or mallet. Can be purchased cracked.

SAUCE:

- ½ cup butter, softened
- 2 tablespoons finely minced parsley
- 2 tablespoons finely minced chives
- 2 tablespoons lemon juice

Blend butter, parsley and chives in a small bowl. Add lemon juice, a little at a time. Turn out onto wax paper, shape into a 1½-inch roll. Wrap tightly and refrigerate until firm. Cut into slices on each serving of steak.

BLUE CHEESE OR ROQUEFORT BUTTER:

- ½ cup blue or Roquefort cheese
- 4 tablespoons (½ stick) butter, softened
- 2 tablespoons sherry, white wine, brandy or cream

Remove cheese and butter from refrigerator. Crumble the cheese. Allow both to stand at room temperature about 2 hours, or until soft. Mash cheese with the butter in a small bowl. Use a fork first, then a spoon. Stir in sherry and mix to a smooth paste. Spoon over meat. This may be prepared ahead of time and refrigerated covered.

Pearl Cohn, Lake County Region

BEEF AND PEPPERS WITH SPAGHETTI

- 2 pounds round steak, cut into thin strips
- ½ cup flour
- ¼ cup butter
- ⅓ cup olive oil or vegetable oil
- 4 medium green peppers, cut into strips
- 2 small onions, sliced
- 4 cloves garlic, minced
- 2 19-oz cans tomatoes
- 2 8-oz. cans tomato sauce
- 1½ teaspoons salt
- 1½ teaspoons basil leaves
- ½ teaspoon oregano
- ⅛ teaspoon ground black pepper
- 2 tablespoons salt
- 4-6 quarts water
- 1 pound spaghetti

Coat beef strips with flour; brown in butter and oil in large skillet. Remove meat; sauté green peppers and onions about 5 minutes. Return meat. Add garlic, tomatoes, tomato sauce, salt, basil, oregano and pepper. Simmer covered 1 hour stirring occasionally. Add 2 tablespoons salt to rapidly boiling water. Gradually add spaghetti, cook until tender. Drain in colander. Serve with beef and pepper sauce. Makes 8 servings.

Lee Bateman, Lake County Region

CHUCK 'N SAUERKRAUT

- 4 to 5-lb. chuck roast
- 2 large onions, sliced
- 1 16-oz. can sauerkraut
- 1 16-oz. can tomatoes
- 2 tablespoons lemon juice
- 1 cup water
- Salt
- Pepper
- 4 to 6 tablespoons apricot or peach preserves

Brown seasoned meat in lightly oiled Dutch oven. Add onions, sauerkraut, tomatoes, lemon juice and water. Cover and cook slowly until meat is nearly tender. Add preserves. If thicker gravy is desired, mix 2 tablespoons chicken fat and 2 tablespoons flour together and add to sauerkraut and tomato gravy.

Ruth Ostreicher, Chicago Region

SPICY PRUNE POT ROAST

- 4 to 5-lb. chuck or rump roast
- 2 teaspoons salt
- 2 cups dried prunes, pitted
- 2 cups boiling water

Sauce:

- ½ cup cider vinegar
- ½ cup water
- 1 cup light brown sugar
- ¼ teaspoon ground cloves
- 1 teaspoon cinnamon

Salt meat and brown in dutch oven or heavy skillet; add dried prunes and 2 cups boiling water. Cook slowly about 3 hours. Remove meat to dish and add rest of ingredients to pot; cook until thickened. Slice meat, reheat in pot and serve. Makes 4 to 5 servings.

Gert Kaufman, Northern Illinois Region

SHISH KEBAB

- ½ cup water
- 2 tablespoons sugar
- ½ cup catsup
- ¼ cup vinegar
- ¼ cup salad oil
- 1 tablespoon dry mustard
- Dash hot pepper sauce
- 1½ pounds chuck or round steak, cut into 1-inch cubes
- Cherry tomatoes
- New potatoes, cooked and peeled or canned
- Green peppers, cut into quarters
- Fresh mushrooms

In a saucepan, combine first 7 ingredients; bring to boil and simmer 20 minutes. Cool. Add to meat and marinate 5 hours or overnight. Thread meat, green pepper, potatoes (cooked and peeled) tomatoes and mushrooms on their own skewers and broil or grill 10 minutes on each side. Reserve marinade and brush on meat and vegetables while broiling. Broil tomatoes last 5 minutes so they do not become too soft. Serve with crisp greens and corn on the cob. Can be prepared in advance.

Joan Gaan, Northern Illinois Region

BRISKET OF BEEF I

- 1 4-lb. beef brisket
- 3 onions, quartered
- 1 teaspoon salt
- 1/4 teaspoon pepper
- 1/2 teaspoon garlic powder
- 1 1/2 teaspoons paprika
- 1/2 teaspoon soy sauce
- 1/4 teaspoon Angostura bitters
- 1/3 cup mustard
- 1/4 cup chili sauce
- 1/4 cup brown sugar
- 1 tablespoon Parmesan cheese

Cut up onions. Place with brisket in roasting pan and bake at 350° about 45 minutes, until brown on the top. Add about 1/2 cup water, cover, and bake 1 hour. Add spices, spreading mustard over top. Mix chili sauce and brown sugar together. Spread over top and sprinkle with Parmesan cheese. Cover and bake until tender. Makes 6 to 8 servings.

Lynn Forrest, Northern Illinois Region

BRISKET OF BEEF II

- 1 2 to 3-lb. beef brisket
- 1 onion, sliced
- 1 can tomato soup
- 1/2 can water
- 1/2 cup red cooking wine
- 1/2 teaspoon salt
- 1/2 teaspoon monosodium glutamate
- 1/4 teaspoon garlic powder
- 1/2 teaspoon paprika
- 2 bay leaves

Brown meat thoroughly in oil. Remove and add onions. Brown. Return meat to pan with onions and seasonings and bring to a boil. Transfer to a roaster; cover tightly and bake at 325° for 2 to 3 hours until tender. Remove bay leaves. Can be prepared in advance.

Mrs. Hal Levin, Des Moines Chapter-at-Large

GERMAN STYLE BRISKET OF BEEF

- 1 4-lb. beef brisket
- 2 onions, sliced
- 1 16-oz. can tomatoes
- ½ cup raisins
- ¼ cup sugar
- 1 lemon, peeled, quartered, seeded
- 1 garlic clove, minced

Dust brisket with flour and sear on both sides in hot oil. Add sliced onions and sauté. Pureé tomatoes in blender and combine with remaining ingredients. Pour sauce over meat and simmer, covered for 2 to 2½ hours, until tender. Can also be baked in 325° oven. Slice diagonally and serve with sauce. Makes 8 to 10 servings.

Ellie Lieb, Chicago Region

HOT AND SPICY FONDUE SAUCE

- 1 cup chili sauce
- ½ cup chopped onion
- 3 tablespoons lemon juice
- 2 tablespoons salad oil
- 1 teaspoon brown sugar
- 2 teaspoons vinegar
- 1 clove garlic, crushed
- ½ teaspoon Tabasco sauce
- ½ teaspoon dry mustard
- ½ teaspoon salt

Combine all ingredients in a small saucepan. Heat to boiling; lower heat and simmer for 10 to 15 minutes. Prepare in advance if you wish, refrigerate and reheat before serving. Makes about 1½ cup sauce.

Debbie Wilner, Northern Illinois Region

BELGIAN BRISKET OF BEEF

- 1 5-lb. beef brisket
- 2 teaspoons salt
- ¼ teaspoon pepper
- 2 onions, sliced
- 4 celery ribs, sliced
- 1 cup chili sauce
- 1 can beer

Place beef in roasting pan. Season. Place onion, celery, chili sauce on beef. Add ¼ cup water to bottom of pan. Roast uncovered at 325°, basting often for 2½ hours. Then pour on beer and roast covered for 1 more hour.

Phyllis Frankel, Chicago Region

SLOPPY JOES

3 medium onions, chopped
2 tablespoons oil
3 pounds ground beef
2 cups finely chopped celery
1 green pepper, chopped
¼ cup brown sugar
1 tablespoon salt
1 tablespoon worcestershire sauce
1 12-oz. bottle chili sauce
2 tablespoons vinegar

Cook onion in oil until translucent. Remove onion and add beef; cook until browned. Add remaining ingredients and simmer 30 minutes. Spoon on buns or spaghetti. Makes 10 servings.

Betty Bornstein, Chicago Region

STUFFED CABBAGE I

1 large head cabbage

Sauce:
Marrow bones
1 pound chuck steak
3 ripe tomatoes
1 16-oz. can tomatoes
Shredded end of cabbage
3 onions, sliced
Salt
1 tablespoon sugar

Filling:
4 tablespoons rice
½ tablespoon lemon juice
1 tablespoon sugar
Salt
3 lbs. chopped meat
3 eggs
1 onion
Salt
½ 8-oz can tomato sauce
1 tablespoon sugar

In large saucepan, heat water to boiling. Add whole cabbage and let stand for 3 minutes. Remove from water; cool and carefully remove each leaf. For sauce, clean bones under hot water. Place in pot with diced chuck steak, tomatoes, cabbage, onion, salt, sugar and 2 glasses of water. Simmer for 2 hours. For filling: Cook rice; add lemon juice, sugar and salt. Combine with remaining ingredients which have been chopped and mixed together. Taste and adjust seasonings. Spoon mixture onto each cabbage leaf; roll up, tucking in all sides. Add stuffed cabbage to sauce; cook for 1½ hours over low heat.

Miriam Faust, Lake County Region

CHUCK WAGON STEAK WITH CRACKED PEPPER

- 1 round bone chuck roast or boneless round roast
- 2 teaspoons meat tenderizer
- 2 tablespoons instant minced onion
- 2 teaspoons thyme
- 1 teaspoon marjoram
- 1 bay leaf, crushed
- 1 cup wine vinegar
- ½ cup salad oil
- 3 tablespoons lemon juice
- 2 tablespoons cracked pepper

Sprinkle meat evenly on both sides with meat tenderizer (use no salt). Pierce deeply all over with fork; place in shallow baking pan. Mix onion, thyme, marjoram, bay leaf, vinegar, oil and lemon juice in a small bowl; pour over meat and let stand at room temperature 1 to 2 hours, turning meat every ½ hour. When ready to grill, pound half of pepper into each side. Grill 15 minutes on each side for rare and serve sliced in ½ inch slices.

Susan Zagorin, Northern Illinois Region

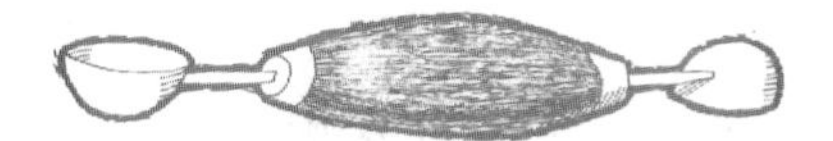

MEAT BALLS WITH CRUSHED PINEAPPLE

- ½ medium green pepper, chopped
- 1 medium onion, chopped
- Oil
- Paprika, salt, garlic salt, pepper
- 1½ pounds ground beef, made into meat balls
- 1 8-oz. can tomato sauce
- 1 8-oz. can crushed pineapple, drained

Saute pepper and onion in oil. Add paprika, salt, garlic salt and black pepper and cook until brown. Broil meatballs. Place in a large pan. Cover with vegetables, drained pineapple and tomato sauce. Cover and cook for 45 minutes. Makes 4 to 6 servings.

Sylvia Mashkes, Chicago Region

STUFFED CABBAGE II

- 2 pounds lean ground beef
- ¾ cup chopped onion
- 1 cup diced celery
- 1 cup cooked rice (optional)
- 2 eggs
- 2 teaspoons horseradish
- 2 tablespoons prepared mustard
- 9 cabbage leaves
- 1 16-oz. can sauerkraut
- 1 8-oz. can tomato sauce

Brown beef without additional grease in pan. Add chopped onions and celery and cook until onions become translucent. Drain off fat. Add salt and pepper to taste, then rice, eggs, horseradish and mustard; blend well. Scald cabbage leaves. Fill with meat and roll. Spread sauerkraut in bottom of 2-quart casserole; arrange cabbage on top of sauerkraut. Pour tomato sauce over all. Cover casserole and bake at 325° for 45 minutes. Makes 4 to 6 servings.

Jayne Schwartz, West Suburban Region

SPAGHETTI MEAT SAUCE

- 1 large onion, chopped
- 1 green pepper, chopped
- 2 ribs celery, chopped
- 2 tablespoons shortening
- 1½ pounds ground beef chuck
- 1 8-oz. can tomato sauce
- 1 teaspoon salt
- 1 teaspoon garlic salt
- 1 teaspoon oregano
- Dash of nutmeg
- Dash pepper
- 1 16-oz. can stewed tomatoes
- 2 bay leaves
- 1 4-oz. can mushrooms, drained

In large skillet or dutch oven, brown onion, celery and green pepper in shortening. Add meat, cook and stir until browned. Add remaining ingredients. Cover and simmer for 2 to 3 hours. Remove bay leaves before serving. The sauce can be made in advance and frozen. Makes 4 to 6 servings.

Aileen Melnick, Northern Illinois Region

CHEESE FILLED MEAT LOAF

1½ pounds ground beef
1 8-oz. can tomato sauce
¾ cup quick cooking rolled oats
¼ cup chopped onion
1 egg
1 tablespoon worcestershire sauce
1½ teaspoons salt
1½ teaspoons monosodium glutamate
½ teaspoon oregano
¼ teaspoon pepper
1 6-oz. package sliced Mozzarella cheese

Combine all ingredients except cheese and mix well. Divide meat into thirds. Pat ⅓ in bottom of loaf pan. Cover with half the cheese. Repeat layers ending with meat. Bake at 350° for 1 hour. Can be frozen or prepared in advance. Makes 5 to 6 servings.

Mrs. Hal Levin, Des Moines Chapter-at-Large

MY BABYSITTER'S MEAT LOAF

2 eggs
⅔ cup milk
2 teaspoons salt
¼ teaspoon pepper
3 slices bread, crumbled
1 tablespoon minced onion
¼ cup shredded raw carrot
1 cup shredded Cheddar cheese
1½ pounds lean ground beef
¼ cup catsup
¼ cup brown sugar
1 tablespoon prepared mustard

Beat eggs with milk; add salt, pepper and bread and mix until the bread absorbs the milk. Add carrots, cheese and beef; blend. Place in 2-qt. baking dish. Mix catsup, brown sugar and mustard and spread over top of loaf. Bake at 350° for 1 hour. Can be frozen or prepared in advance. Makes 6 servings.

Jill Kneeter, Des Moines Chapter-at-Large

PIZZA MEAT PIE

- 1 pound ground beef
- ½ cup powdered cream substitute
- ½ cup dry bread crumbs
- 1 teaspoon salt
- ¼ teaspoon pepper
- 1 clove garlic, minced
- 1 cup water
- 1 cup (4 oz.) shredded Cheddar cheese
- 1 6-oz. can tomato paste
- 1 4-oz. can undrained mushrooms
- 1 teaspoon leaf oregano
- 1 teaspoon grated onion or instant minced onion
- ⅓ cup (1½ oz.) grated Parmesan cheese

Preheat oven to 350°. In medium bowl, combine ground beef, powdered cream, bread crumbs, salt, pepper, garlic and water. Mix well. Pat into a deep 9-inch pie pan or casserole. Combine remaining ingredients, except Parmesan cheese, blend. Spoon over meat. Sprinkle with Parmesan cheese. If desired, cover with cooked sausage, green pepper, mushrooms or olives. Bake 30 to 40 minutes. Makes 4 to 6 servings.

Sheila Schwartz, West Suburban Region

STUFFED PEPPERS

- ½ cup rice
- 1 cup water
- 1 onion, diced
- 1 pound ground beef
- 1 8-oz. can tomato paste
- 1 4-oz. can mushrooms
- ½ cup Parmesan cheese
- 6 green peppers
- 1 8-oz. can tomato juice

Cook rice in water. Saute onion; add beef and brown; add tomato paste, mushrooms, rice and cheese. Blend well. Spoon stuffing into peppers and place in a deep dish. Pour tomato juice to almost cover peppers. Sprinkle with Parmesan cheese. Cover and bake at 350° for 3 hours. Remove peppers with large spoon. Serve with tossed salad and hard rolls. Makes 6 servings.

Myra Ladley, Lake County Region

GIANT STUFFED HAMBURGERS

- 2 tablespoons butter
- 1¼ cups herb seasoned stuffing mix, crushed (about ¾ cup)
- 1 egg, beaten
- 1 3-oz. can chopped mushrooms, drained
- ⅓ cup beef broth
- ¼ cup sliced green onions
- ¼ cup chopped parsley
- 1 teaspoon lemon juice
- 2 pounds ground beef
- 1 teaspoon salt

In medium saucepan, melt butter. Remove from heat, add stuffing mix, egg, mushrooms, beef broth, onion, parsley and lemon juice. Mix well and set aside. Combine beef and salt. Divide meat in half on sheets of wax paper; pat each half into 8-inch circles. Spoon stuffing over 1 circle of meat to within 1 inch of edge. Top with second circle of meat. Peel off paper and seal edges. Invert meat patty onto well greased broiler pan. Peel off remaining paper. Broil about 10 to 12 minutes on each side. Cut into wedges and serve with warmed catsup, if desired. Can be grilled over charcoal. Makes 8 servings.

Lee Bateman, Lake County Region

PIZZA NOODLE CASSEROLE

- 1 8-oz. package broad noodles
- 1 pound ground beef
- ½ teaspoon fennel seed
- Salt and pepper, to taste
- 2 16-oz. cans stewed tomatoes
- 1 6-oz. can tomato paste
- 1 6-oz. can pizza sauce
- Garlic salt, to taste
- ½ pound grated Mozzarella cheese
- Oregano

Cook noodles and drain. Brown beef in skillet with fennel and salt and pepper; drain off fat. Combine tomatoes, tomato paste and pizza sauce with garlic salt to taste; heat to simmering. Layer ingredients in a 13 x 9-inch casserole in this order: ½ noodles, ½ meat, ½ cheese, ½ tomato sauce. Repeat layers; sprinkle with oregano. Bake at 350° for 45 minutes. Makes 6 to 8 servings.

Gail Festerstein, Northern Illinois Region

STROGANOFF CASSEROLE

- 2 pounds lean ground beef
- 1 tablespoon dried onion flakes
- 1 teaspoon parsley flakes
- 2-3 dashes Tabasco sauce
- 1 teaspoon salt
- ¼ teaspoon pepper
- 1 4-oz. can mushroom stems and pieces
- 1 10½-oz. can mushroom soup
- 2 cups dairy sour cream
- 1 8-oz. tube prepared biscuits
- 1 3½-oz. can french fried onion rings
- 2 eggs
- 1 teaspoon celery salt

In skillet, brown beef; add onion flakes, parsley flakes, Tabasco, salt and pepper. Drain mixture; add drained mushrooms and place in 3-qt. casserole. Mix 1 cup sour cream and soup; pour over meat mixture. Cut biscuits in half, arrange cut side down over meat mixture. Place onion rings on top of biscuits. Mix remaining sour cream, eggs and celery salt in blender; pour over all. Bake 375° for about 30 minutes, until golden brown and puffy. Makes 6 to 8 servings.

Jayne Schwartz, West Suburban Region

HUNGARIAN GOULASH

- 1 large onion, sliced
- 2 tomatoes, quartered, or 1 16-oz. can tomatoes
- 3 pounds beef chuck, cut into 1-inch cubes
- 1 teaspoon salt
- ½ teaspoon pepper
- 1 tablespoon paprika
- 1 teaspoon garlic powder (optional)
- 7 new potatoes, quartered

Saute onion and tomatoes until soft. Add meat and seasonings. Cover tightly and cook slowly for about 2 hours (During cooking check to see there is enough liquid left, otherwise add 2 tablespoons water.) Add potatoes and simmer 30 minutes. Prepare in large kettle. Makes 6 servings.

Karyl Mandel, Chicago Region

CHILI

- 1/4 cup oil
- 2 cups diced onions
- 3 cloves garlic, minced
- 2 pounds ground beef
- 1 16-oz. can tomatoes
- 2 15-oz. cans chili beans
- 1 1/2 tablespoons chili powder
- 1/2 teaspoon red pepper
- 1/2 teaspoon oregano
- Salt

Heat oil and saute onions and garlic until translucent. Add beef and brown. Add tomatoes and beans; stir in seasonings, cover and simmer 1 hour. Can be frozen. Makes 6 servings.

Sandi Martin, Omaha Chapter-at-Large

STEAK MARINADE

- 1/2 cup catsup
- 1/2 cup barbecue sauce (Open Pit)
- 1/2 teaspoon garlic powder
- 1 tablespoon cider vinegar
- 1 tablespoon steak sauce
- 1 tablespoon sugar
- 1 tablespoon worcestershire sauce
- 1/4 cup water

Combine all ingredients; pour over steak which has been seasoned with salt, garlic salt and monosodium glutamate. Refrigerate several hours or overnight. A good marinade for skirt steaks.

Diane Segal, Lake County Region

LASAGNE

- 1 pound ground beef
- 1 cup chopped onion
- 2 cloves garlic, minced
- 2 teaspoons oregano
- 2 10 3/4-oz. can tomato soup
- 1/2 cup water
- 1 1-lb. package lasagne noodles
- 1 pint dry cottage cheese
- 1 pound mozzarella cheese, grated

In large skillet, brown ground beef with onion, garlic and oregano. Add soup and water; simmer for 30 minutes. Cook and drain noodles. In 13 x 9-inch baking dish layer 1/3 of noodles, cottage cheese, Mozzarella and tomato sauce. Repeat two more more times. Bake at 350° for 1 hour. Let stand 20 minutes before cutting. Makes 6 to 8 servings.

Carole Butwinick, Twin Cities Region

SPANISH TONGUE

- 1 pickled tongue, 3 to 3½ pounds
- 1 cup diced celery
- 1 whole green pepper, chopped
- 1 medium onion, chopped
- 2 8-oz. cans tomato sauce
- 1 16-oz. can mushrooms
- 1 8-oz. can peas, drained

Simmer tongue in water to cover until tender, about 2 to 2½ hours. Cool and peel. Saute celery, green pepper and onions until soft. Add tomato sauce, mushrooms and peas. Slice tongue and add to sauce. Serve on rice. May be prepared in advance. Makes 4 to 5 servings.

Mildred Rubenstein, Chicago Region

LIVER AND ONIONS

- 1 pound sliced liver
- 2 tablespoons flour
- 2 tablespoons cooking oil
- 1 10½-oz. can onion soup
- ¼ cup chili sauce or catsup

Dust liver with flour. Brown in oil. Combine onion soup and ¼ chili sauce or catsup and add to liver. Cover and simmer about 30 minutes or until liver is tender. Uncover, cook for a few minutes to thicken sauce. Makes 4 servings.

Jean Goldrosen, Northern Illinois Region

MEAT BALL STEW

Meat Balls:

- 1 pound lean ground beef
- ½ cup bread crumbs
- 1 egg
- ¼ cup tomato sauce
- 1 teaspoon salt
- ⅛ teaspoon allspice
- ⅛ teaspoon pepper
- 1 teaspoon onion juice

Sauce:

- 3 cups water
- ¾ cup tomato sauce
- 1 1¼-oz. package onion soup mix
- 1½ cups sliced carrots
- 1 10-oz. package frozen peas
- ½ cup chopped green pepper
- 3 medium potatoes, cubed

Mix ingredients for meat balls. Brown in 2 tablespoons hot fat in large pot. Add remaining ingredients. Bring to a boil and cook over low heat until meat and vegetables are tender, about 1 hour. Makes 6 servings.

Florence Purnell, Des Moines Chapter-at-Large

GREEK MOUSSAKA

1 eggplant (approximately 1¼ pounds
¼ cup butter

Meat Sauce:
1 tablespoon butter
½ cup finely chopped onion
1 pound ground beef chuck or lamb
½ clove garlic, minced
¼ teaspoon oregano
½ teaspoon basil
⅛ teaspoon cinnamon
½ teaspoon seasoned salt
1 8-oz. can tomato sauce

Cream Sauce:
1 tablespoon butter
1 tablespoon flour
¼ teaspoon salt
Dash of pepper
1 cup milk
1 egg
1 cup ricotta cheese
¼ cup grated Parmesan cheese
1 tablespoon dry bread crumbs

Cut unpared eggplant in half lengthwise. Slice crosswise ½ inch thick. Brown the slices quickly in melted butter. For meat sauce: In hot butter, saute onion, meat and garlic until brown, about 10 minutes. Add herbs, spices and tomato sauce; simmer uncovered 30 minutes. For cream sauce: Melt butter, blend in flour, salt and pepper with wire whisk. Add milk gradually. Bring to boil stirring constantly until thickened. Remove from heat; cool slightly. Add well beaten egg and ricotta cheese to cream sauce; mix well. In 10x6x1½-inch baking dish, arrange layers of eggplant and meat sauce sprinkling each layer with Parmesan and bread crumbs. Pour the ricotta cheese sauce over the top. Bake at 350° for 1 hour, or until top is golden brown. Can be frozen, flavor improves by standing one day. Makes 4 to 6 servings.

Barbara Rubenstein, Northern Illinois Region

ROAST RACK OF LAMB WITH MARMALADE

8 chop rack (or rib) of lamb
Salt
Pepper
½ cup orange marmalade

Bring lamb to room temperature and rub on all sides with salt and pepper. Preheat oven to 325°. Place lamb bone side down on rack in shallow pan. Bake for 30 minutes. Remove from oven and spread with orange marmalade. Bake 20 minutes longer. Makes 4 servings.

HONEYED LAMB KEBABS

1 pound boneless lamb, cut into 1½-inch cubes (leg or shoulder)
¼ cup pineapple juice
¼ cup vinegar
3 tablespoons oil
1 teaspoon worcestershire sauce
⅛ teaspoon pepper
1 teaspoon salt
¼ cup honey
1 clove garlic, minced
Dash of oregano
¼ teaspoon ginger

Mix all ingredients except lamb; pour over lamb and marinate for 4 to 6 hours. Arrange on skewers with tomatoes and pineapple chunks that have been marinated in oil and green peppers, mushrooms, onions and potatoes that have been marinated in a mixture of salt, pepper and paprika. Turn and baste frequently. Broil or grill over charcoal 3-4 inches from heat about 15 to 25 minutes. Makes 2 to 3 servings.

Irene Kaplow, Lake County Region

SAVORY LAMB SHANKS

4 lamb shanks
½ cup flour
Fat
1 teaspoon paprika
2 teaspoons salt
¼ teaspoon ginger
½ teaspoon pepper
½ teaspoon celery salt
¼ teaspoon cloves
½ teaspoon garlic salt
3 cups water or 1 16-oz. can tomatoes

Wipe shanks with damp cloth. Dredge in flour and brown in hot fat. Place shanks in casserole. Pour off all but 2 tablespoons fat. Add seasonings and balance of flour to water. Cook slowly until slightly thickened and pour over shanks. Cover and bake at 350° for 1½ hours or until tender. Add more water if necessary. Canned tomatoes can be substituted for water. Makes 4 servings.

Rosabelle Perrye, Chicago Region

LAMB SHANKS WITH MINT JELLY

- 1 large onion, chopped
- 1 clove garlic, minced
- 1 cup catsup
- 3 tablespoons butter
- 1 cup water
- ½ cup mint jelly
- 2 tablespoons lemon juice
- ¼ cup brown sugar
- 1 tablespoon vinegar
- 4 lamb shanks

Brown onion and garlic in butter. Add remaining ingredients. Place shanks in dutch oven and cover with sauce. Bake at 300° for 2½ to 3 hours. Makes 4 servings.

Sandy Rosen, Northern Illinois Region

LAMB CHOPS ORIENTAL

- 6 lamb shoulder chops, about 1-inch thick
- ½ cup soy sauce
- ½ cup peach syrup
- ¼ teaspoon garlic powder or 1 clove garlic, minced
- 6 peach halves, canned

Score fat edges of chops; place in shallow baking dish. Combine soy sauce, peach syrup and garlic in measuring cup; pour over lamb. Cover with plastic wrap and marinate, refrigerated several hours or overnight. Arrange chops on rack in broiler pan or over charcoal grill. Broil about 10 minutes on one side. Turn and place peaches, hollow side up on rack with chops. Brush chops with remaining marinate. Makes 4 to 6 servings.

Mrs. Jerome Segal, Indianapolis Chapter-at-Large

LAMB AND VEGETABLE CASSEROLE

- 4 onions, sliced
- 2 tablespoons cooking oil
- 1½ pounds lamb, cubed
- 3 green peppers, diced
- 1 teaspoon salt
- 1 teaspoon pepper
- 1 teaspoon paprika
- 2 small potatoes
- 1½ cups green beans
- 1½ cups peas
- 1½ cups tomatoes

Fry onions in oil until brown. Place in casserole with lamb and peppers. Season and bake at 325° until lamb is tender, about 30 to 40 minutes. Add vegetables, cover and bake 30 minutes longer. Makes 4 to 6 servings.

Rosabelle Perrye, Chicago Region

SHELLEY'S LAMB CURRY

- 3 pounds lamb, cut into cubes (use leg of lamb or chops)
- 2 tablespoons flour
- 2 tablespoons curry powder
- 1 teaspoon salt
- 2 onions, sliced
- 1 apple (with skin), chopped
- 1/2 teaspoon garlic powder
- 2 1/2 teaspoons brown sugar
- 2 tablespoons ginger
- 1 tablespoon worcestershire sauce
- 1 lemon with rind, sliced
- 1/3 cup walnuts
- 2 cups water

Dredge lamb in mixture of flour, curry powder and salt. Brown in skillet; add remaining ingredients and simmer 1 hour. May be served over rice, or with bowls of chopped peanuts, coconut and chutney. Makes 8 to 10 servings.

Gert Kaufman, Northern Illinois Region

LAMB CHOPS WITH VEGETABLE SAUCE

- 1/2 cup flour
- 1 teaspoon salt
- 1/4 teaspoon pepper
- 8 shoulder lamb chops
- 3 tablespoons butter
- 2/3 cup diced celery
- 2/3 cup sliced carrots
- 2/3 cup chopped chives
- 2 16-oz. cans stewed tomatoes

Mix flour, salt and pepper and lightly coat chops. Using butter, saute celery, carrots and chives for 5 minutes. Brown lamb in same pan. Add tomatoes and cook over low heat for about 45 minutes, or until tender. Can be baked at 350° in a roaster layering meat, vegetables and tomatoes. Serve with rice or mashed potatoes. Makes 8 servings.

Diana Saunders, Lake County Region

VEAL STEAKS

- 10 veal steaks
- 1/3 cup peanut oil
- 1 1/2 cups consomme
- 3/4 cup Sherry
- 2 teaspoons dry onion soup mix
- 2 tablespoons flour mixed with water to a smooth paste

Brown veal in oil and arrange in casserole. In skillet, blend oil, consomme, Sherry, onion soup mix and flour. Cook until thickened. Pour over steaks and bake at 350° for 1 hour. Serve over noodles or rice. Can be frozen or prepared ahead. Makes 8 to 10 servings.

Diana Saunders, Lake County Region

VEAL PAPRIKA

- 2 slices veal steaks, paper thin
- 1 onion, sliced
- Butter
- 4 tablespoons flour
- 1 teaspoon salt
- 1 teaspoon paprika
- ½ teaspoon dry mustard
- ½ teaspoon garlic powder
- ⅛ teaspoon ginger
- ¼ teaspoon pepper
- 3 teaspoons catsup
- ¼ cup water
- ¼ cup white wine
- ½ cup dairy sour cream

Saute onions in butter until translucent. Cut veal into serving portions and dredge in flour, salt and paprika. Add veal to pan with onions and brown. Add seasonings and ¼ cup water. Cover and simmer for 12 minutes. Add wine and sour cream and cook 5 minutes longer. Prepare in large skillet. Makes 4 servings.

Rosalie Gellman, Milwaukee Region

VEAL JULIENNE

- 1½ pound veal steak cut into strips
- 4 tablespoons butter
- ½ cup water
- 1 teaspoon basil
- 1 green pepper, diced
- 1 cup thinly sliced onions
- 1 6-oz. can sliced mushrooms, drained
- 1 15-oz. can tomato sauce
- ½ cup sliced water chestnuts
- Few drops hot pepper sauce
- 1 teaspoon worcestershire sauce
- Salt
- Pepper
- ½ cup dry Sherry
- 1 cup dairy sour cream

Brown veal strips slowly in 2 tablespoons of butter, stirring often to prevent sticking. Add water and basil; simmer 20 minutes. Meanwhile, cook green pepper and onions in remaining 2 tablespoons butter until soft, but not brown; add to veal with mushrooms, tomato sauce and water chestnuts. Mix well. Simmer 15 minutes longer. Stir in hot pepper sauce, worcestershire sauce, salt, pepper and Sherry. Simmer 5 minutes over low heat. Stir in sour cream slowly. Makes 6 servings.

Claire Palmer, Lake County Region

VEAL CUTLETS

- 2 pounds veal cutlets
- 2 tablespoons butter, melted
- 1/4 cup olive or other oil
- 1 cup chopped celery
- 1 cup diced carrots
- 2/3 cup chopped onion
- 1 tablespoon chopped parsley
- 1 cup dry Sherry
- 1 tablespoon tomato paste
- Salt
- Pepper

Combine melted butter and oil in hot skillet. Place cutlets in skillet and brown on both sides. Add celery, carrots, parsley, salt and pepper. Cover and simmer 10 to 15 minutes. Mix Sherry and tomato paste and stir mixture into pan. Cover and simmer gently until cutlets are tender. If desired, gravy can be thinned with a little soup stock. Makes 6 servings.

Lee Bateman, Lake County Region

VEAL PARMESAN

- 6 veal cutlets
- 1 green onion, chopped
- 2 tablespoons oil
- 1 8-oz. can tomato paste
- 1 tablepoon sugar
- 2 tablespoons oregano
- 2 tablespoons basil
- 1 teaspoon salt
- 1/4 teaspoon pepper
- 1 cup boiling water
- 1 egg
- 1/2 cup bread crumbs
- 1/2 teaspoon salt
- 1/4 teaspoon pepper
- 3 tablespoons Parmesan cheese
- 4 tablespoons oil
- Mozzarella cheese

Cook onion in oil. Add tomato paste; stir for 5 minutes. Add sugar, seasonings and water. Simmer 30 minutes. Blend bread crumbs with seasonings and cheese; dip veal into egg and then into bread crumbs. Brown in oil. Pour tomato sauce over top. Cover and bake at 350° for 1 hour. Arrange mozzarella cheese slices over top and bake until melted. Makes 6 servings.

Myra Ladley, Lake County Region

VEAL SCALLOPINE WITH PEPPERS

1 pound veal scallops
¼ cup flour
2 tablespoons olive oil
¼ cup dry white wine
4 green or red peppers, sliced thin and lightly sauteed
1 8-oz. can tomatoes, drained
1½ teaspoons salt
¼ teaspoon freshly ground pepper
⅛ teaspoon oregano

Pound the veal very thin. Dip in flour. Heat oil in skillet; brown veal on both sides. Add the wine; cook over medium heat until evaporated. Add peppers, tomatoes, salt, pepper and oregano. Cook over low heat for 20 minutes. Can be prepared in advance and reheated. Makes 4 servings.

Joyce Goodman, Chicago Region

VEAL SCALLOPINE

1½ pounds veal cutlets
Sugar
¼ cup flour
Salt
Pepper
2 tablespoons olive oil
1 clove garlic
½ cup sauterne or chablis
½ cup water
2 teaspoons lemon juice

Cut ¼ inch thick cutlets into small pieces. Roll in flour seasoned with salt and pepper. Heat oil with garlic in heavy pan. Saute meat until browned. Remove garlic. Add wine, water and lemon juice, cover and simmer until tender, about 30 minutes. Serve with steamed rice. Garnish with parsley. Makes 4 servings.

Rosabelle Perrye, Chicago Region

DELUXE VEAL PARMESAN

- 1 package dry spaghetti sauce mix
- 1 8-oz. can tomato sauce
- 1½ cups water
- 1 teaspoon seasoned salt
- 1½ lbs. veal round steak, ¼ inch thick
- 2 eggs, beaten
- ¼ cup grated Parmesan cheese
- ¼ cup cracker crumbs or matzo meal
- ¼ cup salad oil
- ½ lb. Mozzarella cheese, sliced thin
- 1 8-oz. package spaghetti, cooked

Place spaghetti sauce mix in saucepan. Add tomato sauce, water and seasoned salt. Mix thoroughly; simmer 20 minutes. Cut meat into serving portions. Dip into egg that has been beaten, then into Parmesan cheese mixed with cracker crumbs. Fry coated veal in salad oil until golden brown.

Place pieces in a 12x8-inch baking dish. Pour sauce over meat and top generously with slices of Mozzarella cheese. Bake at 350° for 15 minutes. Move meat to one side and add cooked spaghetti. Spoon sauce over spaghetti. Continue baking 15 minutes longer or until meat is tender. Makes 6 servings.

Mrs. Jerome Segal, Indianapolis Chapter-at-Large

SPECIAL BARBECUE SAUCE I

- 1 teaspoon vanilla
- 1 teaspoon salt
- 1 teaspoon pepper
- 2 teaspoons dry mustard
- 1 small onion, grated
- 5 tablespoons brown sugar
- 3 tablespoons worcestershire sauce
- ½ cup vinegar
- ½ bottle catsup
- 1 10½-oz. can tomato puree
- 1 cup water
- 1 teaspoon horseradish

Combine all ingredients in a 3-quart heavy saucepan. Heat to boiling; lower heat and simmer for 30 minutes. Keeps well in refrigerator.

Temie Greenberg, Lake County Region

BAKED LEMON CHICKEN

- 1 2½-3 lb. broiler-fryer
- ½ cup flour
- 1¼ teaspoons salt
- 1 teaspoon leaf tarragon, crumbled
- 1 stick butter or margarine
- ⅓ cup lemon juice
- 1 tablespoon minced onion
- 1 clove of garlic, mashed
- ⅛ teaspoon pepper

Cut chicken in serving pieces. Combine flour, 1 teaspoon salt and tarragon in a plastic bag. Shake chicken in flour to coat; tap off excess. Melt butter in a 13x9-inch baking pan. Coat chicken on all sides in butter, then turn piece skin-side up. Bake at 350° brushing often with pan drippings, 30 minutes. Meanwhile make lemon baste: Mix lemon juice, instant minced onion, garlic and remaining salt and pepper in a small bowl. Brush chicken pieces with part of the lemon baste. Bake, brushing occasionally with remaining lemon baste, 30 minutes or longer, or until chicken is tender.

Mrs. Selwyn Schwartz, West Suburban Region

CHERRIED CHICKEN

- 2 large fryers, cut up
- Seasoned salt
- 2 12-oz. jars cherry preserves
- 1 can water
- 1 6-oz. can concentrated orange juice
- ¾ stick margarine
- ½ cup dry vermouth

Season chicken with seasoned salt. Combined ingredients for sauce in saucepan. Bring to boil and simmer for 15 minutes (stirring). Place chicken skin side down in shallow roasting pan. Bake, uncovered, at 350° for 45 minutes. Baste, turn chicken and bake additional 30 to 40 minutes. Baste every 10 minutes. Makes 8 servings.

Bonnie Kaplan, West Suburban Region

CHICKEN ITALIANO

1 chicken, cut into serving pieces
½ cup Italian dressing
Dash of paprika
Salt and pepper
14-oz. can sliced mushrooms, drained
⅓ cup grated Parmesan cheese

Brush chicken pieces with about 2 tablespoons of Italian dressing. In large baking pan, place chicken skin side down; cover with remaining dressing and sprinkle lightly with paprika, salt and pepper. Bake at 350° for 30 minutes. Turn chicken, add cheese and paprika. Bake until brown 20 or 30 minutes. Then add mushrooms and bake another 10 or 15 minutes. Makes 4 servings.

Lillian Neimark, Northern Illinois Region

CHICKEN APRICOT

1 chicken, cut up
⅔ cup water
12-oz. jar apricot preserves
1 envelope dry onion soup
1 jar Wishbone Russian Dressing

Put chicken in shallow baking pan skin side down. Combine rest of ingredients. Spread half of sauce on chicken. Bake at 325° for 25 minutes. Turn chicken over and add rest of sauce. Continue baking about 50 to 60 minutes or until done. Can be frozen or prepared in advance. Makes 4 servings.

Mrs. Hal Levin, Des Moines Chapter-at-Large

CHICKEN CURRY

1 3-lb. chicken, cut up
2 teaspoons sugar
2 tablespoons butter
½ large onion
2 garlic cloves
2 tablespoons curry
1 tablespoon pepper
½ tablespoon salt
½ cup pineapple juice
½ cup raisins
1 tablespoon orange peel
¼ cup cooking sherry

Brown sugar, add butter, onion, garlic, curry powder, salt and pepper. Fry chicken separately until golden brown, mix with the sauce and add remaining ingredients; cook until chicken is tender. Serve with curry rice. Excellent party dish. Makes 4 servings.

Dina Kijner, Milwaukee Region

CHICKEN CASHEW

3 fryers, cut up
1 tablespoon monosodium glutamate (MSG)
½ onion

Sauce:
½ cup honey
¼ cup soy sauce
1 tablespoon wine vinegar
1½ cups peach juice, from can of peaches
Peach slices
12-oz. salted cashews

Bake chicken, sprinkled with MSG, with onion and small amount of water ½ hour at 350 degrees. Pour sauce made by combining honey, soy, vinegar and peach juice, over chicken and bake another ½ hour. Place peach slices on chicken, baste from time to time for ½ hour; add cashews and bake ½ hour, basting occasionally. This recipe reheats well either in oven or in saucepan. Makes 10 to 12 servings.

Mrs. Murray Peshkin, West Suburban Region

CHICKEN CASSEROLE DIVAN

1 fryer, cut up
1¼ teaspoons salt, divided
2 tablespoons margarine
1½ cups shell macaroni, cooked
1 10-oz. package broccoli, thawed
1 can cream of mushroom soup
1 cup milk
2 tablespoons grated Parmesan cheese

Sprinkle chicken with 1 teaspoon salt. Heat margarine in skillet, add chicken and brown both sides. Put shell macaroni in 2½-qt. casserole. Add thawed broccoli and sprinkle with remaining salt. Top with browned chicken pieces. Pour blend of soup and milk over mixture in casserole. Bake, covered, in 375° oven for 50 to 60 minutes, until chicken is tender. Serve sprinkled with grated Parmesan.

Patricia Kaplan, St. Louis Region

CHICKEN CACCIATORE

3 pounds chicken pieces
¼ cup olive oil
2 cloves garlic, split
½ cup chopped onions
1 16-oz. can Italian peeled tomatoes
1 8-oz. can tomato sauce
1 6-oz. can tomato paste
½ cup dry white wine
1 bay leaf
½ teaspoon thyme
¼ teaspoon margarine
1 teaspoon salt
Dash pepper

Saute chicken in oil and garlic until golden brown. When chicken is brown, remove garlic and add the remaining ingredients. Cover and simmer for 1 hour, or until chicken is tender. Remove cover and allow sauce to reduce somewhat. Serve with spaghetti. Makes 4 servings.

Audrey Rosenberg, Des Moines, Chapter-at-Large

HONEYED CHICKEN

¼ cup butter
½ cup honey
¼ cup prepared mustard
1 teaspoon salt
1 teaspoon curry powder
1 3-lb. fryer, cut up

Melt butter in a shallow 3-quart baking dish over moderate low heat. Stir in honey, mustard, salt and curry. Roll chicken pieces in mixture and arrange in a single layer in the baking dish. Bake in pre-heated 375° oven for 1 hour, or until fork tender. Makes 4 to 5 servings.

Jean Goldrosen, Northern Illinois Region

LEMON CHICKEN

1 chicken, cut up
1 tablespoon butter
Salt and pepper
⅓ cup fresh lemon juice
2 cloves garlic, crushed
1 tablespoon dried oregano

Preheat oven to 375°. Wash chicken, towel dry. Place chicken in a shallow pan; dot with butter. Sprinkle with ½ teaspoon salt, dash of pepper. Bake uncovered 1 hour in small container; mix remaining ingredients, pour over chicken. Bake 15 minutes or longer until tender. Spoon drippings over chicken. Makes 4 servings.

Phillis Wexler, Milwaukee Region

CHICKEN VESUVIO

2 chickens, cut up
4 potatoes, cut lengthwise into ½ strips
½ cup olive oil
1 cup sauterne wine
½ cup chicken stock
1 teaspoon oregano
2 cloves garlic, finely chopped

In a baking pan saute chicken and potatoes in olive oil until golden brown, strain off oil. Pour a mixture of wine, chicken stock, oregano and garlic over chicken. Cover and place in 425° oven 1 hour, or until tender. This recipe can be prepared in advance.

Elaine Achler, Northern Illinois Region

SAVORY CHICKEN BARBECUE SAUCE

½ cup salad oil
1¼ cups water
2 tablespoons chopped onion
1 clove garlic, crushed
1½ teaspoons sugar
1 teaspoon salt
1 teaspoon chili powder
1 teaspoon paprika
1 teaspoon pepper
½ teaspoon dry mustard
Dash of cayenne
2 tablespoons vinegar
1 teaspoon worcestershire sauce
1 teaspoon Tabasco sauce

Combine all ingredients in a saucepan; simmer for 30 minutes. Use as basting sauce for broiled or rotisseried chicken.

Karen Harris, Chicago Region

CHIPPER CHICKEN

1 medium bag of potato chips
¼ cup butter or margarine
1 teaspoon garlic salt
1 teaspoon salt
⅛ teaspoon pepper
1 3-lb. cut up fryer

Crush chips finely. Melt butter in frying pan and add seasonings. Roll chicken in seasoned butter, then in chips. Place chicken in shallow pan (oblong) skin side up; do not turn. Bake at 350° for 1½ hours. Can be prepared in advance. Makes 4 servings.

Ilene Levin, West Suburban Region

CHICKEN PINEAPPLE

- 1 chicken, cut up, or 6 chicken breasts
- Seasoned salt
- ½ stick butter
- 1 15-oz. can crushed pineapple
- 1 8-oz. can mushrooms and juice
- 1 green pepper (sliced)
- Dash of ginger
- 1 tablespoon soy sauce

Season chicken with salt and dot with butter. Broil until browned on both sides. Place chicken in casserole; add pineapple, mushrooms, green pepper, a dash of ginger and soy sauce. Bake at 350° for 45 minutes, or until tender. This recipe can be frozen. Makes 4 servings.

Mrs. Jerry Harper, Kansas City Region

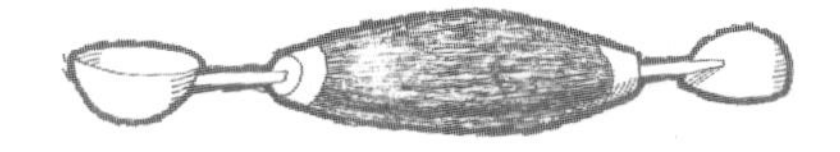

CHICKEN WITH RICE

- 1 3-lb. frying chicken, cut up
- 1 10½-oz. can cream of chicken soup
- 1¼ cans water
- 1 cup Converted rice (Uncle Ben's)
- 1 medium onion, diced
- 1 rib celery, diced
- 1 teaspoon margarine
- 1 teaspoon dry onion soup mix

Season chicken as you wish. Blend soup with water and rice. Saute onion and celery in margarine; add dry onion soup mix for flavoring. Combine with rice mixture and turn into a 12x9-inch baking dish. Top with chicken, skin side up. Bake at 350° for 1½ hours. About 10 minutes before chicken is done, remove from oven, brush skin of chicken with margarine for crisp skin. Can be prepared in advance. Makes 4 servings.

Mrs. Rae Marks, Milwaukee Region

EASY OVEN BAKED CHICKEN

2 3-lb. fryers, cut up
1 stick butter or margarine, melted
Seasoned salt
½ cup orange juice
½ cup brown sugar
½ cup catsup
½ cup sherry
1 can pineapple chunks

Dip chicken pieces in melted shortening. Season with seasoned salt. Place in shallow roasting pan (do not crowd). Bake in 325° oven for 1 hour. Combine rest of ingredients and simmer for about 5 minutes. Turn chicken skin side up, pour on sauce and fruit and bake another half hour, or until done. Can be frozen or prepared in advance. Makes 8 servings.

Ann Kalnitz, Chicago Region

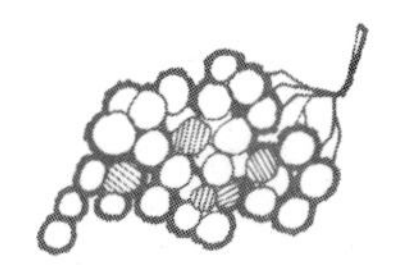

GOURMET BAKED CHICKEN

1 10½-oz. can cream of chicken soup
1 10½-oz. can cream of mushroom soup
1 soup can water
1¼ cups uncooked rice
1 3½-lb. chicken, disjointed or 6 chicken breasts
Salt
Pepper
¼ cup blanched, slivered, toasted almonds

Blend soups with water. Reserve 1 cup of mixture. Blend remaining soup mixture with rice and turn into a greased 2½-quart shallow baking dish. Arrange chicken over rice; season with salt and pepper. Top with reserved soup mixture. Bake at 350° for 1¾ hours (uncovered), or until rice is cooked and chicken is tender. Top with almonds and serve. Makes 4 to 6 servings.

Phyllis Galst, Milwaukee Region

HERBED CHICKEN

3 large chicken breasts, split, or 6 legs and thighs
Salt
Pepper
Garlic salt
1/4 cup butter

Sauce:
1 can condensed cream of chicken soup
3/4 cup sauterne
1/4 teaspoon thyme
1 5-oz. can water chestnuts
1/4 lb. mushrooms
2 tablespoons minced green pepper

Season chicken parts; brown in butter. Blend sauce ingredients. Mix into chicken drippings. Bake 350° for 25 minutes covered. Bake for 35 minutes uncovered. Makes 6 servings.

Carol Linch, Lake County Region

SHERRY CHICKEN

1 3-lb. fryer, cut up
1/2 cup flour
Salt
Pepper
Oil
1 package onion soup mix
1 cup water
1 cup cream Sherry
Garlic powder
Mushrooms (optional)

Coat chicken with seasoned flour. Brown in oil. Remove chicken from pan and drain oil. Mix water, soup mix and garlic powder to taste. Heat to boiling in skillet and then add cream Sherry; return chicken to pan with mushrooms. Simmer 1 hour or until chicken is tender. Serve over plain or wild rice. Sauce will thicken.

Sharon Sak, Indianapolis Chapter-at-Large

OVEN BARBECUED CHICKEN

- 2 frying chickens, quartered
- 1 cup each: catsup, orange juice
- 2 tablespoons each: brown sugar, salad oil, worcestershire sauce
- 1 4-oz. can sliced mushrooms
- 2 teaspoons salt
- 1 clove garlic, mashed
- 1 tablespoon prepared mustard

Place chicken pieces, skin sides up, in a shallow pan. Combine remaining ingredients; cook until it boils. Pour half of sauce over chicken. Bake in a 350° oven uncovered for 30 minutes, pour remaining sauce over chicken. Bake 30 minutes longer. Makes 8 servings.

Fay Nicholas, Northern Illinois Region

SWEET AND SOUR CHICKEN

- 2 fryers, cut up
- 1 small bottle Open Pit barbecue sauce
- 1 small can pineapple juice
- 3/4 cup brown or white sugar

In a saucepan, mix barbecue sauce, pineapple juice and sugar. Simmer and add more sugar to taste. Simmer until all sugar dissolves. Pour sauce over chicken that has been put in baking pan (single layer). Bake uncovered for 2 hours at 350°. (The sauce adheres to chicken better if made ahead and reheated before putting on chicken.) Variation: Chicken can be cut into bite-size pieces and used as an appetizer. (Bake for 1½ hours.)

Enid Schultz, Lake County Region

SWEET AND TART CHICKEN

- 2 chickens, cut up
- Salt, pepper, garlic powder
- 1 jar Reese sweet & tart sauce
- 3/4 cup white wine
- 1/4 cup catsup

Season chickens. Brown in frying pan. Mix the sauce, wine and catsup in a small pot. Heat through and add to chicken. Simmer for 1 hour, covered. Makes 8 servings.

Elaine Achler, Northern Illinois Region

OVEN FRIED CHICKEN WITH LEMON

- 2 frying chickens, cut up
- Salt
- 2 eggs, beaten
- 1 cup crumbs*
- ½ cup grated Parmesan cheese
- ¼ teaspoon ginger (optional)
- ½ cup vegetable shortening
- Lemon wedges

Rub chicken pieces with salt. Dip pieces in egg and then a mixture of crumbs, cheese and ginger. Chill for about 30 minutes. Heat shortening in deep heavy skillet; brown chicken pieces. Transfer chicken to roasting pan or cooky sheet and complete baking at 400° for 20 to 25 minutes. Serve with lemon wedges. Lemon juice should be pressed over the chicken at the table. The flavor is delicious.

*Grated french bread crumbs add a gourmet touch. They are commercially available.

Gilda Lesser, Lake County Region

OVEN GLAZED CHICKEN

- 2 frying chickens, cut up
- ½ cup salad oil
- 1 tablespoon grated orange rind
- ½ cup orange juice
- 1 teaspoon salt
- 1 teaspoon dry mustard
- 1 teaspoon paprika
- ¼ teaspoon Tabasco sauce

Arrange chicken in single layer in large shallow baking pan; brush well with mixture of salad oil, orange rind and juice and seasonings. Bake at 425°, basting often with orange mixture for 45 minutes, or until chicken is tender and glazed a rich golden color. Can be frozen or prepared in advance. Makes 6 to 8 servings.

Anne Ring, Lake County Region

CHICKEN BREASTS SUSANNE

- 1 egg
- 1 cup of packaged herb stuffing mix
- 1 tablespoon lemon juice
- 2 teaspoons worcestershire sauce
- 1 teaspoon prepared mustard
- ½ teaspoon salt
- ½ can condensed cream of mushroom soup
- ¼ cup sherry (more if needed to thin out stuffing)
- 1 7-oz. can crabmeat
- 8 boned chicken breasts
- Salt
- Pepper
- 1 stick butter, melted

Beat egg lightly and add next 7 ingredients. Flake crab meat and toss together with the stuffing mixture. Divide equally on each of the 8 chicken breasts. Roll up and secure with thin bamboo skewers. Baste each breast with melted butter or margarine and put on baking pan in 400° oven for approximately 45 minutes, basting occasionally with the pan drippings or more melted butter as needed. During the last 10 minutes pour some of the mushhroom sauce over each breast. Serve with remaining sauce on the side. Can be prepared in advance by stuffing breasts early in the day but not cooking ahead of time. Makes 8 servings.

Mushroom Sauce:

- ½ pound chopped fresh mushrooms
- 1 can condensed cream of mushroom soup plus remaining ½ can from stuffing
- Sherry, enough to give sauce desired thinness

Heat 1½ cans soup, undiluted. Add chopped mushrooms and cook, covered 5 minutes. Add Sherry as needed, stir and heat gently before serving. Use heavy 2-qt. saucepan with lid. Can be prepared day ahead.

Ruth Weissman, Lake County Region

CHICKEN GRANDE'

- 3 chicken breasts, skinned and boned
- 1 egg
- 2 tablespoons evaporated milk
- 1½ cup corn flake crumbs
- ½ cup flour
- ¼ teaspoon garlic powder
- Salt
- Pepper
- 1 can cream of celery or cream of chicken or cream of mushroom soup
- ½ cup milk
- 6 oz. Mozzarella or Swiss cheese, sliced

Place boned chicken breasts between two sheets wax paper and flatten by pounding gently with edge of plate. Mix egg and evaporated milk. Mix crumbs and flour and seasonings. Dip breasts in egg mixture, then in corn flake mixture. Brown in small quantity of shortening on both sides. Place browned chicken in shallow Pyrex dish. Combine soup and milk, pour over chicken. Bake in 350° oven for about 30 minutes. Then cover with slices of cheese and place back in oven until cheese melts and serve. Makes 6 servings.

Ruth Ostreicher, Chicago Region

CHICKEN VERONIQUE

- 2 tablespoons flour
- ½ teaspoon salt
- ½ teaspoon black pepper
- 8 chicken breasts, boned if desired
- ¼ cup oil
- 1 cup dry white wine
- ⅔ cup orange juice
- 4 tablespoons honey
- 2 tablespoons chopped parsley
- 4 tablespoons slivered orange peel
- 2 cups seedless white grapes

Combine flour, salt and pepper. Use to lightly dust chicken. Brown chicken in oil in large skillet. Place chicken in a single layer in a large pan. Combine wine, honey, juice and parsley. Pour over chicken. Bake in 325° oven for 1½ hours, or until golden. Baste often with sauce. Remove chicken to platter and add orange peel and grapes to sauce in pan. Cook 5 minutes. Then pour over chicken. Garnish with grapes and orange slices. If desired, prepare extra sauce and serve with chicken. Makes 4 to 5 servings.

Beverly Braun, Northern Illinois Region

ROYAL FRIED CHICKEN

- 4 chicken breasts, split
- 1 teaspoon salt
- 1/4 teaspoon pepper
- 1/3 cup flour
- 1 egg, well beaten
- 2 cups coarse fresh bread crumbs
- 1/4 cup salad oil
- 1/4 cup butter

Sauce:

- 3/4 cup butter or margarine
- 1 clove garlic, minced
- 1 teaspoon rosemary
- 1 tablespoon minced parsley
- 2 tablespoons minced green onions and tops
- 1 teaspoon worcestershire sauce
- 1/2 teaspoon salt
- 1/4 teaspoon pepper

Remove skin and bone chicken. Dredge in seasoned flour. Mix egg and water; dip chicken in mixture. Coat with bread crumbs. Brown on both sides in oil and butter. Place in a shallow baking pan. Baste with sauce once while baking. Pour remaining sauce over chicken before serving. Bake in 350° oven for 45 minutes. Can be frozen or prepared in advance. Makes 4 servings.

Jane E. Sanders, Northern Illinois Region

CHICKEN BASQUE

- 1 lb. hot Italian sausage
- 1 cup water
- 2 green peppers julienned
- 2 cloves crushed garlic
- 1 32-oz. can whole tomatoes, drained
- 1 8-oz. can tomato sauce
- 2 teaspoons paprika
- 1 teaspoon oregano
- 1 teaspoon salt
- 1/4 teaspoon pepper
- 3 cups cooked chicken, cut into large pieces

Prick sausage skins; place in large skillet and cover with water; bring to a boil and cook 10 minutes. Drain and cut into 1/4-inch slices. Return to skillet and cook over medium low heat 10 minutes, until lightly browned. Add green peppers and garlic; cook 5 minutes until peppers are tender. Stir in tomatoes, tomato sauce and seasonings. Mix well, then add chicken; mix well to blend. Cover and cook 15 minutes, serve over noodles. Makes 6 servings.

B. Rosen, Northern Illinois Region

CHICKEN CURRY

- 3 tablespoons butter
- 1/4 cup minced onion
- 1-1 1/2 teaspoons curry powder
- 4 rounded tablespoons flour
- 3/4 teaspoon salt
- 3/4 teaspoon sugar
- 1/8 teaspoon ground ginger
- 1 cup chicken broth
- 1 cup milk
- 2 cups diced cooked chicken
- 1/2 teaspoon lemon juice
- 4 cups cooked rice
- Slivered almonds

Melt butter in 3-quart saucepan. Saute onion and curry in melted butter. Blend in flour and seasonings. Cook over low heat until mixture is smooth. Remove from heat. Stir in chicken broth; add milk gradually to keep smooth consistency. Bring to a boil, stirring constantly, and boil 1 minute. Add chicken and lemon juice. Heat; serve on bed of rice. Garnish with slivered almonds. Sauce may be prepared in advance. Add chicken and lemon juice before serving and heat. Makes 4 servings.

Mrs. Ervin Colton, Milwaukee Region

CHICKEN PILAF

- 1/8 cup cooking Sherry
- 1 10 1/2-oz. can condensed cream of mushroom soup
- 1 1/2 cups boiling water
- 1 package dry onion soup mix
- 1 1/2 cups quick-cooking rice
- 1 2-oz. jar chopped pimento
- 5 small chicken breasts (can substitute with any parts you desire)
- 1/4 stick butter
- Seasoned salt
- Monosodium glutamate
- Garlic salt or powder
- Salt
- Pepper
- Paprika

In a casserole (big Corningware roasting pan works out well) combine first 6 ingredients (DO NOT COOK RICE FIRST). Lay chicken out on a cookie sheet or platter. Brush with melted butter and season with above seasonings using paprika last. Place chicken on top of rice mixture in roasting casserole. Cover casserole with aluminum foil and bake at 375° for about 1 1/4 hours, or until chicken and rice are tender. When it is done rice will not be fluffy so expect it to be of mushy consistency. Makes 4 to 5 servings.

Roberta Jacobson, Chicago Region

CHICKEN CASSEROLE ELEGANTE

- 6 lbs. - 7 lbs. chicken
- 1 cup dry Sherry
- 1 pound fresh mushrooms
- ¼ cup butter
- 2 packages long grain and wild rice with seasoning
- 1½ teaspoon salt
- ½ teaspoon curry powder
- 1 medium onion, shredded
- ½ cup diced celery
- ¼ cup sliced water chestnuts
- 1 can mushroom soup
- 1 cup dairy sour cream

Simmer chicken 1 hour in water with 1 cup Sherry. Retain and strain the broth. Bone chicken and cut in bite size pieces. Saute mushrooms in ¼ cup butter. Cook rice according to directions, using chicken broth as liquid. Combine the chicken, rice, most of the mushrooms, salt, curry powder, onion, celery, water chestnuts, undiluted mushroom soup and sour cream. Garnish casserole with remaining mushrooms. Place in buttered casserole. Bake at 350° for 1 hour. This can be prepared the last minute simply by adding the sour cream before baking. Everything else can be done early. Makes 8 servings.

Toni Urban, Des Moines Chapter-at-Large

CHICKEN ENCHILADA CASSEROLE

- 12 corn tortillas, quartered and deep-fried crisp
- ½ lb. grated Cheddar cheese
- 2 cans green chili, chopped
- 2 cups cubed chicken
- ¼ cup chopped onion
- 1 10½-oz. can mushroom soup
- 1½ cups chicken broth

Mix cheese, chili and onion. Mix chicken, soup, broth; add to first mixture. Alternate layers of tortillas and mixture in large greased casserole; bake at 350° until bubbly, about 45 minutes. Makes 6 to 8 servings.

Jerelyn Eisenberg, Northern Illinois Region

ISRAELI STUFFED CHICKEN

- 1 whole chicken fryer
- 1 tablespoon oil
- 1 small onion, chopped
- 4 mushrooms, chopped
- 3 tablespoons toasted almonds, chopped
- 1 slice white bread
- 1 chicken liver, broiled and chopped
- 1 small apple, grated
- 1 tablespoon parsley, chopped
- 1 teaspoon salt
- ½ teaspoon paprika
- ½ teaspoon mustard
- 1 egg, separated
- ½ cup orange juice

Heat oil in skillet; add onion and cook until tender; add mushrooms and almonds and simmer for 5 minutes. Soak bread in small amount of water, press out excess and add bread and liver to sauteed mixture. Add apple, parsley, salt, paprika, mustard and egg yolk; blend. Beat egg white and add to mixture. Rub chicken inside and out with orange juice. Stuff chicken. Sprinkle chicken with remaining salt, pepper and paprika. Place chicken in roasting pan, pour orange juice over all, cover with foil and bake covered 1 hour in a 375° oven. Makes 4 servings.

Florence Sager, Lake County Region

TURKEY CURRY WITH GRAPES

- ¾ cup chopped onion
- ½ cup chopped celery
- ¼ cup margarine
- ¼ cup flour
- 1 to 2 teaspoons curry powder
- ¼ teaspoon ginger
- 2 cups turkey or chicken broth
- 2 cups slivered cooked turkey or chicken
- Salt and pepper
- ½ cup halved seeded green grapes
- Hot cooked rice
- Grapes for garnish

Saute onion and celery in margarine until tender. Stir in flour and spices; add broth. Cook, stirring constantly, until thickened. Add turkey, salt and pepper to taste. Simmer about 5 minutes; stir in halved grapes. Serve over rice; garnish with more grapes. Makes 4 to 6 servings.

Lee Bateman, Lake County Region

CHICKEN LIVERS SUPREME

1½ pounds chicken livers
¼ cup sifted flour
½ teaspoon salt
⅛ teaspoon pepper
1 onion, sliced
2 tablespoons margarine or oil
1 4-oz. can sliced mushrooms, undrained
1½ teaspoons worcestershire sauce

Coat chicken livers with seasoned flour. In skillet, saute onion in oil. Add mushrooms and cook a few minutes. Remove from pan; add chicken livers and cook until brown. Return onions and mushrooms to pan, add worcestershire, cover pan and cook slowly for 10 minutes. Makes 4 servings.

Elaine Achler, Northern Illinois Region

BEER-BASTED DUCKLING

1 4-5 lb. duckling
1 clove garlic
1 teaspoon salt
2 tablespoons curry powder
¼ teaspoon pepper
6-oz. beer
¼ teaspoon salt
⅛ cup brown sugar

Prepare 2 pans (broiler pan with rack and small roaster) by lining with heavy foil. Thaw duckling, rinse and dry. Put necks and giblets in saucepan with water and seasonings as you wish. Simmer to make fine, rich broth. Crush the garlic in the salt and add curry and pepper. Rub duck inside and out with mixture. Tie the feet and bind wings with string. Place on rack in pan. Roast at 350° for 1 hour. Remove from oven; transfer to roaster. Baste with sauce combining beer, salt and brown sugar. Return to oven, roast 1¼ hours; baste occasionally. Duck should be beautifully brown and leg joints should move easily. Add broth from giblets and drippings in pan to make desired amount of gravy. Stir and simmer until slightly thickened.

Patricia Kaplan, St. Louis Region

DUCK WITH ORANGE SAUCE

1 duckling seasoned with salt, pepper and garlic salt
1/3 cup packed brown sugar
1/3 cup granulated sugar
1 tablespoon cornstarch
1 tablespoon grated orange rind
1 cup orange juice
1/4 teaspoon salt

Roast seasoned duck on rack in large pan at 325° for 3 to 3½ hours, pricking often. For sauce: Mix sugars, cornstarch and remaining ingredients. Stir over low heat until sugar dissolves. Cover and simmer until transparent and thickened, about 3 to 5 minutes. Makes 3 to 4 servings.

Arleen Dopkin, St. Louis Chapter-at-Large

EASY BARBECUED DUCK

1 duckling, quartered
1/2 cup catsup
1/2 cup orange juice

Prick duck with fork and broil to take off excess fat. Turn once and take off fat. Place duck in baking pan and cover with a mixture of orange juice and catsup. Bake, uncovered, at 350° for 2 hours, basting frequently. Can be prepared in advance. Makes 4 servings.

Mrs. H. Lindauer, Northern Illinois Region

ALMOND PRUNE RICE STUFFING

1/2 cup chopped almonds
1/2 cup sliced celery
1/4 cup chopped onion
1/4 cup butter or margarine
1 6-oz. package long grain & wild rice
2 1/4 cups water
1/4 cup port wine
1 cup diced cooked prunes
1/2 teaspoon grated lemond rind

Cook almonds, celery and onion in butter until almonds are lightly toasted. Add contents of rice and seasoning packets, water and wine; stir. Bring to a boil. Cover and cook until liquid is absorbed, about 25 minutes. Stir in prunes and lemon rind. Use to stuff or serve with Rock Cornish hens, as desired. Makes 6 servings or enough stuffing for 6 1-pound Rock Cornish hens.

CORNISH GAME HENS

6 rock cornish hens
2 oranges
Chicken fat
Salt and pepper
1 jar currant jelly
1-2 tablespoons lemon juice

Clean hens thoroughly. Tie legs and wings back. Slice oranges in thirds and place one slice in each hen. Rub outside of hens with chicken fat. Sprinkle with salt and pepper. Roast for 1 hour at 350°. To make sauce: heat currant jelly in small pan until melted. Add lemon juice to taste. Spoon oven hens and pass the rest in a gravy boat. Serve with wild rice. Makes 6 servings.

Florence Purnell, Des Moines Chapter-at-Large

CORN FLAKE STUFFING

2 onions, chopped
2-3 green peppers, chopped
1 rib celery, chopped
2-3 tablespoons cooking oil
4-6 cups chicken bouillon
1½ teaspoons garlic salt
½ teaspoon pepper
1 jumbo box corn flakes
2 eggs

In oil saute onions, green peppers and celery, until tender, but not brown. Make 4-6 cups of chicken bouillon. Add seasoning to sauteed vegetables. Add vegetables and 4 cups bouillon to corn flakes; mix; add beaten eggs and toss until completely mixed. Add more bouillon if needed. Texture of stuffing should be wet, but not mushy. You can either stuff a turkey or chicken or bake in casserole for 1½ hours.

Mrs. Norman J. Katz, West Suburban Region

TURKEY DRESSING

¼ cup melted butter
4 cups cubed bread
1 cup canned whole cranberry sauce
2 tablespoons sugar
½ cup raisins
1 teaspoon salt
1 teaspoon cinnamon
2 teaspoons grated lemon rind
¼ cup water

Combine all ingredients lightly. Place in 2-quart casserole and bake in a 350° oven for 45 minutes, or use to stuff a 3-lb. chicken.

Rosabelle Perrye, Chicago Region

BAKED FISH WITH CRABMEAT STUFFING

1 3-lb. whitefish or lake trout
¼ cup butter
¼ cup chopped onion
¼ cup chopped celery
½ teaspoon salt
Dash of black pepper
¼ teaspoon lemon rind
1 cup soft bread crubs
1 6½-oz. can crabmeat, drained
2 tablespoons butter or margarine

Have fish boned and dressed for stuffing. Melt butter in saucepan; add onion and celery and cook until onion is transparent. Add seasonings, lemon rind and crumbs. Remove from heat and add flaked crabmeat. Fill fish lightly with stuffing. Close with poultry pins or small wooden skewers; lace together with string. Arrange in shallow baking dish; dot with margarine. Bake at 375° until fish flakes easily with a fork. Makes 6 servings.

Gloria Dorne, Chicago Region

BROILED PUFFED FISH

1½ pounds sole, turbot or haddock fillets
Salt and pepper, to taste
½ cup shredded Cheddar cheese
½ cup mayonnaise
Cayenne pepper
1 egg white

Season fish with salt and pepper. Broil 4 inches from heat for 10 minutes. Combine cheese, mayonnaise and cayenne. Beat egg white until stiff; fold into cheese mixture. Spread on top of fish and broil 4 to 5 minutes longer, until puffed and light brown. Makes 4 servings.

Mrs. Herman Strifling, St. Louis Region

BAKED FISH WITH SALMON STUFFING

1 4 to 5-lb. fish for baking
½ cup soft butter
2 egg yolks
6 slices bread, trimmed and crumbled
½ cup milk or salmon liquid
1 1-lb. can salmon, drained and flaked
1 teaspoon salt
½ teaspoon white pepper
2 tablespoons chopped chives or parsley
1 small onion, chopped
1 small carrot, chopped
Pinch of thyme
1 cup chicken stock
½ cup dry white wine
Garnish:
12 mushroom caps
1 tablespoon butter
Parsley
Lemon wedges

Sauce:
Fish liquid
1 cup cream
3 tablespoons each: soft butter, flour
Salt and pepper, to taste
Lemon juice

Wash fish well; with sharp knife make deep slits along sides of the backbone; cut the bone at neck and tail ends and remove. This will leave a pocket down the back. Combine butter with egg yolks, crumbs, liquid, salmon, salt, pepper and chives. Stuff fish down back as well as underside. Butter a large baking dish and sprinkle vegetables and thyme over bottom of dish. Arrange fish on top and add stock and wine. Cover baking dish with buttered brown paper or foil; bake at 350° for 45 minutes. Meanwhile, saute mushroom caps in butter; keep warm. For sauce: Strain cooking liquid from baking dish into a saucepan. Add cream and heat to boiling. Thicken with a blend of butter and flour, adding bit by bit and stirring constantly. Season with salt, pepper and lemon juice. Serve separately with fish, garnished with mushroom caps, parsley sprigs and lemon wedges. Makes 6 servings.

Lee Bateman, Lake County Region

BAKED STUFFED FISH WITH SHERRY

1 3 to 4-lb. whitefish or lake trout
2½ cups pulled bread crumbs
1 medium onion, minced
2 tablespoons minced parsley
½ cup chopped celery
½ cucumber, grated
¼ cup melted butter
2 eggs, slightly beaten
½ cup milk or cream
Salt and pepper, to taste
½ cup melted butter
½ cup Sherry

Wash and clean fish; dry with paper towel; season with salt and pepper. Mix bread crumbs with onion, parsley, celery, cucumber, ¼ cup melted butter, eggs, cream and seasonings. Stuff fish lightly with mixture and arrange in a greased baking dish. Mix remaining melted butter and wine, and use for basting fish during baking. Bake at 375° for 45 to 50 minutes. Makes 4 to 6 servings.

Norma L. Platt, Chicago Region

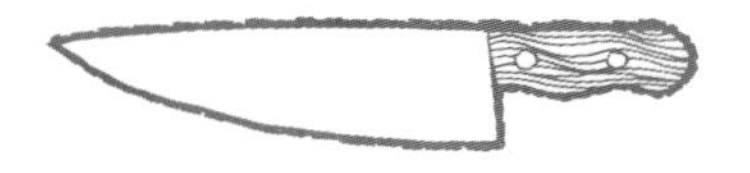

CREOLE BAKED FISH

2 tablespoons chopped onion
½ cup minced green pepper
2 tablespoons butter
1½ cups cooked or canned tomatoes
¼ cup sliced fresh mushrooms
¼ cup sliced pimento-stuffed olives
¼ teaspoon salt
¼ teaspoon pepper
2 tablespoons Sherry
1½ pounds fish steaks or fillets

Cook onion and green pepper in butter until tender. Add tomatoes, mushrooms, olives and seasonings; cook for 2 minutes. Add wine. Pour sauce over fish arranged in shallow baking dish. Bake at 375° for 20 to 25 minutes. Thicken sauce if you wish. Makes 6 servings.

Rosabelle Perrye, Chicago Region

BROILED SALMON STEAK

4 salmon steaks
$\frac{1}{4}$ cup butter
3 tablespoons lemon juice
1 teaspoon salt
$\frac{1}{2}$ teaspoon pepper
1 teaspoon chopped fresh mint or parsley
1 tablespoon paprika

Arrange steak in broiler pan. Melt butter; add lemon juice, salt, pepper and $\frac{1}{2}$ teaspoon mint or parsley. Brush on steaks; sprinkle with paprika. Broil 10 minutes on each side. Sprinkle with parsley or mint just before serving.

Mabelle Schero, Chicago Region

BROILED WHITEFISH WITH SOUR CREAM

6 whitefish fillets
$\frac{1}{2}$ cup corn flake crumbs
6 tablespoons dairy sour cream
Onion powder
Garlic powder
Salt
Paprika

Arrange fish in broiling pan, skin side down. Sprinkle crumbs on each fillet; with knife spread a layer of sour cream over crumbs. Sprinkle with seasonings. Broil without turning at moderate heat until fish flakes with a fork, about 20 minutes. Makes 6 servings.

Ida Zelman, Chicago Region

CREOLE RED SNAPPER

$\frac{1}{2}$ cup chopped celery
$\frac{1}{2}$ cup chopped carrots
$\frac{1}{2}$ cup black olives, chopped
$\frac{1}{2}$ cup chopped green pepper
$\frac{1}{2}$ cup chopped onion
1 cup stewed tomatoes
$\frac{1}{2}$ cup tomato sauce
2 pounds red snapper
Butter

Mix vegetables, olives and tomato sauce. Place $\frac{1}{2}$ of mixture in bottom of shallow baking pan. Arrange fish on top and dot with butter. Top with remaining sauce. Bake at 350° for 45 to 60 minutes. Makes 6 servings.

Mildred Rubenstein, Chicago Region

FLORENTINE SOLE

- 3 10-oz. package frozen chopped spinach
- 2 cups dairy sour cream
- 3 tablespoons flour
- ½ cup minced green onion
- Juice of 1 lemon
- 2 teaspoons salt
- 1½ to 2 pounds sole fillets
- 2 tablespoons margarine
- Paprika

Cook spinach according to package; drain well. Blend sour cream with flour, onions, lemon juice and salt. Combine half of sour cream mixture with spinach and spread evenly over bottom of shallow baking dish. Arrange fish on spinach; Dot with margarine. Spread remaining sour cream over fish, leaving a border to show spinach. If you wish, refrigerate until ready to bake. When ready to serve, bake at 375° for 25 minutes, or until fish flakes easily. Makes 6 to 8 servings.

Patricia Kaplan, St. Louis Region

HALIBUT STEAKS SUPREME

- 3 pounds halibut steaks
- ½ cup French dressing
- 2 tablespoons lemon juice
- ¼ teaspoon salt
- 1 3-oz. can french fried onions
- ¼ cup grated Parmesan cheese

Arrange fish in shallow pan; blend dressing, lemon juice and salt. Pour over fish and let stand for 30 minutes, turning once. Remove fish from sauce and place in a shallow greased baking dish. Crush onion and mix with cheese. Sprinkle over fish. Bake at 350° for 20 to 30 minutes.

Sybil Kaplan, Lake County Region

ORANGE FILLET OF SOLE

- 4 sole fillets
- 1 onion, sliced thin
- 1 rib celery, sliced
- Grated rind of 1 orange
- ¾ cup dairy sour cream
- 1 teaspoon salt
- ½ teaspoon paprika
- ¼ teaspoon pepper

Arrange onion and celery in shallow baking pan. Top with fish fillets. Bake at 400° for 20 minutes. Combine remaining ingredients; spoon over fish and bake at 300° 10 minutes longer. Makes 4 servings.

Mabelle Schero, Chicago Region

ITALIAN STYLE FISH WITH BROCCOLI

1 pound frozen fish fillets
1 10-oz. package frozen broccoli spears
Salt and pepper
Melted butter
2 tablespoons butter
¼ cup minced onion
½ teaspoon salt
⅛ teaspoon pepper

Sauce:
¼ cup melted butter
⅓ cup flour
1½ cups hot milk
½ teaspoon salt
½ teaspoon oregano
¼ teaspoon pepper
¼ cup grated Parmesan cheese
2 tablespoons dry white wine

Thaw fish and broccoli. Season fish with salt and pepper; brush with butter and broil at 450° about 2 inches from heat for 10 to 12 minutes, or until fish flakes. Saute onion in butter; add broccoli and season with salt and pepper. Cook 7 to 8 minutes, or until just tender. Arrange cooked broccoli in shallaw baking pan. Top with fish; cover with sauce, spreading evenly. Sprinkle with paprika; bake at 400° for 25 minutes. Brown top under broiler just before serving. Prepare sauce as for white sauce. Let stand about 15 minutes before pouring over fish. Makes 4 servings.

Michele Gutter, South Bend Chapter-at-Large

WHITE CLAM SAUCE

¼ cup butter
½ cup olive oil
2 cloves garlic, minced
2 medium onions, chopped
1 teaspoon basil
1 teaspoon oregano
Small bunch parsley, chopped
3 8-oz. cans minced clams
1 10-oz. can whole baby clams
Salt and freshly ground pepper, to taste

Melt butter with oil in large skillet; add garlic and onion and cook on medium heat until golden. Add herbs and cook, covered, on low heat for 10 minutes. Add clams and heat through. Season to taste. Serve over hot, cooked linguini. Makes enough for 6 servings.

Ruth Weissman, Lake County Region

RED SNAPPER PARMESAN

- 6 red snapper fillets
- 1 cup dairy sour cream
- 1/4 cup grated Parmesan cheese
- 1 tablespoon lemon juice
- 1 tablespoon grated onion
- 1/2 teaspoon salt
- Paprika

Arrange fish in a greased shallow baking dish. Combine remaining ingredients except paprika. Spread over fish; sprinkle with paprika. Bake at 350° for 25 minutes. Makes 6 servings.

Eenie Frost, Lake County Region

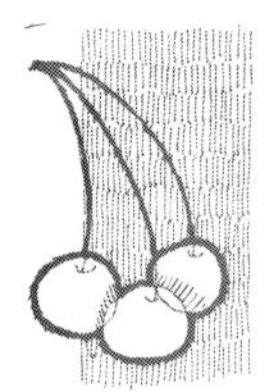

CRAB CASSEROLE I

- 1 7 1/2-oz. can king crabmeat
- 1 cup uncooked macaroni shells
- 1 4-oz. package shredded Cheddar cheese
- 2 hard-cooked eggs, coarsely chopped
- 1 10 1/2-oz. can cream of mushroom soup
- 1 cup milk
- 1 tablespoon frozen chopped chives
- Paprika

Drain crabmeat; flake coarsely. Combine with remaining ingredients except paprika. Turn into a deep 1-quart casserole. Cover and refrigerate for at least 8 hours. Bake, covered, at 350° for 1 hour. Sprinkle with paprika. Casserole can be frozen if you wish. Makes 4 to 6 servings.

Ceil Berger, Northern Illinois Region

CRABMEAT CASSEROLE II

1 7-oz. can crabmeat, drained and flaked
2 10½-oz. cans cream of celery soup
1 9-oz. package frozen peas, thawed
1 2-oz. jar pimento, drained
1 6-oz. can water chestnuts, drained and sliced
1 4-oz. can mushrooms, drained
½ cup minced onion
1 cup garlic croutons

Combine all ingredients except croutons; turn into a 1½ to 2-quart casserole. Top with croutons. Bake at 350° for 30 minutes. Makes 6 servings.

Peg Weissman, Chicago Region

CRABMEAT CREPES

2 eggs, beaten
1 cup milk
½ teaspoon salt
1 cup flour
2 teaspoons worcestershire sauce
¼ teaspoon Italian seasoning

Filling:
1 cup crabmeat plus liquid
1 8-oz. package cream cheese, softened

Sauce:
1 8-oz. package cream cheese, softened
1 cup milk
2 teaspoons worcestershire sauce

Combine ingredients for crepes. Using less than ¼ cup batter for each crepe, cook in greased 6-inch skillet about 1 minute on both sides. Stack with wax paper. Store in refrigerator for 1 to 2 days or freeze for 1 week. Combine filling ingredients. Spread 2 heaping tablespoons down center of each crepe. Roll and place seam side down in ovenproof baking dish. If you wish, refrigerate several hours or overnight. Combine sauce ingredients and pour over crepes. Sprinkle with paprika. Bake at 350° for 30 minutes. Makes 4 servings.

Lola Stoll, West Suburban Region

CRAB IMPERIAL

- 2 6-oz. packages frozen crabmeat
- ¼ cup butter
- ½ cup chopped green pepper
- ½ cup mayonnaise
- 1 egg, slightly beaten
- 1 tablespoon minced parsley
- 2 teaspoons worcestershire sauce
- ¼ cup cream
- 1 teaspoon prepared mustard
- ⅛ teaspoon nutmeg
- ½ teaspoon salt
- ½ teaspoon pepper
- 8 frozen patty shells, baked
- ½ cup buttered bread crumbs

Remove boney pieces from crabmeat. Flake crab, keeping pieces large. Cook green pepper in butter for 5 minutes. Gently mix with crabmeat and remaining ingredients except patty shells and bread crumbs. Turn into patty shells; top with crumbs. Bake at 350° for 20 minutes.

Launa Annes, Lake County Region

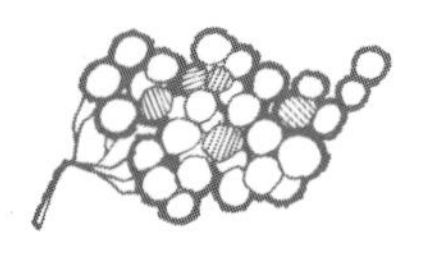

CRAB-MUSHROOM CASSEROLE

- 2 4-oz. cans sliced mushrooms
- 1 6½-oz. can crabmeat
- 2 tablespoons lemon juice
- 3 tablespoons butter
- 3 tablespoons flour
- 1½ cups milk
- 2 tablespoons Sherry
- 2 egg yolks, beaten
- 1 10¾-oz. can Cheddar cheese soup

Drain mushrooms and arrange in casserole. Drain and flake crabmeat and place on top of mushrooms. Sprinkle with lemon juice. Prepare sauce by melting butter in saucepan; blend in flour. Add milk and cook, stirring, until thickened and smooth. Blend in Sherry and egg yolks; cook for 1 minute. Blend in cheese soup. Pour over crabmeat. Bake at 350° for 20 minutes. Makes 2 to 4 servings.

Mrs. Melvin Gilbert, Milwaukee Region

CRAB-SHRIMP DELIGHT

- 1 can cream of shrimp soup
- ½ cup half and half
- 1 6-oz. roll garlic cheese
- ¼ cup butter
- ½ pound shrimp, cooked and cut into small pieces
- 1 6½-oz. can crabmeat, drained and flaked
- 1 4-oz. can sliced mushrooms

Combine soup, half and half, cheese and butter in top of double boiler. Cook and stir until heated through and blended. Add shrimp, crabmeat and mushrooms. Serve over crisp noodles or rice.

Barbara Solomon, Chicago Region

SHRIMP CASSEROLE

- 2 cans cream of shrimp soup
- 1¼ cups milk
- 2 tablespoons dry Sherry
- 1 4-oz. jar pimento, drained and diced
- 2 1-lb. bags frozen shrimps, cooked
- ¼ cup butter
- 2 cups coarse soft bread crumbs or crumbled croutons
- 1 stalk celery, chopped
- 1 tablespoon minced parsley
- ½ teaspoon salt
- 1 8-oz. package shell macaroni
- 1 cup shredded sharp Cheddar cheese

Combine soup, milk, Sherry and pimento in saucepan; cook and stir until mixture is heated and smooth. Remove from heat. In large skillet, saute shrimp in butter. Remove from heat. In same pan combine bread crumbs, celery, parsley and salt. Cook macaroni according to package directions; drain. In large casserole, layer sauce mixture, noodles, shrimp and crumbs, ending with soup. Bake at 350°, uncovered, for 25 minutes. Top with cheese and bake 5 minutes longer. To freeze; layer all ingredients except cheese in casserole; cover well and seal. About 1¾ hours before serving, place in cold oven and set temperature at 350°. Bake for 1½ hours. Sprinkle with cheese and bake 5 minutes longer.

Norma Glass, Lake County Region

SHRIMP DE JONGHE

- 2 pounds shrimp
- ½ cup butter (1 stick)
- 1 clove garlic, minced
- ¾ cup butter (1½ sticks)
- 2 cloves garlic, minced
- 1 cup bread crumbs
- ½ cup Sherry
- Salt and pepper
- 3 tablespoons parsley flakes
- Parmesan cheese

Cook shrimps; drain well. Saute garlic in butter; pour over shrimp and let stand while you prepare butter-crumb mixture. In electric mixer, blend remaining butter with garlic, crumbs, Sherry, seasonings and parsley. Divide butter soaked shrimp among 8 individual greased shells or 1 shallow baking pan (do not layer). Top with crumb mixture; sprinkle with Parmesan. Bake at 350° for 20 to 30 minutes. Makes 8 servings.

Anita Ruttenberg, Chicago Region

SHRIMP-SCALLOP CASSEROLE

- 1 pound shrimp, cooked and cleaned
- 1 pound scallops
- 1 cup water
- 3 tablespoons butter
- 3 tablespoons flour
- 1 10½-oz. can cream of mushroom soup
- ½ pound fresh mushrooms, sliced
- 2 tablespoons butter
- ¼ teaspoon salt
- Pepper
- ¾ cup grated Cheddar cheese
- ¼ cup dry Sherry

Cook shrimp; clean and devein. Heat scallops with water to boiling; cover and simmer for 15 minutes. Drain, reserving liquid. Melt butter in saucepan; blend in flour. Gradually add soup and reserved scallop liquid. Cook until thickened and smooth. Saute mushrooms in remaining butter. Add to sauce with seasonings, cheese and wine. In a 2-quart casserole, arrange alternate layers of scallops, shrimp and mushroom sauce, ending with sauce. Bake at 350° for 30 minutes.

Francine Cantor, St. Louis Region

WILD RICE SHRIMP CASSEROLE

- 1 6-oz. package long grain and wild rice
- 1 10½-oz. can cream of mushroom soup
- 2 tablespoons chopped onion
- 2 tablespoons chopped green pepper
- 2 tablespoons melted butter
- ½ teaspoon dry mustard
- ¼ teaspoon pepper
- 1 tablespoon lemon juice
- ½ teaspoon worcestershire sauce
- ½ cup grated sharp Cheddar cheese
- 1 pound cooked shrimp

Cook rice according to package directions; blend with soup and remaining ingredients. Turn into a greased 1½-quart casserole. Bake at 375° for 40 to 45 minutes. Makes 4 servings.

Myra Ladley, Lake County Region

SALMON ROLL-UPS

- 1 16-oz. can salmon, drained and flaked
- 2 eggs, beaten
- 2 teaspoons dried parsley flakes
- 2 teaspoons instant minced onion
- 1 8-oz. package refrigerated crescent rolls (8)
- 2 tablespoons softened butter

Cheese Sauce:

- 2 tablespoons butter
- 1 tablespoon flour
- Salt and pepper
- 1 cup milk
- 2 ounces American cheese, shredded
- 2 egg yolks, beaten
- 1 tablespoon lemon juice

Mix salmon in bowl with eggs, parsley and onion. Separate rolls; spread with softened butter; spread about 2 tablespoons salmon mixture on each roll. Roll-up each roll, starting with wide end. Place on ungreased cooky sheet and bake at 375° for 15 to 20 minutes. Serve hot with cheese sauce. Melt remaining butter in saucepan; blend in flour and seasoning. Gradually add milk and cook and stir until thickened. Add cheese; cook and stir until melted. Stir a little of hot mixture into beaten egg yolks. Return to hot mixture. Add lemon juice and cook 2 minutes longer. Makes 4 servings.

Florence Bolker, Chicago Region

BAKED SALMON BALLS

- 1 16-oz. can salmon
- 1 small onion, grated
- 1/4 teaspoon pepper
- 3 eggs, slightly beaten
- 1/4 cup cooked rice
- 2 10 1/2-oz. cans cream of mushroom soup
- 1 soup can water
- Paprika

Drain salmon, reserving liquid. Flake salmon and mix with onion, pepper, eggs, rice and enough salmon liquid to moisten. Shape into balls. Blend soup and water and pour into a shallow baking dish. Arrange balls in sauce. Bake at 350° for 1 hour. Sprinkle with paprika and serve. Makes 4 servings.

Helen Yedlin, Chicago Region

SALMON LOAF SOUFFLE

- 1 16-oz. can salmon
- 2 eggs, separated
- 2 tablespoons butter, melted
- 2 tablespoons bread crumbs
- 1/2 cup dairy sour cream
- 2 teaspoons finely chopped onion

Remove bones and mash salmon. Beat egg whites until stiff. Add beaten egg yolks to salmon with butter, bread crumbs, sour cream and onion. Gently fold in egg whites. Turn into a greased loaf pan. Bake at 350° for 1 hour. Makes 4 servings.

Hilary Elsinger, Northern Illinois Region

SALMON SOUFFLE

- 1 16-oz. can salmon, drained and flaked
- 1 13-oz. can evaporated milk
- 3 eggs
- 1/2 teaspoon pepper
- Dash of monosodium glutamate

In large bowl, mix salmon with evaporated milk, eggs and seasoning. Beat for 15 minutes. Pour into an 8-inch glass baking dish. Place in a pan of hot water and bake at 350° for about 1 hour. Serve hot or cold.

Golda Jacobs, Northern Illinois Region

HAITIAN LOBSTER

8 small rock lobster tails
2 cups bread crumbs
½ cup chopped almonds
1 cup mayonnaise
1 teaspoon chives
⅛ teaspoon crushed garlic

Shell uncooked lobster tails. Mix bread crumbs and almonds; set aside. Roll lobster in mixture of mayonnaise, chives and garlic. Dip into crumb-nut mixture. Fry lobster in deep fat heated to 370° until crisp and golden brown. Serve with tartar sauce. Makes 8 servings.

Erika Brodsky, Lake County Region

LOBSTER NEWBURG

2 packages rock lobster tails
Water
Vinegar
1 4-oz. can mushrooms, drained
3 tablespoons butter
½ cup milk
¼ cup Sherry
3 egg yolks
2 teaspoons flour
¼ teaspoon salt
¼ teaspoon hot pepper sauce
1½ cups light cream
Heated patty shells

Cook lobsters in boiling water with a small amount of vinegar for 20 minutes. Drain and cool lobster; cut into bite-size pieces. Saute mushrooms in butter. Add lobster and cook a few minutes. Blend in milk and Sherry; simmer for 3 minutes. Beat egg yolks with flour and seasonings. Stir in cream. Add to lobster and cook, stirring, until sauce thickens. Serve in patty shells. Makes 4 servings.

Linda Kline, Des Moines Chapter-at-Large

TUNA RATATOUILLE

- 2 medium onions, sliced thin
- 1/4 cup butter
- 2 small zucchini, sliced
- 1 small eggplant, pared and cubed
- 1 teaspoon salt
- 1/4 teaspoon pepper
- 1/2 teaspoon oregano
- Garlic salt (optional)
- 1 15-oz. can tomato sauce
- 2 7-oz. cans tuna, drained and in chunks

In large skillet, saute onion in butter. Layer remaining vegetables in skillet, sprinkle each layer with seasonings. Add tomato sauce; cover and cook on low heat for 15 minutes. Add tuna and cook 5 to 10 minutes longer. Makes 4 to 6 servings.

Phyllis Galst, Milwaukee Region

TUNA SOUFFLE

- 1/2 cup butter (1 stick)
- 12 slices white bread
- 2 7-oz. cans tuna, drained and flaked
- 6 slices American cheese
- 3 eggs
- 2 cups milk

Melt butter in 13x9-inch pan. Remove crusts from bread. Arrange 6 bread slices in baking pan; brush with butter. Spread tuna over bread. Top with cheese, then another layer of bread. Brush with remaining butter. Beat eggs with milk; pour over casserole. Cover and refrigerate overnight. Bake at 325° for 1 hour. Makes 6 servings.

Jean Einhorn, Northern Illinois Region

SHRIMP CREOLE

- 1 medium onion, chopped fine
- ½ pound fresh mushrooms sliced
- ⅓ cup butter
- 3 tablespoons flour
- 1 teaspoon salt
- ¼ teaspoon pepper
- 1½ teaspoons chili powder
- Garlic powder
- 1 29-oz. can tomatoes
- 1 green pepper, chopped
- 1½ pounds peeled and deveined cooked shrimps
- Hot Rice
- Minced Parsley

Saute onion and mushrooms in butter; blend in flour and seasonings. Add tomatoes; cook, stirring, until thickened and smooth. Add green pepper and shrimp; simmer for 10 minutes. Serve over rice; garnish with parsley. Makes 6 servings.

Shirley Taussig, Chicago Region

SALMON STUFFED PEPPERS

- 3 large green peppers
- 1 16-oz. can salmon, drained and flaked
- 1 cup cooked rice
- 1 egg, slightly beaten
- 1 cup processed American cheese, cut in ¼-inch cubes
- 1 teaspoon instant minced onion
- ¼ teaspoon salt
- ½ teaspoon worcestershire sauce
- 1 8-oz. can tomato sauce

Cut peppers in half lengthwise. Scoop out seeds and membrane. Cook in boiling salted water for 2 minutes; drain. Combine salmon, rice, egg, cheese, onion, salt and worcestershire. Fill pepper halves with salmon mixture; arrange in a shallow baking pan. Pour tomato sauce over all. Bake at 350° for 30 minutes. Makes 4 to 6 servings.

Mrs. Leonard Karm, Chicago Region

TUNA ASPARAGUS CASSEROLE

2 10-oz. packages frozen asparagus spears, cooked and drained
4 hard-cooked eggs, sliced
2 10½-oz. cans golden cream of mushroom soup
4 7-oz. cans tuna, drained and flaked
2 cups crushed potato chips

Arrange asparagus in the bottom of a buttered 10x6x2-inch casserole. Cover with half the egg slices. Heat soup until smooth; blend in tuna. Spread ½ this mixture over eggs; cover with 1 cup potato chips. Repeat layers. Bake at 350°, covered, for 30 minutes. Uncover and bake 10 minutes longer.

Rosalie Gellman, Milwaukee Region

TUNA LASAGNE

⅓ cup minced onion
½ cup chopped green pepper
1 4½-oz. jar sliced mushrooms
¼ cup butter
1 6-oz. can tomato paste
2 8-oz. cans tomato sauce
½ teaspoon Italian herbs
1 teaspoon oregano
2 7-oz. cans tuna, drained and flaked
¼ pound lasagne noodles
½ pound shredded Mozzarella cheese
½ cup grated Parmesan cheese

Saute onion, green pepper and mushrooms in butter until tender but not brown. Add tomato paste, tomato sauce and seasonings. Stir in tuna. Cook lasagne according to package directions; drain. In an 8-inch square baking dish, layer noodles, tuna mixture, Mozzarella and Parmesan cheese. Repeat layers. Bake at 375° for 25 to 30 minutes. Makes 6 servings.

Maxine Weindruch, Lake County Region

RICE AND CHINESE NOODLE CASSEROLE

- 1 pound rice
- 1/4 pound butter (1 stick)
- 1 10 1/2-oz. can chicken consomme
- Salt, pepper, onion salt, to taste
- Fresh or canned mushrooms (optional)
- 1 3-oz. can chinese noodles

In saucepan, brown uncooked rice in butter; turn into 2-quart casserole with cover. Add chicken consomme and seasonings to taste. If you wish, add canned or sauteed fresh mushrooms. Cover casserole and bake at 350° for 1 hour. Uncover and add chinese noodles. Bake uncovered for 45 minutes longer. Makes 8 to 12 servings.

Mrs. Martin Fishkin, Chicago Region

CHINESE RICE

- 2 medium onions, chopped
- Oil
- 3 eggs
- 1 cup ground beef (optional)
- 1 pound fresh mushrooms, sliced
- 1 teaspoon sugar
- 3 to 4 tablespoons soy sauce
- 1 cup bean sprouts, drained
- 3 cups cooked rice

In large skillet, cook onions in oil until brown, about 5 minutes. Push onions to one side of skillet; add slightly beaten eggs and cook, stirring, until firm. Add ground beef, mushrooms, sugar, soy sauce to taste and then add bean sprouts. Cook and stir for about 10 minutes. Mix with cooked rice. Turn into casserole and bake, uncovered, at 375° for 30 to 45 minutes. Mixture may be frozen or prepared in advance and baked when needed. Makes 10 servings.

Lois Fingerman, Des Moines Chapter-at-Large

HOT AND SOUR SOUP MANDARIN STYLE

- **6 cups chicken stock**
- **1 whole chicken breast, boned and shredded**
- **3 teaspoons salt**
- **1 teaspoon cornstarch**
- **2 tablespoons oil**
- **½ cup bamboo shoots, sliced**
- **3 dried mushrooms, soaked in water**
- **2 pieces fresh bean curd, cut in 1-inch slices (optional)**
- **1 tablespoon vinegar**
- **1 teaspoon pepper**
- **2 tablespoons soy sauce**
- **3 tablespoons cornstarch**
- **6 tablespoons water**
- **3 eggs, beaten**

Heat chicken stock to boiling in a large heavy pan. Season chicken with mixture of ½ teaspoon salt and 1 teaspoon cornstarch. In skillet, quickly stir-fry in oil. Add chicken to stock with bamboo shoots and sliced mushrooms. Simmer for 10 minutes. Add bean curd, remaining salt, vinegar, pepper and soy sauce. Blend cornstarch and water; add to stock and cook until thickened and clear. Add beaten eggs to soup, stirring constantly for about 1 minute. Serve immediately. If you wish to prepare in advance, follow recipe to the point of thickening with cornstarch. Just before serving add cornstarch and eggs. Makes 6 servings.

Joan Dicker, West Suburban Region

SOY SAUCE CHICKEN

- **2 chickens, cut up**
- **⅔ cup Kikkoman soy sauce**
- **¼ cup white wine**
- **½ cup catsup**
- **2 tablespoons salad oil**
- **1 teaspoon ground ginger**
- **2 cloves crushed fresh garlic**

Combine ingredients and marinate chicken pieces overnight. Drain, broil chicken on both sides until brown. Pour remaining marinade over chicken and bake uncovered at 300° until tender, about 1 hour. Baste occasionally.

Arleen Levy, Lake County Region

BEEF CHOW MEIN

- 1 beef flank steak
- 3 tablespoons oil
- Garlic powder, to taste
- Dash of ginger
- Onion powder, to taste
- 1 16-oz. can Chinese vegetables
- 1 16-oz. can bean sprouts
- 1 8-oz. can water chestnuts
- 1 4-oz. can sliced mushrooms
- 1 green pepper, sliced
- 1 small onion, chopped
- 2 tablespoons cornstarch
- Water
- ½ cup soy sauce
- 2 tablespoons sugar
- Fried or white rice

Tenderize flank steak and cut into thin strips. Brown well in large dutch oven in oil. Season to taste with garlic, ginger and onion. Drain canned vegetables and add to meat with green pepper and onion. Prepare sauce in 1-qt. measure by blending cornstarch with a small amount of water; blend in soy sauce, sugar and water to make 2 cups liquid. Add sauce to meat and cook, stirring occasionally, until thickened and clear. Cover pan and simmer for 10 minutes. Serve with rice. Makes 4 to 6 servings.

Adrienne Mintz, Indianapolis Chapter-at-Large

HONG KONG STEAK

- 1 beef sirloin steak, cut 1-inch thick
- Soy sauce
- Garlic salt
- Oyster sauce

Vegetables:

- 1 cup chicken broth
- 1 bokchoy
- 1 small onion, sliced
- ½ pound fresh pea pods
- 1 6-oz. can bamboo shoots
- 1 4-oz. can button mushrooms

Marinate steak soy sauce for 1 hour before cooking. Sprinkle with garlic salt. Broil to degree of doneness you prefer, turning once. Spread beef with oyster sauce; then cut into serving pieces over vegetables. To prepare vegetables, heat chicken broth to boiling in saucepan. Cut vegetables into long strips. Add bokchoy, onion and pea pods to broth; simmer for 1 to 2 minutes. Then add bamboo shoots and mushrooms; cook a minute longer. Season to taste; serve with beef. Makes 4 servings.

Diane Segal, Lake County Region

INDONESIAN BEEF EN BROCHETTE

- 2½ pounds beef chuck or round steak, cut 1½ inches thick
- ½ cup soy sauce
- ½ cup lemon juice
- 2 tablespoons brown sugar
- 2 teaspoons ground coriander
- 2 teaspoons ground cumin
- 1½ teaspoons salt
- 1 teaspoon pepper
- 1 large onion, peeled and sliced
- Unseasoned meat tenderizer
- Small canned potatoes
- Canned onions
- Cherry tomatoes or fresh tomato wedges
- 1 green pepper, cut in 1-inch squares

Trim all fat from beef; cut into 1½-inch cubes. Pierce beef all over with a fork. Place in a large shallow pan. Mix soy sauce, lemon juice, brown sugar, coriander, cumin, salt, pepper and onion in a small bowl. Pour over meat. Marinate in refrigerator for 30 minutes, turning several times. Drain marinade from beef and reserve. Sprinkle meat with tenderizer and let stand 30 minutes. Thread beef alternately on 4 to 6 skewers with potatoes, onions, tomatoes and green pepper, using other vegetables if you wish. Grill over charcoal, brushing several times with marinade and turning to cook on all sides. For rare, allow about 20 minutes. Makes 4 to 6 servings.

Liz Fischman, Twin Cities Region

CANTONESE BARBECUE CHICKEN

- 1 cup barbecue sauce, plain or hickory
- ½ cup honey
- ½ cup soy sauce
- ¼ cup lemon juice
- 1 teaspoon ginger
- Garlic powder, to taste
- 3 frying chickens, cut up

Combine barbecue sauce, honey, soy sauce, lemon juice, ginger and garlic powder. Pour over chicken arranged in a shallow pan. Cover and refrigerate overnight. Bake at 350° for 2 hours, basting and turning chicken frequently. Makes 12 to 16 servings.

Barb Livon, Twin Cities Region

WOK PEPPER STEAK

- 1 flank steak, 1¼ to 1½ pounds
- ¼ cup soy sauce
- ¼ cup Sherry or pineapple juice
- ¼ teaspoon garlic powder or 1 crushed clove garlic
- Peanut or vegetable oil
- Garlic powder
- 1 teaspoon ground ginger
- 1 large green pepper, cut into thin strips
- 1 large sweet onion, sliced into rings
- Tomato wedges (optional)
- Pineapple slices (optional)
- Sliced green onions (optional)
- Hot rice

Freeze flank steak for 30 minutes, or until firm. Cut into thin slices on the diagonal. Combine soy sauce, Sherry and garlic. Marinate steak in mixture for 2 hours or overnight, turning occasionally. When ready to serve, heat 2 tablespoons oil in a wok or large skillet. Sprinkle in a little garlic powder and ginger. Add green pepper and cook and stir for 2 minutes. Push pepper aside, add onions and cook and stir until transparent but crisp. Remove vegetables to a warm platter. Add more oil and ginger, if needed. Quickly cook and stir steak until slices are browned. Return peppers and onions to pan with tomato, pineapple and green onions. Cover and cook for 2 minutes. Serve with rice. If you wish, add pea pods, sliced mushrooms and drained bean sprouts. Cook and stir until tender-crisp. Makes 4 servings.

Mrs. Jerome H. Segal, Indianapolis Chapter-at-Large

CHINESE CHICKEN

- 1½ cups 1-inch pieces green pepper
- ¾ cup sliced onion
- 3 tablespoons vegetable oil
- ¼ cup cornstarch
- 2 cups chicken stock
- 3 tablespoons soy sauce
- 2 cups cooked chicken cubes
- 3 tomatoes, peeled and cut into wedges

Cook green pepper and onion in oil in large covered skillet until tender-crisp, but not browned. Blend cornstarch with chicken stock; add soy sauce. Stir chicken stock and chicken into skillet with vegetables. Cook and stir until thickened and clear. Add tomatoes and heat about 1 minute longer. Makes 6 servings.

Phyllis Frankel, Chicago Region

CHICKEN CHOW MEIN

- 1 pound fresh mushrooms, sliced
- 1 green pepper, cut into strips
- 6 green onions and tops, sliced thin
- ¼ cup butter
- 4 cups cooked chicken, cut up (about 4 chicken breasts)
- 1 16-oz. can bamboo shoots, drained
- 1 8-oz. can water chestnuts, drained
- 1 16-oz. can bean sprouts, drained
- 4 cups chicken broth
- 2 teaspoons salt
- ¼ teaspoon pepper
- ¼ cup soy sauce
- 4 cups diagonally sliced celery
- 1 2-oz. jar pimento, drained and chopped
- ¼ cup cornstarch
- Hot rice

Saute mushrooms, green pepper and green onions in butter in large skillet or dutch oven; remove from pan. Add chicken, bamboo shoots, water chestnuts and bean sprouts; blend in 3 cups chicken broth, salt, pepper and soy sauce. Heat to boiling; simmer for 5 minutes. Add sauteed vegetables, celery and pimento; heat again to boiling. Blend cornstarch with remaining 1 cup chicken broth; add to chicken and vegetables and cook, stirring, until thickened and clear. Serve over rice. Makes 12 servings.

Sandi Schiller, Lake County Region

ORIENTAL CHICKEN BAKE

- 1 frying chicken, cut up
- 1 teaspoon salt
- ⅛ teaspoon salt
- 1 cup orange juice
- 1 cup brown sugar
- 2 tablespoons melted butter
- 1 teaspoon dried mustard
- ¼ teaspoon allspice

Arrange chicken in single layer in baking pan. Combine remaining ingredients and pour over chicken. Bake at 350° for 1 hour, basting frequently with sauce. If you wish, thicken sauce with 1 tablespoon cornstarch before serving. Chicken can be frozen. Makes 4 to 6 servings.

Mrs. Morris Caminer, Milwaukee Region

CHINESE HALIBUT WITH PINEAPPLE

- 1½ pounds halibut steaks or fillets
- ¼ cup flour
- 1 teaspoon salt
- ¼ teaspoon pepper
- 3 tablespoons salad oil
- 3 tablespoons vinegar
- 2 tablespoons sugar
- ⅔ cup water
- 3 chicken bouillon cubes
- 1 small green pepper, cut into strips
- 1 8½-oz. can pineapple tidbits
- 1 tablespoon cornstarch
- 1 tablespoon water
- 1 tablespoon soy sauce

Cut fish into 4 serving portions. Roll in flour with seasonings. Heat oil in large skillet. Add fish and cook over moderate heat for 5 minutes; remove from pan and drain on paper towel. Combine vinegar, sugar, water, bouillon cubes, pepper and pineapple. Heat to boiling; simmer for 10 minutes. Combine cornstarch and remaining ingredients. Gradually add to hot sauce and cook, stirring, until thickened and clear. Serve over fish. Makes 4 servings.

Eileen Kiess, Des Moines Chapter-at-Large

CHICKEN WITH TOMATOES AND PEPPERS

- 2 chicken breasts
- 1 clove garlic, minced
- 3 tablespoons oil
- 2 tablespoons soy sauce
- ½ teaspoon salt
- ¼ teaspoon pepper
- 2 teaspoons cornstarch
- 3 green peppers
- 6-8 green onions
- 4 celery ribs
- 2 large tomatoes
- ¼ teaspoon sugar
- ¼ cup cold water

Cut chicken into 1-inch squares. Mix with garlic, 1 tablespoon oil, 1 tablespoon soy sauce, salt, pepper and 1 teaspoon cornstarch. Let stand 20 minutes. Cut peppers, celery, scallions and tomatoes into 1-inch pieces. Heat remaining 2 tablespoon oil in an electric skillet, or 10-inch skillet; saute peppers, onions, celery for 3-5 minutes. Remove vegetables from skillet. Cook chicken for 3 minutes. Mix remaining soy sauce and cornstarch with sugar and water. Add to skillet with sauteed vegetables and tomatoes. Cook over low heat for 3 minutes. Serve on a bed of cooked rice. Makes 4 servings.

Helen Cohen, West Suburban Region

CANTONESE VEGETABLE CASSEROLE

- 1 1-lb. can bean sprouts, drained
- 1 8-oz. can water chestnuts, drained and sliced
- 1 8-oz. can sliced mushrooms, drained
- 1 10-oz. can frozen peas, thawed
- 1 10½-oz. can cream of mushroom soup
- ½ cup milk
- 1 cup grated Cheddar Cheese
- 1 3-oz. can french fried onion rings

Place half of bean sprouts water chestnuts, mushrooms, and peas in 2-qt. casserole. Combine soup and milk; pour half of mixture over vegetables. Repeat vegetable layer; add remaining soup mixture. Top with cheese. Bake at 350 for 30 minutes. Sprinkle onions on top of cheese; bake 5 minutes longer. The casserole can be assembled for baking, then refrigerated until ready to heat and serve. Makes 8 servings.

Janet Frisch, Twin Cities Region

EGG FOO YUNG

- 1 cup cooked meat
- 1 16-oz. can bean sprouts, well drained
- 1 4-oz. can chopped mushrooms, well drained
- ½ cup chopped onion
- ½ teaspoon salt
- 1 tablespoon soy sauce
- 3 eggs
- Oil

Sauce:

- 2 teaspoons cornstarch
- ½ cup plus 2 tablespoons cold water
- ¼ teaspoon salt
- 1 teaspoon soy sauce
- 1 teaspoon bead molasses

Chop or finely shred meat; mix with bean sprouts, mushrooms and onion. Mix salt, soy sauce and eggs; beat eggs and add to meat mixture. Drop mixture by tablespoons into hot oil in a large skillet; turn once to brown both sides. Drain on paper toweling; place on cookie sheet, cover with foil and keep warm in slow oven while preparing remaining batter. Always mix batter thoroughly before spooning into hot oil. Serve with sauce, prepared by blending 2 teaspoons cornstarch and 2 tablespoons cold water; add remaining ingredients and cook, stirring, util thickened and clear. Makes 6 servings.

Mrs. Sheldon Rosen, Milwaukee Region

TUNA CHOW MEIN CASSEROLE

- 1/4 cup butter
- 1 cup diced celery
- 1/2 cup diced onion
- 1 6 1/2-oz. can tuna, drained and flaked
- 1 16-oz. can bean sprouts, drained
- 1 10 1/2-oz. can cream of mushroom soup
- 1 3-oz. can chow mein noodles

Melt butter in skillet or saucepan; add celery and onion and cook until golden. Blend in tuna, bean sprouts and soup. Grease a casserole dish and line with some of the noodles; add tuna mixture, pressing in firmly. Top with remaining noodles. Bake at 350° for 30 minutes. Makes 6 servings.

Enid Schultz, Lake County Region

ORIENTAL BEEF

- 2 pounds beef round steak, cut 1-inch thick
- 2 tablespoons oil
- Water
- 1/3 cup soy sauce
- 2 teaspoons sugar
- 1/4 teaspoon pepper
- 1 clove garlic, minced
- 3 carrots, pared
- 2 green peppers, cut in 1-inch squares
- 8 green onions, cut in 1 1/2-inch pieces
- 1/2 pound fresh mushrooms, halved
- 1 8-oz. can water chestnuts, halved
- 2 tablespoons cornstarch
- 1/4 cup water

Cut beef into strips 1/8-inch thick and 3 to 4 inches long. In large skillet, brown beef in oil. Pour off drippings; measure and add water to make 1 cup. Combine with soy sauce, sugar, pepper and garlic; add to meat. Cover and simmer for 45 minutes. Using vegetable parer, cut carrots lengthwise into thin strips; cut each strip in half. Add carrots, peppers, onions, mushrooms and water chestnuts to meat. Cover and continue cooking for 15 minutes. Combine cornstarch and water; add to meat mixture; cook and stir until sauce thickens and becomes clear. Makes 6 to 8 servings.

Lee Bateman, Lake County Region

EGGS and CHEESE DISHES

BLENDER CREPES

- 1½ cups cold milk
- ½ cup cold water
- 4 eggs
- ½ teaspoon salt
- ¼ teaspoon sugar
- 1¾ cups flour
- ¼ cup melted butter
- ¼ teaspoon vanilla
- 21-oz. cherry or blueberry filling
- Cinnamon sugar
- Whipped cream

Combine milk, water, eggs, salt and sugar in blender container; mix well. Add flour, butter and vanilla; mix well. Chill for several hours. Cook in a buttered 6 or 7-inch crepe pan, allowing about 2 tablespoons batter for each. Brown on both sides. Turn out of pan and keep warm. Fill crepes as you wish with cherry or blueberry pie filling. Sprinkle with cinnamon sugar and top with whipped cream. Makes about 3 dozen.

Debbie Wilner, Northern Illinois Region

DEVILED EGG BAKE

- 8 hard-cooked eggs
- ¼ cup butter
- ½ teaspoon worcestershire sauce
- ¼ teaspoon dry mustard
- 1 teaspoon parsley
- 1 tablespoon minced onion
- ⅓ cup diced shrimp or corned beef

Sauce:

- 3 tablespoons butter
- 4 tablespoons flour
- 1 cup milk
- ¾ cup cream
- 1 cup grated Cheddar cheese
- Salt and pepper

Peel and halve eggs; mash yolks and add remaining ingredients. Fill egg whites with mixture and arrange cut side down into a shallow baking dish. For sauce, melt butter in saucepan; blend in flour. Add milk and cream and cook, stirring, until thickened and smooth. Add cheese and stir until melted. Season with salt and pepper. Pour sauce over eggs; bake at 325° for about 25 minutes. Can be assembled early in the day, covered and refrigerated. Makes 4 to 6 servings.

Florence Purnell, Des Moines Chapter-at-Large

GERMAN PANCAKE

½ cup flour
½ cup milk
Dash of salt
4 eggs
1 pat butter, plus equal amount of lard
Confectioners' sugar
Fresh lemon juice

Mix flour with milk and salt until smooth. Beat eggs; add to mixture, and beat until smooth. Melt butter and lard in a large heavy deep frying pan. Add egg mixture. Fry until golden brown. Carefully turn with spatula and make 4 short criscross cuts. Bake at 450° for 12 minutes. Pancake will begin to rise after about 7 minutes. Top with confectioners' sugar and fresh lemon juice. Makes 2 servings.

Ellen Friend, Lake County Region

BAKED EGGS

½ cup butter (1 stick)
12 eggs
¾ cup milk
1 16-oz. carton small curd cottage cheese
8 slices American cheese

Melt butter in a 12x9-inch baking dish in oven at 350°, being careful butter does not burn. Beat eggs; add milk and cottage cheese, blending well. Pour over melted butter. Bake 15 minutes at 350°—then top with cheese slices. Bake until cheese melts and eggs are solid, about 10 minutes. Makes 6 to 8 servings.

Debbie Wilner, Northern Illinois Region

HUNGARIAN CREPES (POLACHINTIN)

6 eggs
1½ cups sifted flour
¾ cup sugar (scant)
2 cups milk
3 tablespoons melted butter
Grated rind of 1 lemon

Filling:
2 8-oz. packages cream cheese
2 tablespoons sugar
2 to 3 tablespoons milk
2 egg yolks
1 teaspoon vanilla

Beat eggs well. Add remaining ingredients by hand in order given. Cook crepes in 6 or 7-inch buttered skillet, browning on both sides. For filling, beat cheese well. Add remaining ingredients. Place about a tablespoon of cheese filling on each crepe. Roll and arrange on a jelly roll pan. Bake at 375° for 25 minutes, covering loosely with foil during the last 10 minutes of baking. Makes 24 filled crepes.

Elaine Shapiro, Northern Illinois Region

NORWEGIAN PANCAKES

- 1 cup dairy sour cream
- 1 cup small curd cottage cheese
- 4 eggs
- ¾ cup sifted flour
- 1 tablespoon sugar
- ½ teaspoon salt
- ¼ teaspoon cinnamon
- Fresh berries or fruit syrup

Combine sour cream and cheese; add remaining ingredients except fruit and mix well. Bake on hot greased griddle, turning once. Serve with berries or syrup. Makes about 2 dozen pancakes.

Peg Weissman, Chicago Region

BELGIAN WAFFLES

- 1 cake or package active dry yeast
- 1¾ cups milk
- 4 tablespoons sugar
- ⅓ cup butter
- 2 cups flour
- 3 eggs, beaten

Soften yeast in warm water. Heat milk to scalding and add sugar and butter. When mixture is cooled to lukewarm, add yeast and flour. Add eggs and mix well. Let rise for 1½ hours in a warm place. Stir down batter and place, covered, in refrigerator overnight. (If you want to use the batter immediately, let rise another hour.) Bake in hot waffle iron for about 3 minutes. Serve with butter and syrup or whipped cream and strawberries. Makes 6 servings.

Maxine Sprung, Lake County Region

WAFFLES SUPREME

- ½ pint heavy cream
- 2 eggs, separated
- 1 cup flour
- 1 teaspoon baking powder
- Pinch of salt
- 1 teaspoon melted butter

Whip cream. Beat egg whites until stiff; beat egg yolks until thick and lemon colored. Combine whipped cream and egg yolks. Sift flour with baking powder and salt; blend into yolk mixture. Fold in egg whites. Add melted butter. Bake in waffle maker. If batter seems too thick, add milk. Makes 4 servings.

Myra Weis, Chicago Region

ORANGE FRENCH TOAST

- 8 slices French bread, ¾-inch thick
- 4 eggs
- 1 cup milk
- 2 tabelspoons Grand Marnier
- 1 tablespoon granulated sugar
- ½ teaspoon vanilla
- ¼ teaspoon salt
- 2 tablespoons butter
- Confectioners' sugar

In a 12x8x2-inch baking dish, arrange bread in a single layer. Combine eggs with milk, orange liqueur, sugar, vanilla and salt with rotary beater; mix well. Pour over bread; turn to coat slices evenly. Refrigerate, covered, overnight. To cook, heat butter in a skillet. Add bread and saute until golden, about 4 minutes on each side. Sprinkle with sugar. Makes 4 servings.

Rochelle Kroot, Indianapolis Chapter-at-Large

CHEESE SOUFFLE PIE

- Pastry for 10-inch pie shell
- 2 tablespoons flour
- ⅛ teaspoon nutmeg
- ½ teaspoon dry mustard
- 1 cup milk
- ½ pound grated Swiss cheese
- ¼ cup grated Parmesan cheese
- 4 eggs, separated
- ½ teaspoon salt
- ¼ teaspoon cream of tartar

Roll pastry to fit a 10-inch pie plate. Prick well and bake at 450° for 15 minutes. Combine flour, nutmeg and mustard in a saucepan; add milk and cook, stirring, until thickened. Remove from heat; add Swiss and Parmesan cheese. Place over heat; stir until cheese is melted. Remove from heat and add egg yolks and salt. Beat egg whites until foamy; add cream of tartar and beat until stiff. Fold into cheese sauce; carefully pour into pie shell. Bake at 375° for 25 minutes. Do not freeze. Makes 6 servings.

Erika Brodsky, Lake County Region

ORT CHEESE SOUFFLE

- 12 slices white bread
- 9 eggs, well beaten
- 3 cups milk
- 1½ tablespoon oil
- 1 tablespoon onion flakes
- 1 teaspoon salt
- ½ teaspoon pepper
- 1 cup grated Sharp Cheddar cheese

Trim crusts off bread; cut bread into cubes. Combine eggs, milk, oil and seasonings. Blend in cheese. In ungreased 2-quart souffle dish, alternate bread cubes and egg mixture. Refrigerate overnight. Bake at 350° for 1 hour and 10 minutes, or until puffed and brown. Do not freeze. Makes 12 servings.

Erika Brodsky, Lake County Region

ORANGE BLINTZ SOUFFLE

- 12 frozen cheese blintzes
- 6 eggs
- 6 tablespoons melted butter
- 1½ cups dairy sour cream
- 1 teaspoon vanilla
- ¼ teaspoon salt
- ¼ cup sugar
- ¼ cup orange juice

Grease a 13x9-inch baking dish. Arrange blintzes in pan. Beat eggs with remaining ingredients; pour over blintzes. Bake at 350° for 45 minutes. Serve at once. Makes 6 to 8 servings.

Marcia Levy, Lake County Region

ORANGE SOUFFLE

- 4 eggs, separated
- ¼ cup sugar
- ¼ teaspoon salt
- Juice and grated rind of 1 medium orange

Beat egg yolks until thick and lemon colored. Gradually add sugar and salt and continue beating. Add the juice and grated orange rind. Beat egg whites until stiff but not dry. Carefully fold into yolk mixture. Pour batter into a generously buttered souffle dish. Set in another pan of hot water. Bake 1-quart souffle at 350° for 35 to 40 minutes. Serve at once. Makes 6 servings.

Edythe Oleck, Chicago Region

CHICKEN SOUP

- 1 3-lb. stewing chicken or capon
- 3 quarts water
- 3 carrots
- 3 ribs celery
- 1 parsley root with greens
- 3 tablespoons salt
- 2 teaspoons pepper
- 1 small onion

In large soup pot, heat chicken with water to boiling. Skim off top; simmer for 2 hours. Add vegetables and seasonings. Simmer 30 minutes longer. Strain out vegetables. Cut chicken into small pieces; return to soup. Chill soup thoroughly; remove fat from top. Serve hot with matzo balls, noodles or rice. Makes 8 servings.

Rosabelle Perrye, Chicago Region

EASY KREPLACH

- 1½ cups flour
- 2 eggs, beaten
- ¼ cup water
- 1 pound ground beef, cooked
- 1 onion, minced
- 1 egg, beaten
- ½ teaspoon salt
- Dash of pepper

Combine flour, beaten eggs and water; mix to make a soft dough. Knead well and roll into a rectangle about ⅛-inch thick. Cut dough into 2-inch squares. Mix ground beef with onion, egg and seasonings. Place a tablespoon of meat mixture on each square of dough. Fold dough into triangles and press edges together. Place in a pot of boiling salted water; simmer for 15 minutes. Carefully remove kreplach and transfer to a pot of chicken soup. Simmer 5 minutes and serve.

Sheila Schwartz, West Suburban Region

CHALLAH

- 2 packages active dry yeast
- ½ cup warm water
- 4 eggs
- ¾ cup sugar
- 1 tablespoon salt
- ½ cup oil
- 9 cups sifted flour
- 2 cups warm water
- Egg yolk and water
- Poppy seeds

Dissolve yeast in ½ cup warm water. Set aside. Beat eggs; add sugar, salt and oil. Add 1 cup flour and dissolved yeast. Alternately add remaining flour with 2 cups water. Beat well. Dough will be stiff. Turn out on floured pastry cloth and let rest 5 minutes, covered with dish towel. Knead for 12 to 15 minutes, until smooth. (A small amount of flour will be needed to keep dough from sticking.) Place dough in a greased bowl. Set in warm place and let rise until doubled. Turn out on floured cloth, punch down and divide dough into 4 parts. Divide each into 3 pieces. With hands, make 3 ropes of the 3 pieces and braid. Place in greased and floured 8½x3-inch loaf pans and let rise in a warm place, covered, until doubled. Brush with egg yolk wash (add 1 teaspoon water to 1 egg yolk). Sprinkle with poppy seeds, if desired. Bake at 350° for 50 minutes. Turn out of pans immediately. May be frozen. Makes 4 loaves.

Ruth Schwartz, Lake County Region

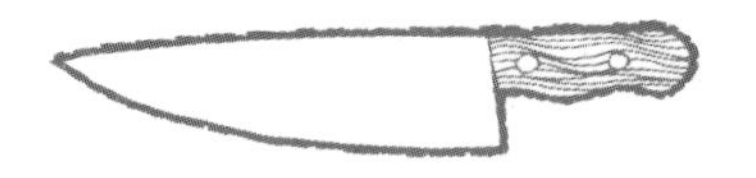

CHOPPED LIVER

- 1 pound liver (chicken, beef or calf)
- 2 large onions, diced
- 3 tablespoons chicken fat
- 3 hard-cooked eggs
- Salt and pepper to taste

Saute onions in fat until translucent. Remove onions from pan and add liver. Saute until browned. Cool. Grind liver, onions and eggs. Add salt and pepper. Moisten with additional fat if necessary. Shape in mold and serve on lettuce leaf. Makes 8 servings.

GEFILTE FISH

- 3 pounds whitefish
- 1 pound each: trout or pickerel, sucker, pike
- 10 cups water
- 2 cups sliced carrots
- 4 large onions, sliced
- 2 ribs celery
- 2 large onions, grated
- 8 teaspoons salt
- 2 teaspoons white pepper
- ¼ cup matzo meal
- 4 eggs
- 1 cup water

Clean fish heads and bones. Place in a large pot with 10 cups cold water. Bring to a boil and add carrots, onion and celery. Bring to a boil again. Grind fish and place in mixing bowl. Add grated onion, seasonings, matzo meal, eggs and water. Beat slowly for 5 minutes. Make fish balls and add to soup mixture. Cover and cook for 2½ hours. Shake pot around often. Let simmer, do not boil. Uncover and cook ½ hour longer. Cool and remove.

Clare Fishman, Chicago Region

GEFILTE FISH MOLD

- 1 1-lb package frozen white fish (fresh may be used)
- 1 1-lb. package frozen pike
- 3 eggs
- 1 teaspoon salt
- Pepper to taste
- 3 medium onions
- 2 tablespoons matzo meal
- 2 tablespoons water

Skin fish; discard skin. Chop fish and onions in meat grinder. Blend in rest of ingredients thoroughly. Liberally grease an 8½-inch ring mold with butter or margarine. Pack mixture into mold; cover with aluminum foil. Place in pan of boiling water, about ⅓ way up the pan. Bake on lower rack in oven at 375° for 2 hours. Remove foil, loosen edges with knife, and immediately turn out on a plate. Cover and allow to cool. Refrigerate. Will keep for a week. Makes 10 servings.

Ruth Schwartz, Lake County Region

MOCK GEFILTE FISH

- 1 7-oz. can white tuna, packed in water
- 3 eggs, beaten
- 7 tablespoons matzo meal
- 1 small onion, grated
- 1/4 teaspoon salt
- 1/4 teaspoon pepper
- 4 glasses boiling water
- 1/4 teaspoon salt
- 1/4 teaspoon pepper
- 1 onion, sliced
- 2 small carrots, sliced

Mix tuna with eggs, matzo meal, onion and seasonings. Tuna should be very fine. If too loose, add more matzo meal. Shape into 6 to 10 balls. In saucepan, combine boiling water with seasonings, onion and carrots; heat to boiling. Remove pan from heat; add tuna balls. Return to heat, cover and simmer for 25 minutes. Serve cold. Makes 6 to 10.

Elaine Achler, Northern Illinois Region

MEAT BLINTZES

- 2 eggs, beaten
- 1/2 cup water
- 1 1/2 cups flour
- 1 teaspoon salt
- Margarine

Filling:

- 1 onion, chopped
- 1 rib celery, chopped
- 2 cups ground cooked meat or chicken
- 1 egg, beaten
- 1 teaspoon salt
- 1/2 teaspoon pepper
- Applesauce

To prepare blintzes, combine well beaten eggs and water. Blend in dry ingredients. Cook blintzes in a 9-inch skillet that has been brushed once with margarine. Pour a small amount of batter into skillet; immediately pour off excess batter. Fry on one side; turn out onto paper toweling. Repeat until all batter is used. For filling, saute onion and celery in a small amount of oil. Add remaining ingredients except applesauce. Fill each blintz with a large tablespoon of meat mixture. Roll. Place on greased cooky sheet, seam side down. Bake at 350° for 30 minutes. Serve hot with applesauce. Makes 12 blintzes.

Meryl Liner, Northern Illinois Region

MEATLESS TZIMMES

- 6 canned sweet potatoes, halved
- 12 dried prunes, soaked in water
- 12 dried apricots, soaked in water
- 1 20-oz. can pineapple chunks
- 1 6-oz can frozen orange juice
- ¼ cup butter
- Brown sugar
- Maraschino cherries
- Chopped pecans

Arrange halved sweet potatoes in a shallow baking dish. Arrange prunes and apricots that have been soaked in water for 30 minutes in open spaces. Drain and reserve pineapple juice; arrange chunks in casserole. Blend pineapple syrup and orange juice; heat with butter until melted. Pour over fruit. Sprinkle with brown sugar. Bake at 350° for 1 hour, basting occasionally. Before serving, garnish with sliced cherries and pecans. Makes 6 servings.

Kay Simons, Lake County Region

CHOLLENT

- 3 pounds beef brisket or short ribs
- 3 tablespoons fat
- 3 tablespoons white sugar
- 1 pound dried lima beans
- 3 onions, sliced
- 3 tablespoons flour
- 2 raw potatoes, grated
- Ginger

Brown beef in fat. Cook sugar in heavy skillet until caramelized. Add lima beans. Add onions to meat. Add flour, potatoes and ginger. Cover with water and simmer over low heat overnight, or cook in oven at 225° overnight. Do not stir. Makes 6 to 8 servings.

Sylvia Zimmerman, Chicago Region

POTATO PANCAKES

- 2 cups grated raw potatoes
- 1 small onion, grated
- 2 eggs, beaten
- 3 tablespoons flour
- 1 teaspoon salt
- ½ teaspoon baking powder
- ¼ teaspoon pepper

Mix potatoes with remaining ingredients; blend thoroughly. Drop by tablespoons into a hot well-greased skillet or griddle, turning once to brown on both sides. Makes 6 servings.

CARROT TZIMMES

- 1½ pounds short ribs or
- 2 to 6-lb. brisket
- 2 pounds carrots
- 1 pound sweet potatoes
- 1 teaspoon salt
- ¼ cup brown sugar
- 1 tablespoon cornstarch

Grate carrots on medium shredder. Cube sweet potatoes (1″ cubes). Place carrots, potatoes, salt and sugar in heavy roasting pan with short ribs or brisket; add enough water to cover and steam on top of stove covered for 20 minutes. Keep covered and roast in 350° oven for 2 hours until meat is tender and water is absorbed. Mix cornstarch with a little cold water and blend carefully into Tzimmes. Simmer on top of stove for 10 minutes.

Sarah Stiebel, Northern Illinois Region

MEAT KNISHES I

- 1½ pounds beef chuck or pot roast
- 3 onions, chopped
- ½ cup margarine (1 stick)
- 2 eggs, separated
- Salt and pepper
- Water
- 1 package refrigerated crescent rolls

Cook meat as you prefer. Chop cooked meat in blender or meat grinder. Brown onion in margarine. Add to meat with egg whites. Season with salt and pepper. Open package of rolls; separate. Cut each in half the long way. Fold the long point over the wide end and form into a rectangle with your fingers. Put a teaspoon of meat mixture in center of each roll; fold the sides over the meat, sealing firmly. Mix egg yolks with about a tablespoon of water. Brush over top of rolls. Bake according to package directions. The knishes can be made ahead and refrigerated before baking. Or bake and freeze, if you wish. Makes 16.

Aileen Melnick, Northern Illinois Region

MEAT KNISHES II

Dough:

- ¾ cup warm water
- 1 package fresh or active dry yeast
- ¼ cup oil
- 1 tablespoon sugar
- 1½ teaspoons salt
- 2 eggs, beaten
- 3¼ cup flour

Filling:

- 1½ pounds ground beef
- 1 cup chopped onion
- 1 tablespoon oil
- 1¼ cups mashed potatoes
- 1½ teaspoons salt
- ½ teaspoon thyme
- ⅛ teaspoon pepper
- Melted margarine

Measure water into a large warm bowl; add yeast and stir until dissolved. Add oil, sugar, salt, eggs and 2 cups flour; beat until smooth. Add enough additional flour to make a soft dough. Turn out onto a floured board and knead until smooth and elastic, about 8 to 10 minutes. Place in an oiled bowl; turn to grease top. Cover and let rise in a warm place until double in bulk, about 1 hour. Punch dough down. On a lightly floured board, roll dough into a 15x22-inch rectangle. Spread filling on dough. Cut into 3 strips, 5 by 22 inches. Roll strips jelly roll fashion. Seal edges well. Cut into 1-inch pieces. Place on oiled baking sheets. Cover and let rise about 30 minutes. Bake at 375° for 20 to 25 minutes until brown. Brush with margarine. For filling: Brown beef and onion in oil. Add beef mixture to mashed potatoes; blend in seasonings. If you wish, freeze baked knishes. To serve, thaw, then heat at 400° for 5 minutes. Makes 5½ dozen.

Enid Schultz, Lake County Region

MILTZ

- Miltz
- 4 tablespoons flour
- 2 tablespoons matzo meal
- ½ cup corn flakes
- 1 small onion, minced
- Salt and pepper
- 2 tablespoons chicken fat, more if need

Make opening through miltz. Mix flour, matzo meal, corn flakes, onion, salt and pepper. Add chicken fat to hold mixture together; stuff miltz. Bake alone or with meat at 350° for 1 hour.

Sylvia Zimmerman, Chicago Region

MOCK KISHKE

- 1 box Tam Tam crackers
- 2 large carrots
- 1 large onion
- 2 large stalks celery
- ¼ pound melted butter or margarine
- Salt and pepper, to taste

Grind crackers. Grind vegetables. Blend crackers and vegetables with melted butter. Season with salt and pepper. Form into 3 rolls; wrap each in aluminum foil. Bake at 350° for 1 hour. If you prefer, pack mixture into an 8-inch round or square pan. Bake at 350° for 10 minutes. Remove from oven and cut into serving portions. Return to oven for 15 minutes when ready to serve.

Adrienne Mintz, Indianapolis Chapter-at-Large

SWEET-SOUR FISH

- 1 medium onion, chopped
- 3 carrots, chopped
- 2 stalks celery, chopped
- Water
- 2 10-¾ oz. cans tomato soup
- ¼ cup raisins
- 1 cup brown sugar
- 4 pounds sliced trout
- Juice of 3 lemons
- 4 crushed gingersnaps

In large pan, cook onion, carrots and celery with water to cover for 15 minutes. Add soup, raisins, and sugar. Heat to boiling. Place fish on top of mixture and simmer for 45 minutes. Add lemon juice and gingersnaps and cook 15 minutes longer. Makes 8 to 12 servings.

Bee Greenstein, Chicago Region

PICKLED FISH

- 6 pounds fish (trout, pickerel or white fish, sliced 1½ to 2 inches thick)
- 1½ pounds onions, sliced
- 5 cups water
- 4 cups vinegar
- 2 tablespoons pickling spices
- 1 lemon, peeled and sliced
- 2 tablespoons salt
- 1¾ cups sugar

Boil onions in water and vinegar for 1 hour, covered. Strain and transfer to large pot. Add remaining ingredients, except fish. Heat to boiling. Add fish, a piece at a time. Cook for 25 minutes or until fish flakes; cool 10 minutes in liquid. Remove fish to a cooky sheet to cool completely. When broth and fish are cold, place fish in a bowl, pour broth over fish and refrigerate.

Betty Grossman, Northern Illinois Region

SWEET AND SOUR TROUT

- 3 pounds trout, cut in slices
- 1 12-oz. jar chili sauce
- 1½ cups water
- 1 bay leaf
- 1 teaspoon salt
- 1 teaspoon ginger
- 1 tablespoon sour salt
- ½ cup brown sugar, or more to taste

Mix chili sauce and water; add bay leaf and salt. Bring to a boil in a large saucepot. Add ginger, sour salt and sugar. Taste should be very sharp sweet-sour. Add fish and simmer gently for about 30 minutes, until fish flakes. Cool in sauce. Refrigerate for about 24 hours. Will keep for about 10 days in refrigerator.

Madlyn Spark, Lake County Region

BAKED FARFEL

- 1 pound toasted farfel
- Boiling salted water
- 1 pound fresh mushrooms, sliced
- 4 tablespoons Kikkoman soy sauce
- 4 large onions, sliced
- ½ cup butter or margarine
- Salt and pepper to taste

Cook farfel in 4 quarts boiling salted water for 10 minutes; drain thoroughly. Steam sliced mushrooms and soy sauce in double boiler for about 10 minutes. Saute onions in butter until golden. Combine farfel, mushrooms and onion; season to taste. Turn into a 13x9-inch pan. Bake at 350° for 45 minutes. Makes 12 servings as meat accompaniment.

Rosabelle Perrye, Chicago Region

PASSOVER RECIPES

PASSOVER BEET BORSHT BISQUE

2 cups mashed potatoes (4 large, pared and boiled)
¼ teaspoon onion powder
¾ teaspoon salt
¾ cup sour cream
1 quart beet borsht, strained or put through blender

Combine all ingredients in order. Blend all ingredients at high speed of electric blender for 30 seconds, using half the ingredients at a time if necessary. Makes 4 to 6 servings.

Jean Goldrosen, Northern Illinois Region

CHREMSLACH (Thick pancakes for Passover)

1 cup matzo meal
1 teaspoon salt
¼ cup sugar
1 cup boiling water
3 eggs

Blend matzo meal, salt and sugar; pour boiling water over mixture and blend well; cool to lukewarm. Beat eggs until creamy; add to matzo meal, blending well. Cover bowl and refrigerate for at least 2 hours. Heat ½-inch oil in large skillet until sizzling. With a large spoon, dipped each time in cold water, scoop mixture into pan and flatten to make thick pancakes. Cook for 5 minutes on one side; turn and cook 3 to 5 minutes longer. Drain on both sides on paper toweling. Serve with cinnamon and sugar or orange marmalade as side dish or dessert. Makes 5 to 7.

Pearl Klotz, Lake County Region

MATZOS WITH EGG & COTTAGE CHEESE

4 large square matzos
Lukewarm water
3 cups (1½ lbs.) cottage cheese
½ cup raisins
4 eggs, well-beaten
2 cups milk
Juice and grated rind of 1 orange
⅔ cup sugar
½ teaspoon salt

Soak matzos, one at a time in lukewarm water. Remove carefully; drain and press between paper toweling to remove excess moisture. Butter 9-inch square pan. Place one soaked matzos into pan, cover with ⅓ of cheese and raisins. Continue layering ending with matzos. Combine rest of ingredients and beat until smooth and well-blended. Pour over matzos. Bake at 375° for 1 hour or until puffed and brown.

Mrs. Bernard L. Shain, Milwaukee Region

MATZO BALLS

2 eggs, separated
½ cup matzo meal
½ teaspoon salt
¼ teaspoon pepper
¼ teaspoon garlic salt
½ teaspoon parsley flakes

Beat egg whites until stiff but not dry. Beat egg yolks. Fold into whites. Blend dry ingredients and fold into egg mixture; let stand 5 to 7 minutes. Using a 1 tablespoon measure, drop mixture into 3 quarts boiling salted water; simmer for 45 minutes. Drain with slotted spoon. Simmer in chicken broth for 5 minutes. Makes 8 balls.

Rosabelle Perrye, Chicago Region

MOCK GEFILTE FISH

1 quart water
1 onion, sliced
1 carrot, sliced
1 stalk celery, sliced
Salt
Pepper
4 eggs, beaten
¼ cup matzo meal
2 7-oz. cans water-packed tuna, drained and chopped

To water in saucepan, add vegetables, salt and pepper. Boil until soft. This is the stock in which the fish is cooked. Combine eggs, matzo meal and tuna; shape into balls. Drop into stock, cover and cook over low heat for 30 minutes.

Renee Goldstein, Chicago Region

PASSOVER WINE GELATIN MOLD

2 3-oz. packages black cherry gelatin
1 16-oz. can pitted sweet cherries
½ cup Passover fruit wine
Walnut pieces

Add 2 cups boiling water to gelatin; stir to dissolve. Drain cherry juice into measuring cup; add wine and enough cold water to make 1½ cups. Add to gelatin. Refrigerate until slightly thickened. Meanwhile, fill cherries with walnuts. Stir cherries into thickened gelatin; pour into 2-quart mold and chill until firm. Unmold and serve on greens.

Aileen Melnick, Northern Illinois Region

APPLE MATZO KUGEL

3 matzos
½ cup hot fat
1 cup matzo meal
5 eggs, separated
¼ cup chopped walnuts
Grated rind of 1 lemon
½ teaspoon salt
2 apples, grated

Soak matzos in water; when dry press out excess liquid. Heat fat in a skillet. Add matzos and fry for 3 minutes. Remove to bowl and add matzo meal, beaten egg yolks, nuts, lemon rind, salt and apples. Fold in stiffly beaten egg whites. Turn into a 2-quart greased casserole; pour hot fat over top. Bake at 350° for 40 minutes, or until brown.

MATZO MEAL PANCAKES

½ cup matzo meal
¼ cup milk, water, orange juice or wine
1 teaspoon salt
4 eggs, separated
2 tablespoons melted fat

Pour water or other liquid on matzo meal; add salt to egg yolks and beat until very light. Add to meal mixture; let stand 5 minutes. Beat egg whites very stiff. Fold lightly into yolk mixture. Drop by spoonfuls onto hot greased skillet. Brown on both sides.

Margaret Goldberg, Lake County Region

PASSOVER ALMOND FRUIT KUGEL

- ½ cup dried apricots
- ⅔ cup blanched whole almonds
- 1 8½-oz. can crushed pineapple
- 2 cups water
- 3 matzos
- 3 eggs, separated
- ⅔ cup sugar
- ¼ teaspoon cinnamon
- ¼ teaspoon salt

Cook apricots in water until tender; drain. Chop almonds; drain pineapple and save juice. Pour pineapple syrup and water over matzos; let stand a few minutes, then squeeze dry. Beat egg yolks; blend in sugar, salt, cinnamon, matzos and fruit. Beat egg whites until stiff and fold into mixture. Pour into 1½-qt. casserole or 9-inch square pan. Bake at 350° for 1 hour, or until browned. Makes 8 servings.

Irma Leone, Chicago Region

PASSOVER FARFEL KUGEL

- 1 cup diced onion
- 1 cup diced celery
- 6 tablespoons chicken fat or oil
- 3½ cups matzo farfel
- 1 teaspoon salt
- ¼ teaspoon pepper
- 2 teaspoons paprika
- 2 eggs, slightly beaten
- 1 can clear chicken soup
- 1¼ cups hot water

Saute onion and celery in fat. Combine remaining ingredients and add to vegetables. Turn into a greased 1½-quart casserole. Bake at 375° for 30 to 35 minutes, or until brown. Makes 6 to 8 servings.

Roz Levin, St. Louis Region

PASSOVER HOLLANDAISE SAUCE

- ½ cup Passover margarine
- 2 egg yolks
- ¼ teaspoon salt
- Dash of pepper
- 2 tablespoons lemon juice

Melt margarine. Beat yolks until thick and lemon-colored; add salt and pepper. Add margarine and lemon juice. Makes ⅔ cup.

Mabelle Schero, Chicago Region

PASSOVER FRUITED MATZO PUDDING

4 cups matzo farfel
2 quarts boiling water
8 eggs, separated
1 cup sugar
2 teaspoons salt
8 tablespoons hot oil
3 cups dried fruit, cut up with kitchen scissors
½ cup chopped nuts

Pour boiling water over farfel which has been placed in a colander and let it drain. Beat egg yolks with sugar until smooth. Add farfel, salt and stiffly beaten egg whites. Use rectangular baking dish. Heat oil in baking dish; drain off excess and add to pudding mixture. Add fruits and nuts. Bake at 350° for 1 hour. Makes 12 servings.

Norma Platt, Chicago Region

POTATO KUGEL

4 large potatoes, grated
1 onion, grated
4 eggs
1 teaspoon salt
Dash of pepper
⅓ cup shortening

Mix potatoes and onions; blend in beaten eggs and seasonings. Preheat oven to 400° and set 11x7-inch glass baking dish in oven with shortening. When fat is melted, add potato mixture. Bake for 1 hour, or until golden brown. Makes 4 servings.

Lillie Feigenbaum, Milwaukee Region

PASSOVER SPINACH SOUFFLE

1 pound spinach
1 tablespoon matzo meal
Salt, pepper
2 eggs, separated
1 tablespoon melted chicken fat or butter

Boil spinach 10 minutes. Drain well, then chop. Add matzo meal, salt, pepper, beaten egg yolks and fat. Beat whites; fold in last. Put by spoonful into greased muffin pans; bake at 350° for 25 minutes.

Sylvia Zimmerman, Chicago Region

PASSOVER EGGPLANT CASSEROLE

- 3 tablespoons butter
- 1 large onion, sliced thin
- 1 medium eggplant, pared and cut into ½-inch cubes
- ½ green pepper, diced
- 1 teaspoon salt
- ¼ teaspoon pepper
- 1 8-oz. can tomato sauce
- 1 4-oz. can mushrooms
- 2 tomatoes, cubed
- 1 pound cream-style cottage cheese
- 1½ cup matzo farfel or 2 matzos finely broken

Saute onion in butter. Combine next 7 ingredients, add to onion, cover, and cook 15 minutes. Stir in tomatoes. Grease 2-qt. casserole and arrange alternate layers of vegetables, cottage cheese and farfel, beginning and ending with vegetables. Bake uncovered at 350° for 20 to 25 minutes. May be put together ahead of time and refrigerated. Makes 6 servings.

Phyllis Galst, Milwaukee Region

PASSOVER BEEF BRISKET WITH TZIMMES

- 1 4-lb. boneless beef brisket
- Meat tenderizer (optional)
- 2 medium onions, thinly sliced
- 1¼ cups water
- 1½ tablespoons brown sugar
- ¼ teaspoon nutmeg
- ¾ cup each: dried apricots and prunes
- 8 small carrots, pared and diagonally sliced
- 4 medium white or sweet potatoes, pared and sliced

If you wish, sprinkle surface of meat with tenderizer. Do not use salt. Pierce meat deeply with fork at ½-inch intervals. Place meat, fat side down, in dutch oven or roaster. Add onions; brown over medium heat, turning frequently. Add water, sugar and spices; cover tightly and simmer over low heat or place in oven at 300° allowing 40 to 50 minutes per pound. About an hour before done, add prunes, apricots, carrots and potatoes in alternate layers; cook until meat, vegetables and fruits are tender. Makes 10 to 12 servings.

Jean Goldrosen, Northern Illinois Region

PASSOVER ORANGE ROAST BRISKET

5 or 6-lb beef brisket
Salt
Pepper
Garlic
Paprika
2 or 3 onions, sliced
1 cup orange juice
½ cup Passover fruit wine
2 tablespoons catsup
1 teaspoon sugar

Rub meat with salt, pepper, garlic, and paprika. Cover and let stand overnight in the refrigerator. Line a roaster pan with half the sliced onions and top with meat, fat side up. Combine juice, wine, catsup and sugar and pour over roast. Top with remaining onions. Roast at 325° for 3 or 4 hours. Remove from oven about ½ hour before carving. Slice against grain. Makes 8 to 10 servings.

Sharon Goldman, Chicago Region

PASSOVER SWEET AND SOUR MEATBALLS

2 pounds ground beef
⅔ cup matzo meal
½ cup water
2 eggs, slightly beaten
½ cup minced onion
1 teaspoon salt
¼ teaspoon pepper
1 large onion, diced
½ cup lemon juice
1 cup sugar
1 11-oz. can tomato-mushroom sauce
½ cup water

Combine beef, matzo meal, water, eggs, onion, salt and pepper. Shape into meatballs. In large pot, combine diced onion, lemon juice, sugar, tomato sauce and water. Bring to a boil; add meatballs, reduce heat and simmer for about an hour. May be prepared in advance. Serves 8 as a main dish or about 16 as an appetizer.

Anne Ring, Lake County Region

PASSOVER CHICKEN CROQUETTES

Small chicken
2 eggs
1 tablespoon grated onion
3 tablespoons matzo meal
Salt
Pepper

Boil chicken. Remove skin. Remove meat from bones and chop chicken fine. Mix with remaining ingredients. Form into patties. Fry in deep fat.

Sylvia Zimmerman, Chicago Region

GLAZED CHICKEN WITH MATZO-NUT STUFFING

1 4-4½ pound chicken
⅓ cup vegetable shortening or chicken fat
⅓ cup minced onion
⅓ cup finely chopped celery
⅓ cup chopped almonds
4 matzos, broken (2½ cups farfel may be substituted)
½ teaspoon salt
⅛ teaspoon pepper
1 egg, slightly beaten
1 can condensed clear chicken soup
1 tablespoon grated orange rind

GLAZE:
1 cup orange juice
2 teaspoons grated orange rind
¼ cup honey
¼ cup peanut oil or chicken fat

Saute onion, celery and nuts in fat until vegetables are tender; add matzos and toss lightly. Combine salt, pepper, egg, chicken soup and orange rind in a large bowl. Add matzo mixture and mix well. Fill chicken. Place chicken on a rack in open roasting pan with breast side down for first half of roasting time. Roast at 325° for 1 hour. Turn chicken. Mix all ingredients for glaze. Baste chicken often. Roast for another 1 to 1½ hours, basting frequently until chicken is done. This recipe must not be made ahead; do not stuff chicken until you are ready to roast it. Makes 4 to 6 servings.

Helen Pollans, Chicago Region

PASSOVER COOKIES

1 cup sugar
2 eggs
½ cup oil
3 tablespoons lemon juice
½ cup potato starch
1 cup cake meal

Optional:
Cut up chocolate bars
½ cup chopped walnuts
Cocoa may be added for chocolate cookies

Cream sugar and eggs. Add oil; then lemon juice and sifted starch and cake meal. Mix with large wooden spoon until well-blended. Blend in one or more of the optional ingredients if desired. Chill until firm. Drop on well-greased cooky sheet or shape into long rolls for mandel bread. Bake at 350° until brown.

Enid Shultz, Lake County Region

PASSOVER CHOCOLATE CHIP COOKIES

½ cup oil
1 cup sugar
4 eggs
2 cups matzo meal
1 teaspoon lemon juice
1 teaspoon salt
1 cup chopped nuts
1 6-oz. package semi-sweet chocolate pieces

Cream oil and sugar. Alternately add eggs and matzo meal, starting and finishing with an egg. Add lemon juice and salt. Mix in nuts and chocolate chips. Drop by teaspoonful on greased cooky sheets. Bake at 350° for 10 to 15 minutes. May be made ahead and/or frozen. Makes 50 to 60 cookies.

Brenda Safer, Milwaukee Region

GINGER CANDY

1 cup granulated sugar
½ cup water
½ cup honey
1 tablespoon ginger
1½ cups matzo meal

In a saucepan, combine sugar, water, honey and ginger; cook until mixture thickens, about 2 minutes. In order to work with it, place the bowl in a pan of water, dip hands in matzo meal and then form the dough into balls, coating well with the meal.

LEMON OR STRAWBERRY MOUSSE (PASSOVER)

- 1 tablespoon gelatin
- ½ cup cold water
- 1 cup boiling water
- 1 cup sugar
- ¼ cup fresh lemon juice
- ½ cup pureed strawberries
- 3 egg whites, stiffly beaten
- A few whole strawberries

Soak gelatin in cold water. Blend into boiling water; stir until gelatin dissolves. Stir in sugar and juice **or** pureed berries. Chill until thickened. Fold in egg whites. Serve in crystal bowl. Decorate with whole strawberries.

Sylvia Zimmerman, Chicago Region

PASSOVER BLUEBERRY MUFFINS

- ⅓ cup shortening
- Scant cup of sugar
- 3 eggs
- ½ teaspoon vanilla
- ½ cup cake meal
- ¼ cup potato starch
- ¼ teaspoon salt
- 1 cup blueberries (frozen, drained)

Cream sugar and shortening. Add 3 eggs, one at a time, beating after each. Add vanilla; mix. Add meal, starch and salt. Fold in blueberries. Bake in muffin pans, using paper liners. Bake at 350° for 45 minutes. May be frozen. Makes 12 muffins.

Mrs. Ronna Locketz, Twin Cities Region

PASSOVER MANDELBROT

- ⅔ cup oil
- 3 eggs
- ¾ cup sugar
- ½ pound chopped almonds or pecans
- 1¾ cups matzo cake meal
- 1 teaspoon almond flavoring or lemon juice

Mix oil, eggs and sugar thoroughly; add nuts and cake meal. Mix until well blended. Divide dough into 2 equal parts; spread each the length of an oiled 15x10-inch pan. Bake at 350° for 20 to 25 minutes. While hot, cover with confectioners' sugar and slice.

Jean Emer, Lake County Region

PASSOVER CHOCOLATE WINE CAKE

- 8 eggs, separated
- 1½ cups sugar
- ¾ cup cake meal
- 2 tablespoons cocoa
- 1 orange (juice and grated rind)
- ¼ cup wine
- ½ teaspoon salt

Beat yolks with sugar until thick and lemon-colored. Sift cake meal with cocoa and stir in. Add grated orange rind, juice, and wine. Mix well. Add salt to egg whites; beat until stiff and fold into mixture. Put in tube pan; bake at 325° for 50 minutes. Cool upside down.

Natalie Sklansky, Chicago Region

PASSOVER HONEY CAKE

- 3 eggs
- 1 cup sugar
- 1 cup honey
- 1 cup hot coffee
- 2 cups matzo cake meal
- ½ cup potato starch
- 2 teaspoons baking soda
- 1 teaspoon ginger
- 1 teaspoon cinnamon
- ½ cup vegetable oil
- 2 tablespoons chopped nuts

Beat eggs well, adding sugar gradually. Blend honey into hot coffee; cool to lukewarm. Add to egg mixture. Sift dry ingredients and add to egg mixture with oil and nuts, blending thoroughly. Pour into an oiled 13x9-inch baking pan (or use 2 9-inch rounds or 2 10-inch tube pans). Bake at 325° for 30 minutes; increase heat to 350° and bake 15 minutes longer. Cool in pan. Freezes well.

Aileen Melnick, Northern Illinois Region

PASSOVER APRICOT JAM

- 1 pound dry apricots
- 6 cups water
- 3 cups sugar

Soak apricots (whole or cut-up) in 6 cups water, overnight. Boil ½ hour, then add 3 cups sugar; boil 15 minutes. Stir continuously, so it does not burn. Pour into sterilized glasses and seal.

Mollie Schwartz, Chicago Region

PASSOVER SPONGE CAKE

12 eggs, separated
1¼ cups sugar
½ cup orange juice and grated rind of 1 orange
1 cup sifted matzo cake meal

Beat yolks with 1 cup sugar. Add juice and grated rind. Fold in cake meal. Beat whites until stiff. Beat in ½ cup sugar. Fold yolk mixture into beaten whites. Bake in large tube pan at 325° for 1 hour. Cool 1 hour inverted. Remove from pan. Freezes well. Makes 12 servings.

Mrs. Marvin Topper, Milwaukee Region

PASSOVER CHOCOLATE NUT CAKE

9 eggs, separated
2 tablespoons lemon juice
2 teaspoons lemon rind
1½ cups sugar
½ cup grated fresh apple or applesauce
2 tablespoons sweet red wine
¾ cup ground walnuts or pecans
2 1-oz. squares unsweetened chocolate, grated
¾ cup cake meal
Dash of salt

Place egg yolks in large bowl; add lemon juice and rind and beat until blended, adding sugar gradually. Beat mixture until thick and lemon-colored, 15 to 20 minutes. After 5 minutes of beating, add apple, wine, nuts and chocolate. Sift in cake meal and fold in well. Add salt to egg whites and beat until stiff but not dry. Add egg yolk mixture and fold gently to blend. Spoon into an ungreased 10-inch tube pan; bake at 325° for 55 to 60 minutes, or until cake tests done. Invert and cool thoroughly before removing from pan.

Florence M. Mayron, Chicago Region

PASSOVER CHERRY MATZO CAKE

6 eggs, separated
2 cups sugar
1 teaspoon cinnamon
Grated rind of 1 lemon
1 cup chopped walnuts
¾ cup matzo cake meal
1 cup drained sour cherries
2 tablespoons cherry juice

In small bowl of electric mixer, beat egg whites until stiff, but not dry. In large bowl, beat eggs and sugar until thick and lemon-colored. Add cinnamon, lemon rind, nuts and cake meal. Fold in cherries and juice. Fold in egg whites. Turn into a 9-inch ungreased spring form pan and bake at 375° for 50 minutes. Serve with whipped cream, if you wish.

Miriam H. Levi, Chicago Region

PASSOVER LEMON CREAM PUFFS

Puffs:
1 cup water
⅓ cup oil
1 cup matzo meal
¼ teaspoon salt
4 eggs

Filling:
2 eggs
¾ cup sugar
1 tablespoon potato starch
Juice of 1 lemon
¾ cup water
1 tablespoon margarine

Topping:
2 tablespoons butter
1 cup sugar
⅓ cup cocoa
¼ cup milk
2 tablespoons butter

For puffs, heat water and fat to boiling in saucepan. Add matzo meal and salt; stir rapidly until dough no longer sticks to pan. Cool slightly. Add unbeaten eggs, one at a time, beating well after each. Drop by tablespoons onto a greased cooky sheet. Bake at 450° for 25 minutes; reduce heat to 325° and bake 40 minutes longer. For filling, beat eggs. Blend sugar and flour; add to eggs. Blend in lemon juice and water. Cook in top of double boiler, stirring, until thick. Add margarine; cool. Slice open shells and insert filling. For topping, melt 2 tablespoons butter in saucepan; add sugar and cocoa. Stir in milk and heat to boiling. Boil for 3 minutes. Add remaining butter; cool. Hand beat until mixture is of pouring consistency. Drizzle over puffs. Makes 12.

Sarah Myers, St. Louis Region

QUICKIE RECIPES

SHRIMP SPREAD

2 8-oz. packages cream cheese
1 teaspoon lemon juice
¼ cup dairy sour cream
4 green onions, minced
Garlic salt
Dash of worcestershire sauce
1 8-oz. package frozen cooked shrimp
2 4½-oz. cans sliced ripe olives, drained

Blend cream cheese, lemon juice, sour cream, onions and seasonings. Fold in shrimp and ripe olives just before serving. Serve with crackers or chips.

Barbara Livon, Twin Cities Region

CRAB-CLAM SPREAD

2 3-oz. packages cream cheese
¼ cup soft butter
¼ cup Miracle Whip salad dressing
1 10½-oz. can minced clams, drained
1 6½-oz. can crabmeat, drained and flaked

Blend cream cheese, butter and dressing in saucepan over low heat. Add clams and crabmeat. Serve hot from chafing dish with crackers or bread sticks.

Mrs. Victor Wexler, Milwaukee Region

GUACAMOLE

2 ripe avocados
1 tablespoon lemon juice
½ small onion, grated
2 tablespoons chili sauce
Dash of Tabasco sauce
Corn chips

Mash pulp of avocado in mixer. Blend in lemon juice, onion, chili sauce and Tabasco. Cover and chill thoroughly. Serve with corn chips. Makes 10 servings.

Jill Kneeter, Des Moines Chapter-at-Large

CHUCK STEAK WITH VEGETABLES

1 3-lb. beef chuck steak
Oil
1 1½-oz. envelope spaghetti sauce mix with mushrooms
2 1 lb. cans small whole potatoes, drained
1 16-oz. can sliced carrots, drained
2 4-oz. cans mushrooms, drained

Brown steak slowly in oil, allowing about 10 minutes on each side. In the meantime, prepare sauce according to package directions. Pour over meat. Cover pan and bake at 350° for 1 hour. Add potatoes, carrots and mushrooms. Cover and bake 30 minutes longer, or until beef is tender. If you wish, substitute fresh pared potatoes for canned potatoes; add to beef with sauce mix. Makes 6 to 8 servings.

Elaine Achler, Northern Illinois Region

COLD MARINATED BEEF

1 pound sliced, cooked roast beef
2 onions, sliced
1½ teaspoons salt
½ teaspoon pepper
3 tablespoons lemon juice
2 cups dairy sour cream

Combine all ingredients; chill several hours or overnight. Makes 12 servings.

Erika Brodsky, Lake County Region

EASY OVEN STEW

2 to 3 pounds beef stew meat, cubed
1 $10\frac{1}{2}$-oz. can cream of mushroom soup
1 $10\frac{1}{2}$-oz. can onion soup
2 soup cans water
3 cups uncooked noodles

Combine beef, soups and water in a casserole with a tight-fitting lid. Bake, covered, at 300° for 2 to 3 hours. An hour before serving, add noodles. This stew can be cooked all afternoon, if you wish. Occasionally check to see if it needs more water. Makes 6 to 8 servings.

Mrs. Bernard L. Shain, Milwaukee Region

HAMBURGER PIE

1 pound ground beef
1 tablespoon minced onion
1 teaspoon salt
Pepper to taste
¾ teaspoon Italian seasoning
1 6-oz. can tomato paste
1 can quick crescent dinner rolls
4 slices mozzarella cheese

In skillet, brown ground beef; pour off drippings. Add onion, seasonings and tomato paste; blend well. Open can of rolls. Unroll and separate dough into 8 triangles. Place in an ungreased 9-inch pie pan, pressing pieces together to form a crust. Turn meat mixture into crust; top with cheese. Bake at 375° for 25 to 30 minutes. Makes 4 servings.

Joyce Kossy, Northern Illinois Region

PRESSURE COOKED BEEF STEW

1 16-oz. can baked beans
1 pound beef chuck, cut in strips
2 tablespoons catsup
1 9-oz. package frozen mixed vegetables

Place beans, beef and catsup in pressure cooker. Cook according to directions for 12 minutes. Open and add vegetables. Stir well. Heat for 2 minutes and serve. Makes 4 servings.

Sharon Graff, West Suburban Region

EASY SPAGHETTI

- 1 pound ground beef
- Salt and pepper
- 1 large onion, chopped
- 1 10¾-oz. can tomato soup
- 1 pound spaghetti
- 1 teaspoon salt
- 1 teaspoon paprika

In a large skillet, brown ground beef over low heat. Season to taste. Add onion; cover and cook until transparent, about 5 minutes. Drain fat. Add soup and 1 soup can of water, blending well. Cover and cook over low heat for 45 minutes, stirring every 10 minutes. Cook spaghetti according to directions; drain. Add spaghetti to sauce. Season. For a small family, freeze half the sauce and cook only half the spaghetti. Makes 6 servings.

Mrs. Arthur Cohen, Chicago Region

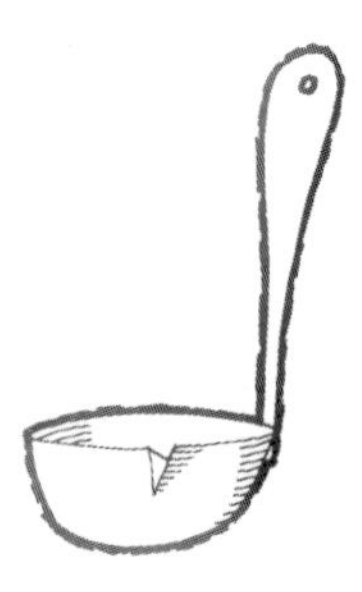

MEATZA-PIZZA

- 1 pound lean ground beef
- ½ cup dry bread crumbs
- ⅛ teaspoon garlic powder
- 1 cup milk
- ¼ teaspoon pepper
- 1 teaspoon salt
- 1 8-oz. can pizza sauce
- ½ pound grated mozzarella cheese
- 1 4-oz. can sliced mushrooms, drained
- 1 small green pepper, sliced thin into strips
- Parmesan cheese

Combine beef, bread crumbs, garlic, milk, pepper and salt; pat into an 8 or 9-inch pie pan as if it were a pie shell. Spread sauce over meat. Cover with mozzarella, mushrooms and green pepper. Sprinkle with parmesan. Bake at 350° for 45 to 60 minutes. Makes 4 servings.

Madlyn Spark, Lake County Region

MARINATED FLANK STEAK

1 beef flank steak, scored
1/4 cup soy sauce
1 cup chopped green onion
1 cup dry red wine
1/2 cup butter (1 stick)
2 tablespoons parsley

Place steak in a glass pan, 13 x 9 inches. Brush with soy sauce on both sides. Pierce with a fork. Refrigerate several hours or overnight, adding soy sauce occasionally. Shortly before serving, combine onion and wine in a saucepan; heat just to boiling. Add butter and parsley; stir until butter is melted. Grill or broil steak, allowing 4 minutes on each side. Slice diagonally into thin slices. Serve with sauce. Makes 4 servings.

Lola Stoll, West Suburban Region

SOUPER MEAT LOAF

2 pounds ground beef
1 10 3/4-oz. can vegetarian vegetable soup
1/2 cup bread crumbs or matzo meal
1/3 cup chopped onion
1 tablespoon worcestershire sauce
1 egg, slightly beaten
1 teaspoon salt
1/2 teaspoon garlic powder
Dash of pepper
1 4-oz. can mushrooms (optional)

Combine all ingredients; mix well. Shape into a loaf in a shallow baking pan. Bake at 350° for 1 hour and 15 minutes. Makes 8 servings.

Dale Madansky, Northern Illinois Region

TUNA BOATS

2 6 1/2-oz. cans tuna, drained
1/2 cup sweet pickle relish
1/2 cup sliced olives
4 hard-cooked eggs, chopped
2 cups shredded Cheddar cheese
1 cup mayonnaise
10 to 12 hamburger buns

Mix tuna with remaining ingredients except buns. Spread on buns. Wrap in foil; bake at 350° for 25 minutes. Makes 10 to 12 servings.

Mrs. Bernard L. Shain, Milwaukee Region

EASY OVEN TURBOT

- 3 pounds fresh turbot
- Garlic salt
- Lemon pepper
- Paprika

Rub seasoning on both sides of fish. Arrange in a lightly greased 13 x 9-inch pan; bake at 350° for 20 minutes. Makes 4 servings.

Francie Rosen, South Bend Chapter-at-Large

QUICK TUNA A LA KING

- 1 10½-oz. can cream of chicken soup
- 1 tablespoon instant minced onion
- ¼ teaspoon garlic powder
- Dash of celery salt
- Dash of basil
- 1 6½-oz. can tuna, drained
- 1 8½-oz. can peas or peas and carrots
- Parmesan cheese

Pour melted butter onto the bottom of a 13x9-inch baking pan. seasonings; simmer for 5 minutes. Break tuna into bite-sized pieces; add to soup with peas. Heat through, stirring often. Sprinkle with cheese. Serve over toast, noodles or rice. Chicken can be substituted for tuna, if you wish. Makes 2 to 3 servings.

Rose Krichiver, Lake County Region

VEAL SCALOPPINE MARSALA

- 2 pounds veal, sliced very thin
- ½ cup flour
- ¼ cup butter
- ⅔ cup dry Marsala wine
- ½ teaspoon salt
- ⅛ teaspoon pepper
- 1 beef bouillon cube

Dip veal slices in flour. Saute veal slices a few at a time in butter in a large skillet; turn once. Remove from pan and keep warm. Add wine to drippings in pan, stirring to loosen brown bits from bottom of pan. Blend in salt, pepper and bouillon cube. Cook and stir for 2 minutes. Return veal to pan. Cover and simmer 5 minutes. Serve with rice or noodles. To increase amount of sauce, add a little more wine, chicken broth or water. Makes 8 servings.

Lily Frandzel, Chicago Region

CRANBERRY CHICKEN

- 2 3-lb fryers, quartered
- 1 1-lb. can whole berry cranberry sauce
- 1 8-oz. bottle french dressing

Place in roasting pan, all pieces flat. Salt delicately over all. Pour the cranberry sauce and the french dressing over chicken. Cover and roast 1½ hours in 350° oven. Chicken will be juicy, tender and flavorful. If more glaze is desired, or dryer chicken pieces, uncover last 15 minutes, making certain that all pieces are moist and coated with sauce. Makes 6 servings.

Pearl Klotz, Lake County Region

MUSHROOM CHICKEN

- 1 can cream of mushroom soup
- 1 package onion soup mix
- 2 cans of water
- ¾ cup of regular rice
- 1 cut up chicken (about 9 pieces)

Combine the two soups and water. Sprinkle the rice on the bottom of the pan. Lay the chicken, skin side up, on top of the rice and pour the soups over. Bake covered for 1½ hours in 350° oven; bake for an additional ½ hour uncovered.

(Pan should be deep enough so that the soup does not run over and large enough so the chicken does not overlap — a roasting pan is good). Makes 4 servings.

Julie Smith, South Bend Chapter-at-Large

WONDER CHEESE PIE

- 1 egg
- ½ teaspoon salt
- ⅛ teaspoon pepper
- ¾ cup flour
- ½ cup milk
- ½ cup grated Cheddar cheese
- ½ cup grated Cheddar cheese

Combine all ingredients except the last ½ cup cheese. Pour into an 8-inch pie pan; bake at 425° for 30 minutes. Sprinkle remaining cheese on top of pie; bake 5 minutes longer. This cannot be frozen. Makes 6 servings.

Erika Brodsky, Lake County Region

QUICK RICE CASSEROLE

1 1/3 cups quick cooking rice
1 10½-oz. can chicken gumbo soup
1 10½-oz. can beef broth
1 soup can water

Combine all ingredients; turn into a well greased casserole. Cover and bake at 350° for 20 to 25 minutes. Uncover and bake about 10 minutes longer, until golden. Makes 4 to 6 servings.

Frances Keno, Chicago Region

PAPER BAG BARBECUED CHICKEN

3 tablespoons each: catsup, brown sugar
2 tablespoons each: vinegar, worcestershire sauce, melted butter
1 tablespoon lemon juice
¼ cup water
1 teaspoon each: salt, mustard, chili powder, paprika
1 3-lb. frying chicken, cut up
Salt and pepper

Heat all ingredients except chicken to boiling. Simmer for a few minutes to blend flavors. Season chicken. Grease inside of a brown paper bag. Dip each piece of chicken in barbecue sauce and place inside of bag. Pour remaining sauce over chicken. Tie end of bag and place in a pan. Bake at 350° for 2 hours.

Audrey Rosenberg, Des Moines Chapter-at-Large

ONION RICE

1 cup long grain rice
2 tablespoons butter
2½ cups boiling water
1 envelope dry onion soup mix

Brown rice in butter in large saucepan or skillet. Add boiling water and soup mix. Cover and simmer for 25 minutes, or until liquid is absorbed. Makes 4 to 6 servings.

Cynthia Glickman, West Suburban Region

THREE BEAN SALAD

- 1 1-lb. can cut green beans, drained
- 1 1-lb. can cut wax beans, drained
- 1 1-lb. can dark kidney beans, rinsed and drained
- ½ cup thinly sliced celery
- 20 small pimento stuffed olives, sliced
- ½ cup bottled Italian dressing (low calorie, if you wish)
- Salad seasoning and onion salt to taste

Combine all ingredients in large bowl, mixing gently but thoroughly. Cover and store in container with tight cover for several hours or overnight. Invert container occasionally to blend. Keeps well in refrigerator. Makes 8 to 10 servings.

Sue Colton, Milwaukee Region

ZUCCHINI PARMESAN

- 2 pounds zucchini
- ¼ cup butter
- 2 cloves garlic, minced or 2 teaspoons garlic powder
- 1 teaspoon paprika
- 1 tablespoon oregano
- Salt and pepper to taste
- ½ cup water
- Grated Parmesan cheese

Wash and slice zucchini crosswise. Melt butter in large skillet; add zucchini and seasonings; cook over moderate heat until zucchini softens; add water and simmer 5 minutes longer. Drain off liquid; sprinkle Parmesan over zucchini. Makes 6 to 8 servings.

Judith Zwirn, West Suburban Region

SAUTEED MUSHROOMS

- 2 pounds fresh mushrooms
- ¼ cup butter
- 1 tablespoon garlic salt

Select mushrooms with caps as tightly closed as possible. Wash thoroughly and drain well. Melt butter in skillet; add garlic salt. Add mushrooms and cook until golden brown, about 10 minutes. Pour off some of extra liquid during cooking. Serve as a vegetable accompaniment or as an appetizer on wooden picks. Makes 8 servings.

Judith Zwirn, West Suburban Region

SPINACH WITH CREAM CHEESE

- 1 10-oz. package frozen leaf or chopped spinach
- 1 tablespoon grated onion or chives
- 2 tablespoons lemon juice
- 1 teaspoon salt
- ¼ teaspoon pepper
- 1 3-oz. package cream cheese, softened

Cook spinach according to package directions; drain well. Carefully blend in onion, lemon juice, salt and pepper; blend in cheese. Makes 4 servings.

Elaine Achler, Northern Illinois Region

BLINTZ SOUFFLE

- ¼ cup butter
- 12 frozen cheese or fruit blintzes
- 4 eggs
- 1 cup dairy sour cream
- 1 teaspoon sugar
- 1 teaspoon vanilla
- 1 teaspoon cinnamon

Melt butter in a 13 x 9-inch baking dish. Add frozen blintzes, folded side down. Beat eggs with sour cream, sugar and flavorings. Pour over blintzes. Bake at 375° for 35 to 45 minutes. Makes 6 to 8 servings.

Debbie Wilner, Northern Illinois Region

QUICK COFFEE CAKE

- ½ cup dairy sour cream
- 1 cup flour
- 1 teaspoon baking powder
- 1 egg
- 1 cup sugar
- 1 teaspoon vanilla

Topping:
- Cinnamon
- Sugar
- Nuts
- Butter pieces

Beat together batter ingredients. Spread in a greased 8-inch square pan and sprinkle generously with topping. Bake at 350° for 20 to 25 minutes. Makes 16 2-inch squares.

Henriette Piel, Northern Illinois Region

CHOCOLATE PISTACHIO CAKE

1 package white or yellow cake mix
4 eggs
¾ cup oil
1 cup dairy sour cream
1 package instant pistachio pudding
1 5½-oz. can chocolate syrup

Mix all ingredients except chocolate syrup with electric mixer. Pour three-fourths of mixture into greased and floured 12-cup Bundt pan. Add syrup to remaining batter. Mix well. Knife into other batter. Bake at 350° for 1 hour. Allow to cool in pan for 1 hour. Makes 16 servings.

Bobbi Katz, West Suburban Region

BLENDER-QUICK CHOCOLATE MOUSSE

1 6-oz. package semi-sweet chocolate pieces
2 eggs
3 tablespoons strong hot coffee
1 to 2 tablespoons rum
¾ cup scalded milk

Combine ingredients. Blend 2 minutes. Chill. Makes 4 servings.

Mildred Weinstock, Chicago Region

MAGIC COOKIE BAR

½ cup butter, melted (1 stick)
1½ cups graham cracker crumbs
1 cup walnuts, coarsely chopped
1 cup (6 oz. package) semi-sweet chocolate or butterscotch pieces
1⅓ cups (3½ oz.) flaked coconut
1⅓ cups (15 oz. can) sweetened condensed milk

Pour melted butter onto the bottom of a 13x9-inch baking pan. Sprinkle crumbs evenly on top. Sprinkle chopped nuts evenly over crumbs. Scatter chocolate or butterscotch pieces over nuts (for better flavor, use 1 cup each of semisweet chocolate **and** butterscotch pieces.). Sprinkle coconut evenly over chocolate pieces. Pour sweetened condensed milk evenly over coconut. Bake at 350° for 25 minutes or until lightly browned on top. Cool in pan 15 minutes. Cut into bars. Makes 2½ dozen.

Mrs. Joel Glabman, Milwaukee Region

STRAWBERRY-PINEAPPLE PARFAITS

1 pint vanilla ice cream
1 package frozen strawberry halves
1 8-oz. can crushed pineapple
½ cup chopped cashew nuts

Garnish:
Whipped topping
Chopped nuts
Maraschino cherries

In parfait glasses, layer ice cream, strawberries, pineapple and cashews. Repeat. Then top with third ice cream layer. Freeze. Remove from freezer 15 minutes before serving to soften. Garnish and serve with cookies. Makes 4 parfaits.

Sally Simon, Northern Illinois Region

QUICK PINEAPPLE PIE

1 20-oz. can crushed pineapple
1 package vanilla pudding mix (not instant)
1 9-inch baked vanilla cookie crumb crust
Sweetened whipped cream topping

Combine pineapple and pudding mix in saucepan. Cook, stirring over medium heat, until brought to boil. Boil 1 minute, stirring constantly. Set aside to cool. Spoon into vanilla cookie crumb crust or another pre-baked crust of your choice. Chill several hours. Serve with sweetened whipped cream topping. Makes 6 to 8 servings.

Lily Frandzel, Chicago Region

BUTTER PECAN MYSTERY CAKE

1 package yellow cake mix
1 pint butter pecan ice cream
3 eggs
⅔ cup water

Combine dry cake mix, ice cream, eggs and water in large bowl. Blend and beat as directed on package. Turn into a well-greased, lightly-floured 13x9-inch pan. Bake at 350° for 40 to 50 minutes. Frost with chocolate frosting or sprinkle with confectioners' sugar. Makes 12 to 15 servings.

Miriam Witt, Chicago Region

PASTA and RICE DISHES

APRICOT NOODLE PUDDING

1 8-oz. package medium noodles, cook and drained
4 eggs, well beaten
1 cup dairy sour cream
Juice and grated rind of 1 lemon
½ cup melted butter (1 stick)
½ cup sugar
1 10-oz. jar peach or apricot preserves

Combine all ingredients except preserves. Turn half of mixture into a buttered 13x9-inch baking pan. Cover with preserves. Top with remaining noodle mixture. Bake at 350° for 1 hour.

Judi Silverman, Indianapolis Chapter-at-Large

APPLE BUTTER NOODLE PUDDING

1 8-oz. package wide egg noodles, cooked and drained
¼ cup butter, melted
1 egg, slightly beaten
Chopped walnuts
1 cup sugar
1 tablespoon cinnamon
1 tablespoon lemon juice
1 1-lb. jar apple butter

Combine cooked noodles and butter. Add eggs, chopped nuts, sugar, cinnamon and lemon juice. Arrange half of noodles in a greased 13x9-inch baking dish. Top with half the apple butter. Add remaining noodles, then remaining apple butter. Sprinkle with additional walnuts. Bake at 375° for 30 minutes. Makes 8 servings.

Betty Gault, Northern Illinois Region

CREAMY NOODLE KUGEL

1 8-oz. package wide noodles, cooked and drained
½ cup butter (1 stick)
1 8-oz. package cream cheese
Salt
6 tablespoons sugar
4 eggs, beaten
1¾ cups milk

Cream butter and cream cheese; add salt, sugar and eggs. Gradually add milk and blend. Stir in noodles. (Mixture will be very liquid.) Pour into a greased 13x9-inch baking dish. Bake at 350° for 1½ hours. Makes 12 servings.

Jeanne Berkowitz, Chicago Region

NOODLE KUGEL

1 8-oz. package wide noodles
3 eggs, separated
½ pint dairy sour cream
1 carton cottage cheese
½ teaspoon salt
½ cup butter, melted (1 stick)
Buttered bread crumbs

Cook noodles according to package directions, adding 1 tablespoon oil to water; drain. Beat egg yolks with sour cream, cottage cheese and melted butter; add noodles to mixture. Beat egg whites until stiff; fold into noodle mixture. Pour into a buttered 13x9-inch casserole. If you wish, top with buttered crumbs. Bake at 350° for 1 hour and 15 minutes. Makes 8 to 10 servings.

Mrs. Marvin Topper, Milwaukee Region

BUTTERMILK NOODLE PUDDING

1 16-oz. package medium noodles, cooked and drained
1 quart buttermilk
½ cup butter, melted (1 stick)
Pinch of salt
4 large or 5 medium eggs
½ cup sugar
1 cup corn flakes, slightly crushed
1 cup brown sugar
2 tablespoons butter

Combine noodles with buttermilk, melted butter, salt, beaten eggs and sugar. Turn into a 13x9-inch baking dish. Bake at 350° for 45 minutes. Remove from oven and top with mixture of corn flakes, brown sugar and butter. Bake 30 minutes longer. Let stand 20 minutes before serving. Makes 12 to 16 strvings.

Ruth Landsman, Chicago Region

CHEDDAR NOODLE PUDDING

1 8-oz. package medium noodles, cooked and drained
1 13-oz. can evaporated milk
½ cup water
2 eggs, beaten
1½ cups grated Cheddar or American cheese
1 cup crushed potato chips

Mix noodles with evaporated milk, water, eggs and 1 cup grated cheese. Turn into a 13x9-inch greased baking dish. Cover with remaining cheese and crushed potato chips. Bake at 400° for 20 to 25 minutes. Makes 8 to 10 servings.

Ann Roman Siegel, Chicago Region

CHEESE NOODLE PUDDING

1 8-oz. package noodles, cooked and drained
6 tablespoons butter
1½ cups dairy sour cream
¾ cup small curd creamed cottage cheese
Salt and pepper, to taste
4 slices American cheese, cut into strips

Mix noodles with butter, sour cream, cottage cheese, seasonings and 2 slices of American cheese. Place in a souffle dish or casserole; decorate top with remaining cheese strips. Bake at 325° for 1¼ hours. Makes 8 servings.

Mrs. Samuel D. Arnstein, Chicago Region

CHERRY KUGEL

1 12-oz. package wide noodles, cooked and drained
2 eggs, slightly beaten
⅔ cup sugar
1 teaspoon vanilla
1 16-oz. can pitted tart cherries, drained

Combine eggs with sugar and vanilla; add noodles. Stir in cherries. Turn into a well-greased 2-quart casserole. Bake at 350° for 35 minutes, or until top is golden brown. Makes 8 to 10 servings.

Linda Kline, Des Moines Chapter-at-Large

CHEESE NOODLE PUDDING

- 1 16-oz. package broad noodles, cooked and drained
- ½ cup butter, melted (1 stick)
- 5 eggs, well beaten
- ¼ cup dairy sour cream
- 3 to 4 tablespoons sugar
- 1½ cups milk
- 1 8-oz. package cream cheese
- 3 tablespoons Cheez Whiz
- 1 16-oz. carton cottage cheese
- Butter
- Corn flake crumbs

Mix noodles and butter. Mix beaten eggs with sour cream and sugar; add to noodles. Heat milk to lukewarm; add cheeses; stir until melted. Add to noodles with cottage cheese, stirring to blend. Melt butter in the bottom of a 3-quart rectangular casserole. Pour in noodle mixture; top with corn flake crumbs. Dot with butter and bake at 350° for 1 hour and 15 minutes. Makes 10 to 12 servings.

Bert Robins, Lake County Region

CHERRY TOPPED KUGEL

- 1 16-oz. package medium or wide noodles, cooked and drained
- 7 large eggs
- ½ cup milk
- ½ teaspoon salt
- 1 13¼-oz. can crushed pineapple in heavy syrup
- ½ cup raisins (optional)
- 1 cup cottage cheese
- ½ cup sugar
- ¼ cup butter, melted
- ¾ cup cornflake crumbs
- 1 20-oz. can cherry pie filling

In large bowl, beat eggs; add milk, salt, pineapple plus syrup, raisins, cheese and sugar. Slowly add cooked noodles. Mix melted butter and crumbs; place in a 13x9-inch baking dish. Carefully add noodle mixture, spreading evenly on top of crumbs. Spread cherries evenly over noodles. Bake at 350° for 40 minutes. Let noodles stand 15 minutes before cutting. Makes 16 servings.

Min Hirsch, Lake County Region

NOODLE PUDDING WITH HOT BRANDY SAUCE

- 1 16-oz. package broad noodles, cooked and drained
- 6 eggs, well beaten
- 1 16-oz. carton creamed cottage cheese
- 1/4 cup butter, melted
- 1 tablespoon dairy sour cream
- 1/2 teaspoon vanilla
- 1/2 cup sugar
- 1 teaspoon salt
- 1/2 teaspoon cinnamon

Brandy Sauce:

- 1 16-oz. can apricot filling
- 1 10-oz. jar apricot or peach preserves
- 3 tablespoons honey
- 1/2 cup boiling water
- Dash of lemon juice
- 3 tablespoons apricot brandy
- 2 tablespoons brown sugar
- Butter

Mix noodles with remaining ingredients; turn into a 13x9-inch greased baking dish and bake at 350° for 1 hour or until brown. Serve with hot brandy sauce, made by combining remaining ingredients. Makes 12 servings.

Norma L. Platt, Chicago Region

ONION NOODLE KUGEL

- 1 package dry onion soup mix
- 1 cup water
- 1 12-oz. package wide noodles, cooked and drained
- 5 eggs, beaten
- 2 tablespoons schmaltz (rendered chicken fat)
- Oil

Blend onion soup mix and water; heat to boiling and simmer until mixture thickens; cool. Add cooled onion mixture to beaten eggs and schmaltz. Blend into noodles. Generously coat a 13x9-inch baking pan with oil. Preheat pan in oven at 325° for 15 minutes. Turn noodle mixture into baking pan. Bake at 325° for 1 hour, or until noodles are browned. Makes 10 to 12 servings.

Debbie Sherman, Twin Cities Region

PEACH KUGEL

- 1 16-oz. package wide noodles, cooked and drained
- 4 eggs
- 1½ cups sugar
- 1 teaspoon salt
- 1 8-oz. carton cottage cheese
- ½ cup butter (1 stick)
- 1 pint dairy sour cream
- 2 16-oz. cans sliced or halved peaches
- ½ cup peach syrup

Beat eggs with sugar and salt. Blend in cottage cheese, butter and sour cream. Combine with noodles and peach syrup. Turn into 2 buttered 13x9-inch baking pans, being careful not to fill too full. Top with peaches. Bake at 350° for 1½ hours. Makes 16 to 20 servings.

Mrs. Charles H. Cell, Twin Cities Region

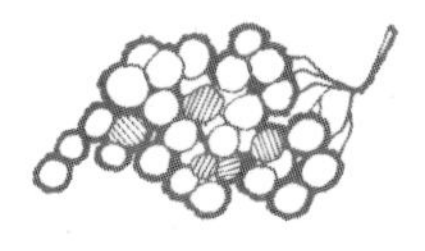

SWEET KUGEL

- 1 16-oz. package noodles, cooked and drained
- 6 eggs, beaten
- 1 8-oz. package cream cheese
- 1½ pounds cottage cheese
- 1 16-oz. can applesauce
- 1 cup white raisins
- 1½ cups sugar
- Nutmeg
- Cinnamon
- ½ cup butter, melted (1 stick)

Mix drained noodles with eggs, cream cheese, cottage cheese, applesauce, raisins, sugar and spices. Melt butter in a 13x9-inch baking pan. Add noodle mixture. Cover and bake at 350° for 1 hour. Uncover and bake 30 minutes longer. Makes 12 to 16 servings.

Mrs. Morris Rosen, South Bend Chapter-at-Large

UPSIDE DOWN NOODLE PUDDING

- 1 8-oz. package wide noodles, cooked and drained
- 4 eggs, beaten
- ½ cup sugar
- ¾ cup dairy sour cream
- ¾ carton creamed cottage cheese
- 1 to 2 tart red apples, grated
- ½ cup butter, melted (1 stick)
- Dark brown sugar

Combine noodles with eggs, sugar, sour cream, cottage cheese and apples. Melt butter in a 13x9-inch glass baking dish. Sprinkle brown sugar evenly over butter. Press down with a fork to make sure bottom of dish is completely covered. Add noodle mixture. Bake at 350° for 1 hour and 10 minutes. Just before serving, turn out onto a serving platter. The brown sugar and butter will be caramelized. Makes 12 servings.

Norma L. Platt, Chicago Region

NOODLE PUDDING SOUFFLE

- 3 eggs, separated
- ½ cup butter melted (1 stick)
- 2 tablespoons sugar
- 1 pound creamed cottage cheese
- 1 cup dairy sour cream
- 1 8-oz. package noodles, cooked and drained
- ½ cup crushed corn flakes
- Butter

Beat egg yolks; add melted butter and sugar. Add cottage cheese, sour cream and noodles. Fold in stiffly beaten egg whites. Place in a buttered 13x9-inch baking dish. Sprinkle with corn flakes. Dot with butter. Bake at 375° for 45 minutes. Makes 8 servings.

Erika Brodsky, Lake County Region

NOODLES WITH PESTO SAUCE

1 8-oz. package noodles
1 tablespoon salt
3 tablespoons butter
1 tablespoon olive oil
1/4 teaspoon crushed garlic
3 tablespoons chopped parsley
1 teaspoon basil
1/2 teaspoon marjoram

Cook noodles in 3 quarts boiling water with salt until tender. In the meantime, make sauce: Melt butter in small saucepan; remove from heat and add remaining ingredients. Mix well. Drain noodles; toss with sauce until well coated. Makes 6 servings.

Mrs. Stanley Palmer, St. Louis Region

SEA SHELLS PARMESAN

1 10 1/2-oz. can cream of mushroom soup
1/4 cup milk
2 tablespoons melted butter
1 teaspoon oregano
1/2 cup ricotta cheese
1/4 cup grated parmesan cheese
1/4 cup dairy sour cream
1 8-oz. package macaroni shells, cooked and drained
1/3 cup sliced stuffed olives (optional)

In saucepan blend soup, milk and butter; heat until blended and smooth. Add oregano, cheeses and sour cream. Cook and stir until heated through. Add macaroni shells and olives; serve at once. Makes 4 to 6 servings.

Arleen Levy, Lake County Region

NOODLES ROMANOFF

1 8-oz. package noodles
1 1/2 cups dairy sour cream
3/4 cup grated American cheese
2 tablespoons Parmesan cheese
1/2 teaspoon salt
1/4 teaspoon garlic powder
1 teaspoon worcestershire sauce
Dash of Tabasco sauce

Cook and drain noodles. Combine remaining ingredients except Parmesan; toss with noodles. Turn into a buttered 2-quart casserole. Sprinkle with Parmesan. Bake at 325° for 35 to 40 minutes. Makes 4 to 6 servings.

Flora Jane Gold, Northern Illinois Region

BAKED TOMATO RICE

- 3 tablespoons butter
- ¼ cup minced onion
- 1 cup long grain rice
- 1 cup tomato juice
- 1 14-oz. can chicken broth
- 2 tablespoons parsley flakes

Melt butter in skillet; add onion and rice and cook over moderate heat for 10 to 15 minutes, or until rice is golden. Stir frequently. Remove from heat; add remaining ingredients. Pour into a 1-quart casserole. Cover and bake at 350° for 30 minutes; stir. Cover and bake about 15 minutes longer, or until rice is tender. Makes 4 to 6 servings.

Miriam Witt, Chicago Region

CURRIED RICE

- ¼ cup butter
- 1½ teaspoons salt
- ½ teaspoon pepper
- ½ teaspoon curry powder
- ¼ cup minced green onions and tops
- 1 8-oz. can whole tomatoes, chopped
- 2 cups water
- 2 chicken bouillon cubes
- 1 cup long grain rice

Melt butter in large suacepan; add seasonings and vegetables. Cook and stir until vegetables are softened. Add water and bouillon cubes; heat to boiling. Stir in rice. Cover and simmer for 30 minutes, or until rice is tender and liquid is absorbed. Makes 4 to 6 servings.

Rosalie Hersh, Northern Illinois Region

OVEN STEAMED RICE

- 1½ cups long grain rice
- 1½ teaspoons salt
- Dash of pepper
- 2 tablespoons butter
- 3½ cups boiling water
- ¼ cup sliced green onions

In 2-quart ungreased casserole with tight-fitting cover, mix rice and seasonings. Dot with butter. Pour boiling water over rice; stir with fork to blend and melt butter. Bake, covered at 350° for 45 minutes. Add green onions, mix lightly and serve. Makes 6 to 8 servings.

June Brody, Lake County Region

VENETIAN RICE

1 medium onion, chopped
3 tablespoons butter
1 cup long grain rice
1 teaspoon leaf basil, crumbled
½ teaspoon seasoned salt
Dash of pepper
1 14-oz. can chicken broth
1¼ cups water
1 10-oz. package frozen peas, cooked and drained
2 tablespoons grated Parmesan cheese

Cook onion in butter until golden in large skillet; stir in rice. Continue cooking, stirring constantly, until rice is golden. Stir in seasonings, broth and water. Heat to boiling. Cover and simmer for 20 to 25 minutes, or until rice is tender and liquid is absorbed. Stir in peas; sprinkle with cheese. Toss lightly and serve. Makes 4 to 6 servings.

Lily Frandzel, Chicago Region

WILD RICE CASSEROLE

1 cup chopped onion
1 cup chopped celery
2 tablespoons butter
1 cup uncooked wild rice
2 10½-oz. cans cream of mushroom soup
1 4½-oz. jar sliced mushrooms
1 2-oz. jar sliced pimento
1½ cups grated Swiss cheese
3 tablespoons Sherry
¾ cup chopped walnuts

Saute onion and celery in butter; wash rice in cold water, drain and add to vegetables. Stir in remaining ingredients. Turn into a 2-quart casserole. Cover and bake at 325° for 1 hour and 15 minutes. Can be assembled in advance. Makes 10 servings.

Ellen Kogen, Lake County Region

MEATLESS LASAGNE

- 1 medium onion, chopped
- 3 cloves garlic, minced
- Oil
- 1 28-oz. can tomatoes
- 2 6-oz. cans tomato paste
- ½ cup water
- 1 teaspoon salt
- ½ teaspoon oregano
- ½ teaspoon basil
- 1 1 lb. package lasagne noodles
- 1½ cups ricotta cheese
- 1½ cups grated Parmesan
- ¾ cup wheat germ
- ½ pound Mozzarella cheese

Saute onion and garlic in oil; add tomato, tomato paste, water and seasonings; cover and simmer for 1 hour. Cook and drain noodles. Spread ¼ of sauce in a 13 x 9-inch baking dish. Cover with ⅓ noodles. Dot with ⅓ ricotta. Sprinkle with ⅓ of Parmesan, then ⅓ of wheat germ. Spread with another ¼ of sauce. Repeat layers, ending with sauce. Top with Mozzarella cheese. Bake at 375° for 30 minutes. Makes 8 to 10 servings.

Bonnie Wallman, Chicago Region

ORANGE RICE

- ¾ cup chopped celery
- 2 tablespoons chopped onion
- 1 cup long grain rice
- 3 tablespoons butter
- 1 teaspoon salt
- 1 teaspoon sugar
- 1 teaspoon grated orange rind
- 1 cup orange juice
- 1 cup water
- 2 sliced oranges
- ½ cup cashews
- Parsley

Saute celery, onion and rice in butter until golden. Add salt, sugar, rind, orange juice and water. Heat to boiling. Stir once, cover and simmer for 25 minutes. Add orange slices and cashews. Toss to mix. Garnish with parsley and serve. Makes 4 to 6 servings.

Erika Brodsky, Lake County Region

LOW-CALORIE BAKED FISH CREOLE

- 2 cups stewed tomatoes
- 1/4 cup thinly sliced onion
- 1/4 cup chopped green pepper
- 1/4 cup chopped mushrooms
- 1 tablespoon lemon juice
- 1/4 teaspoon liquid sweetener
- Pinch of oregano
- 1/8 teaspoon dry mustard
- 2 pounds whitefish fillets
- Salt and pepper, to taste

In a saucepan, combine all ingredients except fish and salt and pepper. Simmer for 15 minutes. Arrange fish in a Teflon-lined baking dish. Season with salt and pepper. Top with vegetables and bake at 350° for 30 minutes. Makes 6 to 8 servings.

Florence Kaplan, Chicago Region

LOW-CALORIE SALMON RING

- 2 16-oz. cans salmon, drained and flaked
- 1 cup skim milk
- 6 eggs
- 2 tablespoons chives
- 2 sprigs parsley
- 1/2 teaspoon salt
- 1/4 teaspoon pepper

Tomato Sauce:

- 1 10 3/4-oz. can tomato soup
- 1 teaspoon worcestershire sauce
- 1/4 teaspoon pepper

Mix salmon with remaining ingredients; divide mixture into 2 parts. Mix well in blender. Pour into a well-oiled 6-cup ring mold. Set mold in a pan of hot water and bake at 400° for 50 minutes, or until knife inserted comes out clean. Let stand for 20 minutes; unmold. For sauce, combine and heat remaining ingredients. Makes 6 to 8 servings.

Sheila Seidmon, Northern Illinois Region

LOW-CALORIE CHICKEN CASSEROLE

- 2 whole chicken breasts
- 1 16-oz. can french style green beans
- 1 8½-oz. can peas
- ½ pound fresh mushrooms, sliced
- 1 cup water
- 2 chicken bouillon cubes
- ¼ cup soy sauce

Arrange chicken and vegetables in a baking dish. Dissolve chicken bouillon in hot water; blend in soy sauce. Pour over chicken and vegetables. Let stand before baking if possible. Bake at 350° for 30 minutes. Makes 2 servings.

Carolyn Lieder, Chicago Region

VEGETARIAN SPAGHETTI AND MEAT SAUCE

- 1 onion, diced
- Ground celery seed
- 1 green pepper, diced
- 1½ pounds ground beef
- 1 4-oz. can mushrooms
- 1 8-oz. can tomato sauce
- 1 6-oz. can tomato paste
- Oregano
- 2 9-oz. packages frozen Italian green beans

In Teflon frying pan, combine onion, celery seed (a couple of good shakes) and green pepper; cook until browned. Add meat and cook until brown. Combine mushrooms plus liquid, tomato sauce, tomato paste and oregano; add to meat mixture and simmer for 30 minutes. Cook beans as directed on package. Drain well. Serve hot meat sauce over green beans. Makes 4 servings.

Florence Kaplan, Chicago Region

DIETERS TUNA SANDWICH

- 1 slice bread
- 2 ounces tuna (packed in oil)
- 4 ounces fresh mushrooms, sliced
- 1 egg
- ½ cup milk
- ¼ cup soy sauce
- Onion flakes, to taste

Place bread in bottom of a small casserole dish. Top with tuna and mushrooms. Combine remaining ingredients and pour over all. Bake at 350° for 30 minutes. Makes 1 serving.

Carolyn Lieder, Chicago Region

CAULIFLOWER-CHEESE CASSEROLE

1 head cauliflower, in flowerets
¼ cup tomato juice
Parsley
Oregano
½ teaspoon garlic powder
1 to 2 slices Swiss or American cheese

Cook fresh or frozen caulifowerets in water until just tender, about 15 minutes. Arrange in casserole. Combine tomato juice and seasonings and pour over cauliflower. Cut cheese into thin strips. Arrange in lattice pattern over cauliflower. Bake at 350° just until heated through and cheese melts.

Natalie Sklansky, Chicago Region

DIETERS CHOP SUEY

1 8-oz. package frozen diced chicken
1 16-oz. can Chinese vegetables, drained and rinsed
Garlic powder
Soy sauce

Combine all ingredients in a Teflon pan, seasoning to taste. Heat through and serve. Makes 1 serving.

Phyllis Silver, Northern Illinois Region

LOW-CALORIE FRENCH DRESSING I

½ cup tomato juice
2 tablespoons vinegar
2 tablespoons minced green pepper
½ teaspoon worcestershire sauce
½ teaspoon salt
½ teaspoon dry mustard
Dash of garlic salt
¼ teaspoon sugar substitute
1 teaspoon onion flakes plus hot water (optional)

Combine all ingredients; blend well. Chill and serve over tossed greens or other salads. For low-calorie egg salad, mix chopped eggs with 1 teaspoon pickle relish and dressing to moisten.

Miriam H. Levi, Chicago Region

LOW-CALORIE FRENCH DRESSING II

- 1/4 cup salad oil
- 1/2 cup water
- 1/2 cup lime juice
- 1/2 teaspoon dry mustard
- 1 teaspoon salt
- 1 teaspoon celery salt
- 1 teaspoon onion powder
- 1/2 teaspoon black pepper
- 1/2 teaspoon oregano

Combine all ingredients; chill well before serving over vegetable or green salad. Makes about 1 cup dressing.

Sheila Seidmon, Northern Illinois Region

APPLE CRISP, LOW-CAL STYLE

- 4 apples, pared, cored and sliced
- 1/4 cup reconstituted lemon juice
- 1 teaspoon lemon extract
- 1/3 cup nonfat dry milk
- 1 teaspoon cinnamon
- 1/2 cup dry sugar substutite
- 1 tablespoon artificial brown sugar

Arrange apples in rows in bottom of 7 x 10-inch baking pan. Sprinkle with lemon juice and extract. Mix dry milk with remaining ingredients; sprinkle on apples. Bake at 350° for 45 minutes. Makes 4 servings.

Mrs. Melvin Gilbert, Milwaukee Region

STRAWBERRY PUDDING, DIET STYLE

- 1 envelope (1 tablespoon) plain gelatin
- 1/2 cup boiling water
- 1/3 cup nonfat dry milk
- 3 teaspoons sugar substitute
- 1 capfull vanilla
- 1/2 cup fresh or non-sweetened frozen strawberries
- 6 ice cubes

Place water and gelatin in blender; mix. Add milk, sweetener, vanilla and strawberries; mix. Add ice cubes gradually. Chill and serve. Makes 1 serving.

Phyllis Bower, Chicago Region

PINEAPPLE SAILBOATS

2 small pineapples
2 medium fresh peaches
2 tablespoons Kirsch or apricot brandy
5 egg whites
Dash of salt
10 tablespoons sugar, or the equivalent in a powdered sugar substitute

Cut pineapple in halves lengthwise, leaving the green ends intact. Remove the meat without cutting the shells. Cube pineapple. Poach peaches in 1 cup water for 10 minutes. Skin, pit and cut in slices. Marinate fruit in Kirsch or brandy in refrigerator for at least an hour. Divide fruit among pineapple shells. Beat egg whites with salt and sugar until stiff. Spread over pineapple, making sure you touch the edges. Place on baking sheet and bake at 450° for 3 to 5 minutes, or until meringue is lightly browned. Serve at once. Makes 4 servings.

Ruth Weissman, Lake County Region

LOW-CALORIE SPONGE CAKE

6 eggs, separated
6 tablespoons sugar
1 teaspoon grated lemon rind
1 teaspoon vanilla
¼ teaspoon baking powder
10 level tablespoons cake flour

Let egg whites stand at room temperature for 1 hour. Beat egg yolks with sugar until thick and lemon colored. Add lemon rind and vanilla; mix well. Add baking powder, blending well again. Beat egg whites until stiff but not dry. Fold into yolk mixture, alternating with spoonfuls of sifted flour. Turn into a buttered and floured 8-inch spring form pan. Bake at 350° for 30 to 35 minutes, or until cake tests done. Cake can be frozen. Makes 10 to 12 servings.

Mrs. S. J. Hiller, Milwaukee Region

BAKED ACORN SQUASH

1 acorn squash
2 teaspoons butter
2 tablespoons brown sugar
½ cup syrup from canned pears, peaches or fruit cocktail

Cut squash in half. Scoop out seeds. Fill each half with a teaspoon butter, a tablespoon sugar and ¼ cup fruit syrup. Place in greased baking dish; bake at 350° for 1½ hours. Makes 2 servings.

Esther Kramer, Indianapolis Chapter-at-Large

ASPARAGUS CASSEROLE

2 1-lb. cans asparagus
3 tablespoons butter
3 tablespoons flour
¾ teaspoon salt
1 cup asparagus stock
2 tablespoons grated American cheese
½ cup milk or cream
2 egg yolks, beaten
Ritz crackers, crushed for topping

Drain asparagus, reserving liquid. Melt butter in saucepan; blend in flour, salt and asparagus liquid. Cook and stir until mixture comes to a boil and thickens. Stir in cheese. Combine milk and egg yolks; stir into sauce. In greased baking dish or casserole, arrange layers of ½ asparagus, ½ cheese sauce and cracker crumbs. Repeat layers. Bake at 350° for 45 minutes, or until bubbly. Casserole can be assembled in advance and refrigerated. Makes 6 to 8 servings.

Susan Langerman, West Suburban Region

ASPARAGUS PARMESAN

- 3 pounds fresh asparagus
- ½ cup flour
- 1 egg
- 2 tablespoons dry white wine
- 1 cup dry bread crumbs
- 1 tablespoon grated Parmesan cheese
- ¼ teaspoon garlic powder
- 1 teaspoon salt
- 1 teaspoon black pepper
- ½ cup olive oil

Wash asparagus well; break off tough ends. Dip asparagus into flour, then into a mixture of egg beaten with wine. Then dip asparagus into mixture of crumbs, cheese and seasonings. Heat olive oil in a large skillet; add asparagus and cook until lightly browned and tender, about 10 minutes. Makes 6 servings.

Myra Weis, Chicago Region

EASY BAKED BEANS

- 2 16-oz. cans baked beans (molasses style)
- Brown sugar
- Dry mustard
- Catsup

Spread contents of one can of beans in casserole. Sprinkle with brown sugar and mustard. Add second can of beans. Spread catsup on top of beans. Bake uncovered at 325° for 2½ hours. Makes 8 to 10 servings.

Jackie Gilbert, Milwaukee Region

BEETS IN ORANGE SAUCE

- 1 tablespoon cornstarch
- ¼ cup sugar
- 2 tablespoons grated orange rind
- 3 tablespoons lemon juice
- ¾ cup orange juice
- ½ teaspoon salt
- ¼ cup butter
- 2 1-lb. cans beets, drained

Mix cornstarch and sugar in heavy saucepan; add remaining ingredients except beets and cook, stirring, until thickened and clear. Add beets and heat through. Makes 6 servings.

Eenie Frost, Lake County Region

LIMA BEAN CASSEROLE

- 1 pound dried large lima beans
- 2 teaspoons salt
- ½ cup butter (1 stick)
- 1 cup catsup
- 1 10¾-oz. can tomato soup
- ¼ teaspoon prepared mustard
- 1 cup brown sugar

Soak beans overnight in cold water. Add salt and simmer beans until slightly soft, about 45 minutes. Combine remaining ingredients in saucepan and heat to boiling. Drain beans; blend sauce with beans and turn into a 2½-quart casserole. Cover and bake at 375° for 2½ hours. Uncover if there is too much liquid and cook 30 minutes longer. Sauce can be made in advance and frozen; casserole can be baked in advance and reheated before serving. Makes 8 to 10 servings.

Sue Colton, Milwaukee Region

HAWAIIAN BEETS SUPREME

- 1 1-lb. can cut beets
- 1 15¼-oz. can pineapple chunks
- 1½ tablespoons cornstarch
- ½ teaspoon salt
- Pinch white pepper
- 3½ tablespoons vinegar
- 3 tablespoons sugar
- ½ teaspoon monosodium glutamate

Drain beets and pineapple, reserving liquid. Mix and measure 1½ cups. Slice or dice beets. In heavy saucepan, blend cornstarch with salt and pepper. Add vinegar, sugar and monosodium glutamate, mixing well. Add reserved liquid and cook, stirring constantly, until mixture thickens and becomes clear. Add beets and pineapple; heat through. Sauce will thicken when standing. Makes 4 to 6 servings.

Emma Oesterreicher, Chicago Region

BROCCOLI CASSEROLE 1

- 2 10-oz. packages frozen broccoli
- 1-10½-oz. can cream of mushroom soup
- ½ cup mayonnaise
- 1 tablespoon lemon juice
- ½ cup grated sharp Cheddar cheese
- 1 2-oz. jar chopped slivered almonds
- 2 tablespoons prepared mustard
- 1 2-oz. jar pimento, chopped (optional)
- 1 cup crushed cheese crackers

Cook broccoli according to package directions; drain well and arrange in a shallow greased casserole. Mix soup with remaining ingredients except crackers. Pour over broccoli; top with crackers. Bake at 350° for 45 minutes. Makes 4 to 6 servings.

Esther Kramer, Indianapolis Chapter-at-Large

SAVORY SAUCED BROCCOLI

- 1 pound fresh broccoli (or 1 10-oz. package frozen)
- ¼ cup butter
- 2 tablespoons flour
- ½ teaspoon salt
- ¼ teaspoon allspice
- ⅛ teaspoon oregano
- ¼ cup minced parsley
- ¼ cup chopped almonds
- 1½ teaspoons lemon juice

Cook broccoli until just tender; drain and save 1 cup liquid. In saucepan, blend melted butter, flour, seasonings and parsley; gradually add liquid and cook and stir until thickened and smooth. Add lemon juice; arrange broccoli in pan—cover with sauce—heat and serve. Pour over broccoli. Makes 4 servings.

Sarah Stiebel, Northern Illinois Region

BROCCOLI CASSEROLE II

- 3 10-oz. packages frozen chopped broccoli
- 1 pint dairy sour cream
- 1 envelope dry onion soup mix
- ¼ cup buttered bread crumbs

Cook broccoli according to package directions; drain well. Combine sour cream and onion soup mix; stir in broccoli. Place in a greased 1½-quart casserole; top with crumbs. Bake at 350° for 40 minutes, or until bubbly. Prepare in advance and refrigerate, if you wish. Spinach can be prepared in the same way. Makes 6 servings.

Mrs. John Berkman, Twin Cities Region

BROCCOLI-MUSHROOM BAKE

- 2 10-oz. packages frozen chopped broccoli
- 2 tablespoons butter
- ½ teaspoon salt
- Dash of pepper
- 2 eggs
- ¼ cup herb seasoned bread crumbs
- 1 4-oz. can mushroom pieces, drained
- 1 2-oz. jar chopped pimento
- Bread crumbs
- Paprika

Cook broccoli according to package directions; drain well and leave broccoli in pan. Add butter, salt and pepper. Add beaten eggs, seasoned bread crumbs, mushrooms and pimento. Turn into a greased 1½-qt. casserole. Top with plain bread crumbs and paprika; bake at 350° for 30 minutes. Makes 6 servings.

Mildred Jacobs, Chicago Region

BROCCOLI PARMESAN

- 2 10-oz. packages frozen chopped broccoli (or spears)
- 1 large onion, chopped
- 1 4-oz. can mushrooms, chopped
- 2 tablespoons butter
- 1 tablespoon flour
- 1 6-oz. can tomato paste
- Salt and pepper, to taste
- Grated Parmesan cheese

Cook broccoli as directed on package; drain and reserve ½ cup liquid. Meanwhile, saute onion and mushrooms in butter; blend in flour, tomato paste, broccoli liquid and salt and pepper to taste. Cook and stir until thickened. Arrange broccoli in a greased 1½-qt. casserole. Top with sauce and sprinkle with cheese. Bake, covered, at 350° for 30 minutes; uncover and bake 15 minutes longer. Makes 4 servings.

Sheryl Reinstein, Chicago Region

BROCCOLI PUFF CASSEROLE

- 2 10-oz. packages frozen broccoli cuts
- 1 $10\frac{1}{2}$-oz. can condensed cream of mushroom soup
- $\frac{2}{3}$ cup shredded Cheddar cheese
- $\frac{1}{3}$ cup milk
- 1 egg, beaten
- $\frac{1}{4}$ cup fine dry bread crumbs
- 1 tablespoon butter, melted

Cook broccoli according to package directions, omitting salt; drain thoroughly. Arrange broccoli in a greased $10x6x1\frac{1}{2}$-inch baking dish. Blend soup and cheese. Gradually add milk and egg, stirring until well blended. Pour over broccoli; sprinkle mixture of crumbs and butter evenly over top. Bake at 350° for 45 minutes. Makes 6 servings.

Florence Purnell, Des Moines Chapter-at-Large

GREEN AND GOLD BROCCOLI-RICE CASSEROLE

- 1 medium onion, chopped
- 1 tablespoon butter
- 1 $10\frac{3}{4}$-oz. can Cheddar cheese soup
- 1 6-oz. roll nippy cheese
- $\frac{1}{2}$ teaspoon garlic powder
- 1 8-oz. can chopped mushrooms
- 1 10-oz. package frozen chopped broccoli, cooked and drained
- 3 cups hot cooked rice
- 1 3-oz. can french fried onions

Cook onion in butter until golden; add cheese soup, cheese and garlic. Cook over low heat until cheese melts. Add mushrooms plus liquid, broccoli and rice; arrange in a greased casserole. Top with onions and bake at 350° for 20 minutes. Makes 6 servings.

Sylvia Mashkes, Chicago Region

CARROT AND APRICOT CASSEROLE

- 1 8-oz. package dried apricots
- 1 12-oz. can apricot nectar
- 2 jars tiny whole carrots, drained
- $\frac{3}{4}$ cup brown sugar
- Butter
- $\frac{1}{2}$ cup slivered almonds

Soak apricots in apricot nectar for several hours or overnight. In buttered 2-quart casserole, arrange in layers $\frac{1}{2}$ carrots, $\frac{1}{2}$ apricots and nectar; dot with butter and $\frac{1}{2}$ the brown sugar. Repeat layers. Bake at 350° for 30 to 45 minutes. Makes 8 servings.

Lillian Waldman, Lake County Region

CARROT MOLD

- 1 cup shortening
- ½ cup brown sugar
- 1½ cups grated raw carrots
- 2 eggs
- 1¼ cups flour
- 1 teaspoon baking powder
- ½ teaspoon baking soda
- ¼ teaspoon cloves
- ¼ teaspoon allspice
- ½ teaspoon cinnamon
- Grated rind of 1 lemon
- ½ teaspoon salt
- 2 tablespoons bread crumbs or matzo meal

Cream shortening and sugar in large bowl; add carrots and eggs and beat well. Sift flour with baking powder, soda, spices, lemon rind and salt. Combine with bread crumbs; add to creamed mixture and mix thoroughly. Pour into a well greased 2-qt. mold. Set in a pan of simmering water and bake at 350° for 1 hour. Makes 8 to 10 servings.

Mrs. Morris Caminer, Milwaukee Region

CRUMB-TOPPED CARROT BAKE

- 1½ cups thinly sliced carrots
- 1 teaspoon instant minced onion or onion salt
- 1 cup water
- ½ teaspoon salt
- ¼ cup butter
- 1 tablespoon flour
- ¼ cup grated American cheese
- ⅓ cup fine bread crumbs

Heat carrots, onion, water and salt in saucepan to boiling. Lower heat, cover and simmer for 15 minutes, or until tender. Drain carrots, reserving liquid. Melt 2 tablespoons butter in saucepan; blend in flour. Add carrot liquid and cook and stir until thickened and smooth. Add cheese and stir until melted. Arrange carrots in a 1-quart shallow casserole. Pour cheese sauce over carrots and top with bread crumbs mixed with remaining butter. Bake at 350° for 20 minutes. Makes 3 to 4 servings. Casserole can be assembled in advance and refrigerated.

Susan Langerman, West Suburban Region

ZESTY CARROTS

- 6 large carrots or 1 bunch finger carrots
- ¼ cup butter
- Salt and pepper, to taste
- ¼ cup prepared mustard
- ½ cup honey
- 2 tablespoons chopped chives or parsley

Wash, pare and cut carrots diagonally into 1-inch slices (about 3 cups). Cook, covered, in boiling salted water until tender-crisp; drain well. In small saucepan, combine butter, seasonings, mustard, honey and chives. Cook over medium heat, stirring, until well blended, about 3 minutes. Add carrots; heat for several minutes over low heat. Makes 4 to 6 servings.

Lillian Minkus, Chicago Region

CAULIFLOWER-CHEESE CASSEROLE

- 2 10-oz. packages frozen cauliflower
- 1 10¾-oz. can Cheddar cheese soup
- ¼ cup milk
- 1 3-oz. can french fried onion rings

Cook cauliflower according to package directions; drain. Arrange in shallow baking pan; cover with a mixture of soup blended with milk. Top with onion rings. Bake at 350° for 20 minutes. Makes 6 servings.

Cynthia Glickman, West Suburban Region

CAULIFLOWER CUSTARD

- 2 large heads cauliflower
- 4 eggs, beaten
- 1 tablespoon oil
- 1 tablespoon salt
- 1 teaspoon pepper
- 2 cups half-and-half cream
- 1 teaspoon dried dill
- 1 teaspoon dried parsley flakes

Cook cauliflower in boiling salted water for 20 minutes; drain well and chop. Blend with remaining ingredients and pour into a buttered 2-quart casserole. Bake at 325° for 1 hour. Makes 12 servings.

Erika Brodsky, Lake County Region

CAULIFLOWER FRITTERS

- 1 cup sifted flour
- 1 teaspoon baking powder
- ½ teaspoon salt
- 1 egg, beaten
- ½ cup milk
- 2 tablespoons butter, melted
- 1 cup cooked cauliflower, mashed
- Shortening

Sift flour with baking powder and salt. Blend in egg, milk, butter and cauliflower. Drop by spoonfuls into hot shortening. Cook 3 to 5 minutes on each side. Makes 4 servings.

Ruth Landsman, Chicago Region

CELERY CASSEROLE

- 4 cups diagonally cut celery
- 1 10½-oz. can condensed cream of chicken soup
- 1 5-oz. can water chestnuts, drained and sliced
- 1 cup seasoned stuffing mix (dry)
- 3 tablespoons melted butter

Mix celery, soup and water chestnuts; turn into a 2-quart casserole. Mix stuffing mix and butter; spoon over top of celery. Bake at 350° for 30 minutes. Makes 6 servings.

Eenie Frost, Lake County Region

SOUTHERN CORN CUSTARD

- 1 1-lb. 1-oz. can creamed corn
- 1 5⅓-oz. can evaporated milk
- 3 eggs, slightly beaten
- ¼ cup butter, melted
- 1 tablespoon flour
- Dash of paprika and salt

Mix corn with milk, eggs, melted butter and flour. Pour into a greased casserole. Place in a pan of hot water and bake at 350° for 45 minutes, or until wooden pick inserted near center comes out clean. Makes 4 servings.

Mildren Weinstock, Chicago Region

EGGPLANT CASSEROLE

- 1 eggplant, peeled and sliced
- 2 tablespoons butter
- 2 eggs, slightly beaten
- ¼ teaspoon pepper
- 1 small onion, minced
- ½ teaspoon oregano
- ½ cup salted crackers, coarsely crushed
- ½ cup grated Cheddar cheese
- 6 slices tomato

Cook eggplant slices in boiling salted water for 10 minutes; drain well and mash eggplant. Blend in butter, eggs, pepper, onion, oregano and crackers. Pour into a buttered 1-quart casserole. Cover with tomato slices; sprinkle with cheese. Bake at 375° for 25 minutes. Assemble in advance and refrigerate until ready to bake, if you wish. Makes 6 servings.

Helen N. Cohen, West Suburban Region

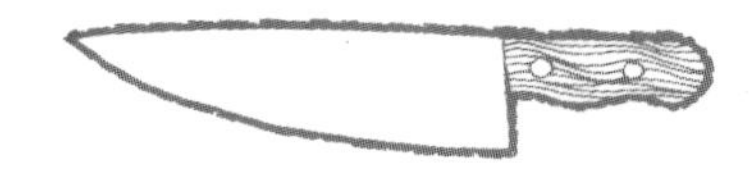

EGGPLANT PARMESAN

- 1 eggplant, peeled and cut into ½-inch slices
- Salt
- Flour
- ¼ to ½ cup olive oil
- 1 15-oz. can tomato sauce with tomato bits
- 8 ounces Mozzarella cheese
- Parmesan cheese

Sprinkle both sides of eggplant slices with salt. Let stand 20 to 30 minutes; pat eggplant dry with paper towels. Dip each slice in flour, shaking off excess. In a heavy skillet, heat olive oil until haze forms over it; add eggplant slices a few at a time and brown. Work quickly to prevent eggplant from soaking up too much oil. Add more oil as needed. Drain browned eggplant on paper towels. Pour tomato sauce into an oiled oven-to-table serving dish. Place a few eggplant slices on top of sauce; add a layer of Mozzarella cheese, then sprinkle with Parmesan. Repeat layers. Cover dish with foil; bake at 325° for 20 minutes. Remove foil and bake 10 minutes longer at 300°. Makes 4 servings.

Judy Davis, Chicago Region

SWEET-SOUR GREEN PEPPERS

- 12 green peppers
- 2 tablespoons salad oil
- 2 tablespoons sugar
- ½ teaspoon salt
- Pinch of pepper and garlic powder

Broil green peppers until skin gets brown. Immediately immerse in cold water; peel. Add salad oil to peppers; combine remaining ingredients and blend with peppers. Chill several hours before serving. Makes 12 servings.

Rose Kaufman, Milwaukee Region

MUSHROOMS AU GRATIN

- 1 pound fresh mushrooms
- 2 tablespoons butter
- ⅓ cup dairy sour cream
- ¼ teaspoon salt
- ⅛ teaspoon pepper
- 1 tablespoon flour
- ¼ cup minced parsley
- ½ cup shredded Swiss or Cheddar cheese

Wash mushrooms; cut lengthwise ¼-inch thick. Heat butter in skillet; add mushrooms and cook 5 to 10 minutes, or until brown. Cover pan for 2 minutes. Blend sour cream, salt, pepper and flour until smooth. Stir into mushrooms and heat. Turn into a shallow baking dish; sprinkle parsley and cheese evenly over top. Refrigerate if you wish before baking at 425° for 10 minutes. Makes 4 to 6 servings.

Barbara Bernstein, West Suburban Region

BLENDER-MADE GRATED POTATO CASSEROLE

- ½ cup milk
- 3 eggs
- ½ teaspoon salt
- ⅛ teaspoon pepper
- 1 cup cubed sharp process American cheese
- 2 tablespoons butter, softened
- ½ small onion, cut in pieces
- 3 medium potatoes, pared and cubed (about 3 cups)
- Green pepper, rings (optional)

Add in order to blender container milk, eggs, salt, pepper, cheese, butter, onion and potatoes. Cover and blend on high speed just until all potatoes are grated. Do not overblend. Pour into a greased 10x6x1½-inch baking dish. Bake at 375° for 35 to 40 minutes. Garnish with green pepper rings, if you wish. Makes 6 servings.

June Minkus, Lake County Region

POTATO PUFF

- 1 envelope instant mashed potatoes
- 1/4 cup chopped pimento (optional)
- 2 tablespoons chopped green onion
- 1 small clove garlic, minced
- 1 teaspoon salt
- 1 8-oz. carton cottage cheese
- 3/4 cup dairy sour cream
- 3 eggs, separated
- 2 tablespoons butter

Mix potatoes with pimento, green onion, garlic, salt, cottage cheese, sour cream and beaten egg yolks. Whip egg whites until stiff; fold into potato mixture. Turn into a greased 2-quart casserole. Dot top with butter. Bake at 350° for 1 hour. Makes 4 servings.

Nancy Lieberman, Indianapolis Chapter-at-Large

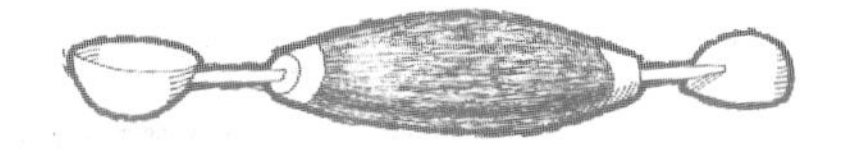

POTATO TORTE

- 6 tablespoons butter
- 6 Idaho potatoes, pared and sliced thin
- 1 cup grated Parmesan cheese
- Salt and pepper, to taste
- 1/2 teaspoon nutmeg
- 1/2 cup grated Swiss cheese
- 1/4 cup heavy cream
- 2 tablespoons chopped chives

Thickly butter a 2-quart mold or heatproof bowl. Layer potatoes into the mold, sprinkling each layer with Parmesan, salt, pepper and nutmeg. Cover tightly with lid or foil and bake at 400° about 1 hour, or until potatoes are done. Unmold on ovenproof serving dish, sprinkle with Swiss cheese and brown quickly under broiler. Pour cream slowly into center of potatoes. Sprinkle with chives. Makes 6 servings.

Lee Bateman, Lake County Region

SWEET POTATO SOUFFLE

4 cups hot mashed sweet potatoes
½ cup sherry
¼ teaspoon salt
½ cup sugar
2 eggs, beaten
½ cup butter (1 stick)
½ cup chopped walnuts

Combine hot sweet potatoes, sherry, salt, sugar, eggs and butter in electric mixer; whip until light. Turn into a lightly greased casserole; bake at 350° for 15 to 20 minutes, or until golden. Sprinkle with nuts before serving. Makes 8 servings.

Jackie Gilbert, Milwaukee Region

SPINACH CHEESE BAKE

2 medium onions, diced
½ pound fresh mushrooms, sliced
½ cup butter (1 stick)
4 10-oz. packages frozen chopped spinach
1 8-oz. package shredded Cheddar cheese

Saute onions and mushrooms in butter; cook spinach according to package directions; drain well. Mix spinach with sauteed vegetables and turn into a 13x9x2-inch baking dish. Top with cheese and bake at 350° for 20 to 30 minutes. Makes 8 to 10 servings.

Phyllis Silver, Northern Illinois Region

BAKED HASH BROWN POTATOES

1 cup milk or cream
2 12-oz. packages frozen hash brown potatoes, thawed
¼ cup butter
¼ cup pimento
1 tablespoon onion flakes
1 teaspoon salt
⅓ cup grated Cheddar or Parmesan cheese

Heat milk to boiling. Add thawed potatoes, butter, pimento, onion flakes and salt; cook until liquid is absorbed, about 5 to 10 minutes. Turn into a greased 2-quart casserole; top with cheese. Cover and bake at 350° for 1 hour, or until brown. Makes 6 to 8 servings.

Arleen Levy, Lake County Region

HOLIDAY MASHED POTATOES

- 4 cups mashed potatoes
- ½ cup heavy cream, whipped
- ¼ cup grated Parmesan cheese
- Paprika
- Parsley flakes

Place potatoes in a greased 1½-quart casserole. Spread whipped cream over potatoes; sprinkle with cheese, paprika and parsley. Bake uncovered at 375° for 15 to 20 minutes, or until lightly browned. Makes 8 servings.

Jackie Gilbert, Milwaukee Region

SPINACH NOODLE PUDDING

- 1 pound broad noodles
- 1 10-oz. package frozen chopped spinach, cooked and drained
- 4 eggs
- ¼ cup butter
- 1 cup half-and-half sour cream
- 1 cup cottage cheese
- ¼ cup chopped green onions
- Salt and pepper, to taste

Cook noodles in boiling salted water until just tender; drain well and combine with remaining ingredients. Turn into a greased large ring mold. Place in a pan of hot water; bake at 350° for 1 hour. Unmold and fill center, if you wish, with a colorful vegetable. Makes 12 servings.

C. Kahn, Lake County Region

SPINACH TOMATO CASSEROLE

- 2 10-oz. packages frozen chopped spinach
- 1 tablespoon vinegar
- 1 10½-oz. can cream of celery soup
- ½ teaspoon salt
- ¼ teaspoon pepper
- 1 3-oz. can french fried onions
- 2 tomatoes, sliced
- ½ cup shredded Cheddar cheese

Cook spinach according to package directions, adding vinegar to water; drain well. Blend soup and seasonings; fold in spinach. Pour into a greased 9-inch square baking dish. Sprinkle with onion rings; add sliced tomato. Sprinkle cheese over all. Bake at 325° for 35 minutes. Makes 6 servings.

Gloria Luxenberg, Lake County Region

SPINACH SOUFFLE

- 2 10-oz. packages frozen chopped spinach
- 4 tablespoons butter
- 3 slices American cheese, cut in pieces
- 1 cup creamed cottage cheese
- 1 egg, beaten
- Salt and pepper, to taste
- Bread crumbs

Cook spinach according to package directions; drain well. Combine with remaining ingredients except crumbs. Turn into a greased casserole; top with crumbs. Bake at 375° for 1 hour. Makes 6 servings.

Cynthia Glickman, West Suburban Region

BAKED TOMATOES

- 6 firm tomatoes
- 1/4 cup butter
- 1/2 cup bread crumbs
- 2 teaspoons seasoned salt
- 1 teaspoon garlic powder
- 2 tablespoons Parmesan cheese

Wash tomatoes and cut top portion off of each. Melt butter in sauce pan and add remaining ingredients. Arrange tomatoes in baking dish; spoon some crumb topping over each. Bake at 350° for 10 to 15 minutes. Prepare in advance and refrigerate before baking if you wish. Makes 6 servings.

Judith Zwirn, West Suburban Region

MIXED VEGETABLE CASSEROLE

- 2 10-oz. packages frozen cauliflower
- 2 10-oz. packages frozen broccoli
- 2 10-oz. packages frozen green beans
- 1 10 3/4-oz. can Cheddar cheese soup
- 1 10 1/2-oz. can cream of mushroom soup
- 1 10 1/2-oz. can cream of celery soup
- 1 3-oz. can french fried onions

Cook vegetables separately according to package directions until just tender. In large casserole, alternate layers of a soup, a vegetable and onion rings, beginning with soup, and ending with onion rings. Bake at 350° for 30 minutes. Makes 12 servings.

Norma L. Platt, Chicago Region

ZUCCHINI AND CHERRY TOMATOES

2 tablespoon butter
2 tablespoons olive or cooking oil
3 anchovy fillets
1 clove garlic
2 medium zucchini
16 cherry tomatoes
Grated Parmesan cheese
Salt and pepper, to taste

In large skillet, heat butter and oil with anchovies and garlic. Cook and stir over high heat until anchovies disintegrate; remove garlic. Slice zucchini lengthwise in quarters; then cut in half (do not pare). Add to skillet and brown quickly over high heat; cook just about 5 minutes so zucchini stays crisp and green. Add tomatoes; cook on low heat until heated through. Sprinkle with cheese and seasonings. Makes 6 servings.

Theresa Weisberg, Chicago Region

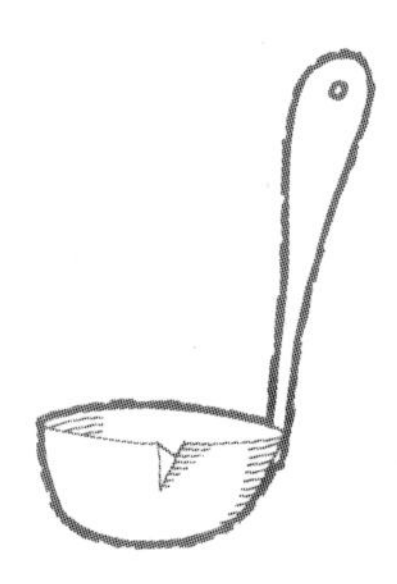

ZUCCHINI-CARROT PUDDING

4 eggs
6 large zucchini, peeled
3 large carrots, peeled
1 large Idaho potato, peeled
1 large onion, peeled
½ cup matzo meal
¾ cup dry bread crumbs
½ cup butter (1 stick)
Salt, to taste
Garlic powder, to taste

Beat eggs in a large bowl. Grate vegetables into bowl. Stir in matzo meal, bread crumbs and melted butter. Season with salt and garlic powder. Turn mixture into an oiled 11 x 7½-inch glass baking dish. Bake at 350° for 1 hour, or until brown. Makes 8 servings.

Miriam Strauss, Chicago Region

ZUCCHINI CASSEROLE

- 1 large Spanish onion, sliced
- Oil
- Salt and pepper, to taste
- Garlic powder
- Paprika
- 6 zucchini, sliced
- 3 tomatoes, sliced
- Fresh mushrooms, sliced (optional)
- 1-6-oz. package Mozzarella cheese

In skillet, saute onion in oil with seasonings. Add zucchini and cook until golden, adding more seasonings, if you wish. Add tomatoes and simmer on low heat for 2 to 3 minutes. If you wish, add mushrooms. Layer vegetables and cheese in a greased 2½-quart casserole, ending with cheese. Bake at 350° for 30 to 40 minutes. Prepare in advance, if you wish; canned tomatoes can be substituted for fresh. Makes 6 servings.

Sue Gingold, Milwaukee Region

ZUCCHINI HALVES WITH CHEESE

- 5 meduim zucchini
- 1 medium onion, sliced thin
- 1 tablespoon oil
- Salt and pepper, to taste
- ½ teaspoon oregano
- 1 8-oz. can tomato sauce
- 1 8-oz. package sliced Mozzarella cheese

Cut zucchini in half lengthwise. In large skillet, cook onion in oil until tender but not brown. Add zucchini halves in one layer (use two pans if necessary). Season with salt, pepper and oregano. Add tomato sauce. Cover and cook over low heat until squash is tender, about 10 minutes. Top with cheese slices. Sprinkle with additional oregano and serve. Makes 6 servings.

Eenie Frost, Lake County Region

MIXED VEGETABLE-RICE MOLD

- $1\frac{1}{3}$ cups converted rice
- Salt
- 1 10-oz. package frozen asparagus cuts
- 1 10-oz. package frozen broccoli spears
- ½ pound fresh mushrooms, sliced
- 1 large onion, diced
- Butter
- 1 2-oz. jar chopped pimento
- 1 $10\frac{1}{2}$-oz. can cream of mushroom soup

Cook rice in $2\frac{1}{2}$ cups water for 15 minutes; drain well and season with salt. Cook asparagus and broccoli in boiling water just until it comes apart; drain well and salt. Saute mushrooms and onion in butter; season with salt. If broccoli is whole, cut in 1-inch lengths. Generously butter a 6-cup ring mold; combine rice with vegetables, pimento and soup; pack into mold. Add additional pats of butter over top. Cover mold with foil and refrigerate for several hours or overnight. Place mold in a shallow pan of hot water; bake at 350° for 1 to $1\frac{1}{2}$ hours. To make mold parev, substitute cream sauce for soup, prepared with 2 tablespoons each of mar parv and flour and ½ cup each of water and cream substitute. Makes 12 servings.

Carol Kaplan, Northern Illinois Region

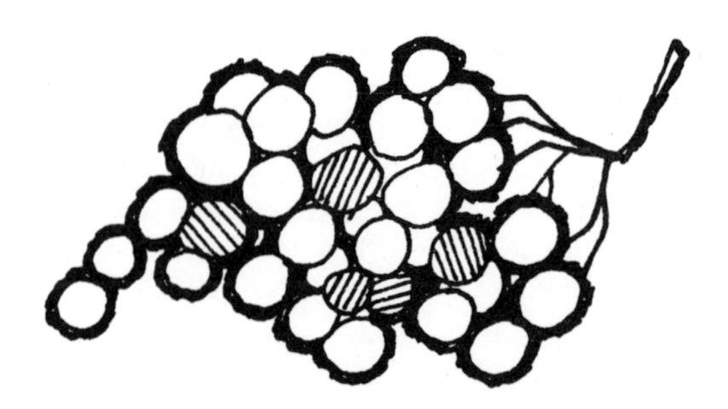

SALADS and SALAD DRESSINGS

CARROT SLAW

4 large carrots, coarsely grated
½ cup raisins or sliced dates
½ cup peanuts or broken pecans
½ 20-oz. can unsweetened pineapple chunks
¼ cup pineapple juice
1 teaspoon sugar
2 heaping tablespoons mayonnaise or salad dressing
2 heaping tablespoons dairy sour cream or yoghurt
1-2 tablespoons peanut butter (optional)
¼ cup shredded coconut (optional)
Shredded lettuce or salad greens

Combine all ingredients except coconut and lettuce. Chill several hours. Top with coconut and serve on greens. Makes 6 to 8 servings.

Ann Roman Siegel, Chicago Region

COLE SLAW

1 large head cabbage, finely sliced
1 medium onion, finely sliced
1 green pepper, finely sliced
1 cup sugar (scant)
¾ cup salad oil
½ cup wine vinegar
1 teaspoon salt
½ teaspoon coarsely ground pepper
½ teaspoon celery seeds

Mix and place sliced vegetables in serving bowl. Combine remaining ingredients in a small saucepan; heat to boiling, Pour hot dressing over vegetables. Mix well and refrigerate until well chilled. Makes 8 to 10 servings.

Renee Drell, West Suburban Region

CREAMY COLE SLAW

- ½ cup sugar
- ⅓ cup cider vinegar
- ¾ cup mayonnaise
- 1 head cabbage, shredded
- 1 package carrots, shredded

Blend sugar, vinegar and mayonnaise. Blend into mixture of shredded cabbage and carrots, mixing well. Chill 2 to 4 hours before serving. Makes 6 servings.

Phyllis Silverman, Lake County Region

CUCUMBERS IN SOUR CREAM I

- 4 cucumbers, pared and thinly sliced
- 1 teaspoon salt
- 1 teaspoon sugar
- ½ teaspoon pepper
- 1 cup dairy sour cream
- 2 teaspoons chopped dill (optional)

Combine all ingredients. Chill well before serving. Makes 8 to 10 servings.

Mabelle Schero, Chicago Region

CUCUMBERS IN SOUR CREAM II

- 3 medium cucumbers
- 1 large sweet onion
- Salt
- Ice Water
- ¼ cup cider vinegar
- ¼ cup salad oil
- 1 cup dairy sour cream
- Dash of pepper
- Paprika

Pare cucumbers; score with a fork; cut into thin slices. Peel onion and cut into thin slices. Arrange alternate layers of cucumbers and onions in a bowl, sprinkling each layer generously with salt. Cover with ice water and refrigerate for 2 to 3 hours. Drain off salt water; rinse cucumbers and onions in water; drain well. Blend vinegar and oil; pour over vegetables and let stand 2 or 3 hours. Drain off vinegar and oil; blend in sour cream. Season to taste with pepper and sprinkle top generously with paprika. Makes 6 to 8 servings.

Miriam Witt, Chicago Region

DILL SOUR CREAM POTATO SALAD

- 4 cups diced cooked potatoes
- 1 cup sliced celery
- 3 to 4 green onions, chopped
- 3 tablespoons vinegar
- 3 tablespoons salad oil
- ½ teaspoon seasoned salt
- ½ teaspoon seasoned pepper
- 2 sprigs fresh dill, or
  1 teaspoon dry dill
- 1 cup dairy sour cream
- Chopped green and red pepper
- Fresh tomato wedges

Combine potatoes, celery and onions. Mix vinegar, oil, salt, pepper and dill; pour over potatoes and mix gently. Refrigerate for several hours. Blend in sour cream and chopped pepper. Garnish with additional dill and tomato wedges. Makes 4 to 6 servings.

Gloria Gordon, Northern Illinois Region

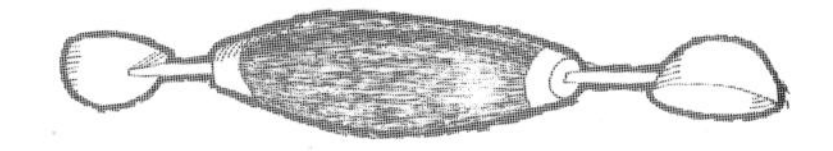

FRESH VEGETABLE SLAW

- 1 head cabbage
- 1 bunch carrots
- 3 cucumbers
- 3 green peppers
- 1 bunch green onions
- ⅔ cup vinegar
- ⅔ cup sugar
- ⅓ cup oil
- 1 teaspoon salt
- ½ teaspoon pepper

Shred cabbage and carrots. Dice cucumbers and green peppers and slice green onions and tops. Mix in large bowl with blend of remaining ingredients. Chill for at least 3 hours before serving. Makes 8 servings.

Sandra Foreman, Lake County Region

GREEN BEAN SALAD

- 3 16-oz. cans whole green beans, drained
- 1½ teaspoons garlic salt
- ¾ teaspoon dry mustard
- 6 tablespoons olive or salad oil
- 4½ tablespoons tarragon or cider vinegar
- 1½ cups sliced celery
- 4 to 6 green onions, sliced
- 3 hard-cooked eggs, sliced

In large bowl, toss beans with seasonings, oil and vinegar. Refrigerate until 1 hour before serving. Add remaining ingredients; chill until ready to serve. Makes 12 to 14 servings.

Roddie Rosenthal, Lake County Region

GREEN BEAN AND PEA SALAD

- 1 cup vinegar
- ½ cup salad oil
- 1½ cups sugar
- 1 tablespoon water
- 1 teaspoon paprika
- 2 1-lb. cans french-cut green beans, drained
- 1 1-lb. can green peas, drained
- 1 small green pepper, chopped
- 1 small onion, chopped
- ¾ cup chopped celery
- 1 large pimento, chopped

Combine vinegar, oil, sugar, water and paprika; pour dressing marinade over mixture of remaining ingredients. Cover and refrigerate several hours or overnight. Keeps well. Makes 8 servings.

Phyllis Frankel, Chicago Region

HAWAIIAN SLAW

- 1 head iceberg lettuce, shredded
- 1 13¼-oz. can crushed pineapple, well drained
- ¼ cup toasted flaked coconut
- ¼ cup chopped maraschino cherries
- Mayonnaise, to moisten
- Pinch of ground ginger

Mix shredded lettuce with crushed pineapple, coconut and maraschino cherries. Add mayonnaise to moisten and ginger. Chill before serving. Makes about 8 servings.

Mrs. E. C. Dratler, Lake County Region

GREEK SALAD

- 1 head iceberg lettuce, torn into bite-size pieces
- 1 8-oz. can sliced beets, drained
- 2 large tomatoes, cut in wedges
- ½ red onion, thinly sliced and separated into rings
- 1 cucumber, sliced
- ½ cup pitted ripe olives
- ¼ pound (1 cup) feta cheese, crumbled
- 1 clove garlic, minced
- 3 anchovy fillets, chopped
- 1 cup olive oil
- ½ cup red wine vinegar
- 1 teaspoon prepared mustard
- ¼ teaspoon salt
- Dash of pepper

Place lettuce in salad bowl. Top with beets, tomatoes, onions, cucumber, olives and cheese. Combine remaining ingredients; whisk with a fork until blended. Pour enough dressing on salad to moisten; toss gently. Makes 12 servings.

Sydell Levinson, Northern Illinois Region

KIDNEY BEAN SALAD

- 4 1-lb. cans kidney beans, drained
- 1 onion, finely sliced
- 1 cup diced celery
- 1 cup sweet pickle relish
- ½ cup mayonnaise
- ½ cup half-and-half sour cream
- 2 tablespoons lemon juice
- 2 tablespoons vinegar
- 2 tablespoons sugar
- Salt and pepper to taste

Mix beans and onion in large bowl. Combine celery, relish, mayonnaise, sour cream, lemon juice, vinegar and sugar, blending well. Add to beans and mix gently, but thoroughly. Refrigerate for 6 hours or overnight. Season with salt and pepper just before serving. Makes 12 to 16 servings.

Dorothy Solomon, Lake County Region

OVERNIGHT VEGETABLE SALAD

- **1 head cauliflower, cut up**
- **1 head iceberg lettuce, in bite size pieces**
- **1 large sweet onion, thinly sliced**
- **1 pound beef fry, cooked and crumbled**
- **¼ cup sugar**
- **2 cups Miracle Whip**
- **⅓ cup grated Parmesan cheese**
- **1 cup seasoned croutons**

In large salad bowl, combine cauliflower, well drained lettuce, onion and beef-fry. Mix sugar and salad dressing and place spoonfuls of mixture over vegetables. Cover and refrigerate overnight. Just before serving, toss ingredients and add cheese and croutons. Makes 8 servings.

Judith Derdiger, Chicago Region

PEA SALAD

- **1 red onion, diced**
- **Grated Parmesan cheese**
- **1 head lettuce, broken into bite-size pieces**
- **1 8½-oz. can Le Sueur peas**
- **½ lb. beef fry, cooked and crumbled**
- **1 cup Miracle Whip**
- **½ teaspoon salt**
- **¼ teaspoon sugar**
- **¼ teaspoon pepper**
- **1 teaspoon paprika**
- **1 clove garlic, minced**

Layer salad ingredients in bowl, beginning with diced onion. Sprinkle with cheese, then add ⅓ of lettuce. Add all of well drained peas, then sprinkle again with cheese. Top with ⅓ lettuce, then add beef fry. Sprinkle with cheese, add remaining lettuce, and sprinkle again with cheese. Refrigerate for 2 hours. Combine remaining ingredients for dressing; chill. Just before serving, toss salad, add dressing and toss again. Makes 6 to 8 servings.

Susan Gordon, Lake County Region

MEDITERRANEAN SALAD

- 4 4-oz. cans button mushrooms
- 2 8-oz. cans pitted black olives
- 2 6-oz. cans marinated artichoke hearts
- 1 8-oz. jar cocktail onions
- 1 bottle Italian dressing
- 2 8-oz. cans cocktail beets
- 2 large cucumbers, finely diced
- Salt, pepper and garlic salt to taste

Combine mushrooms, olives, artichokes and onions in bowl. Add dressing to cover; cover and refrigerate several hours or overnight. Marinate beets separately with additional dressing. Add beets and diced cucumber to other ingredients just before serving. Adjust seasonings to taste. Makes 8 to 12 servings.

Launa Annes, Lake County Region

SOUR CREAM POTATO SALAD

- 6 cups sliced cooked potatoes (about 7 medium)
- ⅓ cup clear French or Italian dressing
- ¾ cup sliced celery
- ⅓ cup sliced green onions
- 4 hard-cooked eggs
- 1 cup mayonnaise
- ½ cup dairy sour cream
- 1½ teaspoons prepared horseradish mustard
- Salt and celery seed to taste

While potatoes are warm, pour dressing over them, mix gently; cover and chill for 2 hours. Add celery and onions to potatoes. Chop egg whites and add to potatoes. Sieve yolks and reserve some for garnish. Combine remaining egg yolk with mayonnaise, sour cream and mustard. Fold into salad. Add salt and celery seed. Chill for 2 hours. Garnish with sieved egg yolk just before serving. Makes 8 to 10 servings.

Audrey Rosenberg, Des Moines Chapter-at-Large

TOMATOES VINAIGRETTE

- 1 clove garlic, minced
- ½ teaspoon salt
- ¼ teaspoon pepper
- 1 teaspoon oregano
- 2½ tablespoons wine vinegar
- ¼ cup salad oil
- ¼ cup olive oil
- 2 to 4 tomatoes, sliced
- Minced onion
- Minced parsley

Blend garlic, salt, pepper, oregano, wine vinegar and oil. Arrange sliced tomatoes in serving or refrigerator dish. Cover with dressing and refrigerate 4 hours or ovenight. Ganish tomatoes with minced onion and parsley and serve on lettuce. Makes 4 to 6 servings.

Rosalie Gellman, Milwaukee Region

TOSSED SALAD GOURMET

- 1 medium head Boston lettuce
- 1 medium head romaine lettuce
- 2 large ripe tomatoes, peeled and cut into bite-size pieces
- 1 onion, thinly sliced
- 2 cloves garlic, minced
- 2 tablespoons minced chives
- 1 tablespoon chopped fresh basil, or 2 teaspoons leaf basil, crumbled
- 12 large pitted green olives
- 12 large pitted black olives
- 1 teaspoon prepared hot mustard
- 2 tablespoons red wine vinegar
- 6 tablespoons olive oil
- Salt and freshly ground pepper to taste
- 6 large red radishes, thinly sliced

Prepare the salad greens 2 to 4 hours ahead of time. Wash and core; tear into bite-size pieces into salad bowl. Cover and chill. When ready to serve, add tomatoes, onions, garlic, chives, basil and olives. Stir mustard into vinegar and sprinkle over salad; toss. Sprinkle with oil, salt and pepper; toss again. Top with radish slices and serve. Makes 6 servings.

Pearl Cohn, Lake County Region

WALDORF SALAD

- 2 cups diced, unpared apples
- 1 grapefruit, sectioned and cut into 1-inch pieces, or ½ can unsweetened pineapple chunks
- ½ cup peanuts, walnuts or pecans
- ½ cup raisins
- 2 heaping tablespoons mayonnaise or salad dressing
- 2 heaping tablespoons dairy sour cream or yoghurt
- 1 teaspoon vanilla, or ½ teaspoon maple flavoring
- Shredded lettuce or curly endive

Combine all ingredients except lettuce; refrigerate for several hours or overnight. Serve on lettuce. Makes 4 to 6 servings.

Ann Roman Siegel, Chicago Region

WINTER SALAD

- 1 head iceberg lettuce, in bite-size pieces
- 4 hard-cooked eggs, chopped
- 1 7-oz. can artichoke hearts, drained and cut in halves
- ½ cup julienne sliced turkey
- ⅓ bottle imitation bacon bits
- 2 cups mayonnaise
- ¾ cup dairy sour cream
- 4 ounces blue cheese, crumbled
- 1 teaspoon instant minced onion
- Garlic salt to taste

Combine lettuce, eggs, artichokes and turkey in bowl; cover and chill several hours. Combine remaining ingredients and chill. When ready to serve, top salad with enough dressing to moisten; toss and serve. Makes 4 to 6 servings.

Lola Stoll, West Suburban Region

ROAST BEEF SALAD

- 5 pound rump or sirloin tip roast
- 1 large sweet onion, chopped
- 2 green pepper, cut in 2-inch strips
- 2 4-oz. jars pimento, drained
- 2 bottles Tomato Marinade (Reese)

Roast meat to degree of doneness you prefer, allowing about 25 minutes per pound at 325°. When cold, cut beef into thin strips. Mix with remaining ingredients and chill at least 8 hours, stirring occasionally. Drain well and serve. Makes about 20 servings.

Esther Balikov, Lake County Region

ANCHOVY DRESSING

1 cup dairy sour cream
½ cup mayonnaise
2 2-oz. cans flat anchovy fillets
2 to 3 tablespoons chopped chives
1 clove garlic, minced
1 tablespoon lemon juice
1 tablespoon tarragon vinegar
Coarsely ground black pepper

Blend all ingredients; chill several hours before serving. Makes about 1 pint.

Sheila Schwartz, West Suburban Region

BLENDER ANCHOVY DRESSING

5 cloves garlic
2 medium onions, chopped
3 ribs celery, chopped
1 2-oz. can anchovies
½ teaspoon pepper
4 eggs (raw)
¼ cup prepared mustard
2 cups salad oil

Combine all ingredients in blender container; blend until smooth. Chill overnight before serving. The dressing is especially good with a salad of romaine lettuce, garnished with Parmesan cheese and croutons. Makes about 1 quart.

Erika Brodsky, Lake County Region

CAESAR SALAD

1 cup salad oil
1 clove garlic, peeled
1 coddled egg
1 teaspoon wine vinegar
Juice of 1 lemon
¼ teaspoon salt
Pinch of pepper
Anchovy fillets, (optional)
1 to 1¼ pounds romaine lettuce
Plain or seasoned croutons

Place first 8 ingredients in blender container; beat for 1 minute. Chill for 3 to 4 hours. In the meantime, wash lettuce carefully and dry thoroughly; tear into bite-size pieces and chill. Just before serving, mix dressing in blender for 1 minute. Pour over lettuce; toss and serve with croutons. Makes 4 to 6 servings.

Anne Hilecher, St. Louis Region

COLE SLAW DRESSING

- 1 cup sugar
- 2 tablespoons flour
- 1 teaspoon salt
- ½ cup salad oil
- ½ cup wine vinegar
- ½ cup water
- ¼ teaspoon celery seeds

Blend sugar, flour and salt in a saucepan. Add oil, vinegar and water. Cook and stir quickly until mixture is thickened. Remove from heat and add celery seeds. Chill before serving. Makes about 1 pint.

Phyllis Silver, Northern Illinois Region

CREAMY BLUE CHEESE DRESSING

- ½ cup mayonnaise
- 1 cup dairy sour cream
- 2 cloves garlic
- 1 teaspoon salt
- 3 to 4 ounces blue cheese, crumbled
- Buttermilk or milk (optional)

Blend mayonnaise and sour cream. Mash garlic and salt with a fork. Add to creamed mixture with blue cheese. The dressing can be thinned, if you wish, with buttermilk or milk. The dressing will keep in the refrigerator for at least a week. Makes 1¾ cups.

Elaine Pollack, Northern Illinois Region

CREAMY PARMESAN DRESSING

- 1 pint salad dressing or mayonnaise
- 1 8-oz. bottle French dressing
- 1 1½-oz. can grated Parmesan cheese
- 2 to 3 garlic cloves, crushed

Blend all ingredients; chill several hours before serving. Makes about 3 cups dressing.

Sheryl Reinstein, Chicago Region

CUCUMBER DRESSING

- 1 pint mayonnaise
- 1 pint dairy sour cream
- 2 medium cucumbers, grated and drained
- 1 small onion, grated
- 1/4 teaspoon garlic powder
- 1/4 teaspoon sugar
- 1/2 teaspoon salt
- 1/2 teaspoon paprika

Place all ingredients in blender; blend until smooth. Makes about 5 cups.

Eenie Frost, Lake County Region

GOURMET CHEESE DRESSING

- 3 ounces (3/4 cup) Roquefort cheese
- 1 3-oz. package cream cheese
- 1 cup dairy sour cream
- 1/4 cup Sherry
- 1 tablespoon grated onion
- 1/2 teaspoon salt
- 1/4 teaspoon paprika
- 1 drop Tabasco sauce

Crumble Roquefort cheese into a bowl. Blend in cream cheese. Add remaining ingredients and blend until creamy. Chill several hours before serving. Makes about 1 pint.

Beatrice Rapkin, Milwaukee Region

GREEN GODDESS DRESSING

- 1 clove garlic
- 4 anchovy fillets
- 2 tablespoons chopped onion
- 1 teaspoon chopped parsley
- 2 teaspoons chopped chives
- 1 teaspoon tarragon
- 1 1/2 teaspoons tarragon vinegar
- 1 1/2 cups mayonnaise

Cut clove of garlic in half; rub cut sides over inside of mixing bowl. Mince anchovy fillets and combine with onion, parsley, chives, tarragon and vinegar. Add mayonnaise and stir until thoroughly blended. Chill before serving. Makes 1 pint.

Mrs. S. J. Hiller, Milwaukee Region

ROQUEFORT DRESSING

1 pint mayonnaise
1 pint dairy sour cream
4 ounces Roquefort cheese, crumbled
1 teaspoon garlic powder
½ teaspoon monosodium glutamate
⅛ teaspoon salt
Snipped chives or parsley flakes for color

Blend all ingredients; cover and chill at least 2 hours before serving. Makes about 1 quart.

Linda Kline, Des Moines Chapter-at-Large

SOUR CREAM DRESSING

⅔ cup dairy sour cream
⅓ cup mayonnaise
⅓ teaspoon garlic salt
⅓ teaspoon white pepper
½ teaspoon dry mustard
½ teaspoon salt
⅓ cup snipped chives or green onion tops
1 tablespoon lemon or lime juice
4 drops worcestershire sauce

Blend all ingredients; chill several hours before serving. If you wish add chopped hard-cooked eggs or crumbled Roquefort cheese. Makes about 1⅓ cups.

Mrs. Marvin Topper, Milwaukee Region

SOUR CREAM DRESSING FOR FRUIT

½ pint dairy sour cream
1 teaspoon vanilla
2 tablespoons confectioners sugar, sifted
Grated or ground nutmeg

Blend sour cream with vanilla and sugar. Sprinkle nutmeg over the top just before serving over fruit or gelatin molds. Makes about 1 cup.

Dorothy K. Moss, Lake County Region

SUMMERTIME FRUIT DRESSING

- 2 eggs
- ½ cup sugar
- ⅓ cup lemon juice
- ⅓ cup pineapple juice
- 1 pint heavy cream

Break eggs into a saucepan; beat well. Add sugar, lemon juice and pineapple juice. Cook, stirring constantly, until mixture thickens and becomes custard-like. Cover and refrigerate until cold. Fold in whipped cream. Serve over fresh fruit salads. Makes about 3 cups.

Norma Glass, Lake County Region

THOUSAND ISLAND DRESSING

- 1 cup mayonnaise
- ¼ cup chili sauce
- 1 slice onion
- ¾ cup diced celery
- ¼ cup stuffed green olives, cut in pieces
- ¼ cup sweet pickle relish
- 2 or 3 sprigs parsley
- 1 slice green pepper
- 1 hard-cooked egg, quartered
- 1 teaspoon paprika

Place all ingredients in blender; blend until fairly smooth. Makes about 1 pint.

Flora Jane Gold, Northern Illinois Region

SALMON MOLD

- 1 10¾-oz. can tomato soup
- 1 8-oz. package cream cheese
- 2 envelopes (2 tablespoons) plain gelatin
- 1 1-lb. can salmon, drained
- 1 cup diced green pepper
- 1 cup diced celery
- 1 small onion, grated
- 1 cup mayonnaise

Heat soup in saucepan; blend in cream cheese, mixing thoroughly. Soften gelatin in ½ cup cold water; add to soup mixture, stirring to dissolve. Add remaining ingredients; mix well. Pour into lightly oiled 5½ to 6-cup mold. Chill several hours or until firm. Unmold on greens and serve. Makes 6 servings.

Phyllis Frankel, Chicago Region

CURRIED SHRIMP SALAD

- 2 pounds medium shrimp, fresh or frozen
- 1/3 cup mayonnaise
- 1 tablespoon lemon juice
- 3/4 teaspoon curry powder
- 1/4 cup chopped green onions
- 4 lettuce leaves

Early in day, cook shrimp; chill thoroughly. About 10 minutes before serving. Combine mayonnaise, lemon juice and curry. Add shrimps and onions. Serve on lettuce. Makes 4 servings.

Mrs. Selwyn Schwartz, West Suburban Region

SHRIMP SALAD I

- 2 cups small shrimp, cooked
- 1 bottle Catalina French dressing
- 2 to 3 hard-cooked eggs
- 1/2 cup diced celery
- 1/2 cup diced green pepper
- 1 bunch green onions, sliced
- 1/3 cup mayonnaise
- Salt to taste

Marinate shrimp in dressing for several hours or overnight; drain off excess dressing. Cut egg with egg slicer and add to shrimps with remaining ingredients. Chill several hours before serving. Makes 4 servings.

Elaine Achler, Northern Illinois Region

SHRIMP SALAD II

- 1 pound shrimp
- 1 cup mayonnaise
- 1/2 clove garlic, minced
- 1 teaspoon chopped parsley
- 1 teaspoon lemon juice
- 1 hard-cooked egg, chopped
- 1 teaspoon prepared mustard
- 1 teaspoon catsup
- Lettuce leaves

Cook shrimps and chill thoroughly. Combine mayonnaise with remaining ingredients, except lettuce. Add shrimp and chill well. Serve on lettuce. Makes 4 to 6 servings.

Lydia Lilienheim, Northern Illinois Region

TROPICAL TUNA SALAD

- 1 7-oz. can white meat tuna, drained and flaked
- 1 8-oz. can pineapple tidbits, drained
- ½ green pepper, diced
- 1 2-oz. jar pimento, chopped
- ¼ cup mayonnaise
- 1 teaspoon soy sauce
- Slivered almonds
- Salad greens

Blend tuna, pineapple, green pepper, pimento, mayonnaise, soy sauce and some of the almonds. Chill well. Serve on salad greens with almond garnish. Makes 4 servings.

Lillian Neimark, Northern Illinois Region

BAKED PEAR-NEPTUNE SALAD

- 1 16-oz. can Bartlett pear halves
- 1 16-oz. can salmon
- 1 cup chopped celery
- ¼ cup chopped onion
- ½ cup chopped green pepper
- 1 tablespoon lemon juice
- ¾ cup salad dressing or mayonnaise
- 1 teaspoon curry powder
- ½ teaspoon salt
- ⅛ teaspoon pepper
- 1 tablespoon melted butter
- ¼ cup cereal flakes

Drain and chop pears, reserving several slices for garnish. Drain salmon; break into bite-size pieces. Combine pears, salmon, celery, onion and green pepper; sprinkle with lemon juice. Combine salad dressing, curry, salt and pepper; gently stir into salad mixture. Turn into a buttered 1½-quart casserole. Mix melted butter and cereal flakes. Sprinkle over salad. Arrange reserved pear slices over top. Bakes at 350° for 40 minutes. Makes 6 servings.

Mrs. Harold Press, Chicago Region

CHICKEN CURRY SALAD

1 cup shredded coconut
1 cup white raisins
1 cup chopped peanuts
1 cup diced banana
1 cup diced apple
1 cup pineapple tidbits
1 cup diced celery
2 cups diced cooked chicken
1 tablespoon curry powder
1 cup chutney
Mayonnaise
Salt to taste

Blend all ingredients with mayonnaise to moisten. Season to taste. Chill several hours or overnight. Makes 4 to 6 servings.

Beatrice Rapkin, Milwaukee Region

CONFETTI EGG MOLD

14 or 16 hard-cooked eggs
1 2-oz. jar sliced pimentos
1 medium green pepper, chopped
2 tablespoons dehydrated chives
1 teaspoon salt
½ teaspoon pepper
½ cup Miracle Whip or dairy sour cream
¼ cup pickle liquid from 6-oz. jar sweet pickles
1 envelope (1 tablespoon) plain gelatin
¼ cup cold water

Crab Dressing:
1 6½-oz. can crabmeat
¾ cup Miracle Whip
⅛ teaspoon minced garlic
¼ cup chili sauce
1 tablespoon dehydrated onion
2 tablespoons sour cream

Chop hard-cooked eggs; blend with pimento, green pepper, chives, salt, pepper and salad dressing. Heat pickle liquid; soften gelatin in cold water; add to pickle liquid and stir until dissolved. Mix with egg salad; turn into an oiled 4½ to 5-cup ring mold. Chill several hours or until firm. Unmold salad and serve with Crab Dressing, prepared by combining remaining ingredients. Makes 12 to 14 servings.

Miriam S. Hoffman, Lake County Region

MOLDED SHRIMP SALAD

3 cups tomato juice
½ cup chopped green pepper
½ cup chopped green onion
2 tablespoons vinegar
2 tablespoons lemon juice
3 tablespoons sugar
Salt and pepper to taste
2 3-oz. packages lemon flavored gelatin
2 12-oz. packages frozen shrimp, thawed
1 cup chopped celery

Simmer tomato juice, green pepper, onion, vinegar, lemon juice, sugar, salt and pepper for 10 minutes. Place gelatin in a deep bowl. Pour liquid mixture over gelatin and stir until dissolved. Grease a 9-inch ring mold with mayonnaise. Pour gelatin mixture into mold and let cool. Add celery and whole shrimp (thawed). Place in refrigerator to firm. Unmold and serve on lettuce, or as an appetizer. Makes 10 servings.

Esther Kramer, Indianapolis Chapter-at-Large

SALMON MOUSSE I

2 tablespoons butter
3 tablespoons flour
1¼ cups milk
2 tablespoons plain gelatin
¼ cup cold water
1 16-oz. can salmon, drained and flaked
1 teaspoon minced onion
2 tablespoons minced celery
Salt and pepper, to taste
1 cup heavy cream

Sauce:

¼ cup mayonnaise
½ cup dairy sour cream
1 teaspoon cider vinegar
1 tablespoon chopped pimento
1 tablespoon chopped celery
1 tablespoon capers
1 tablespoon sweet pickle relish

Prepare cream sauce with first three ingredients; soften gelatin in water; add to cream sauce and stir until dissolved. Cool. Add salmon, onion, celery and seasonings to sauce. Fold in whipped cream. Pour into an oiled mold and chill until firm. Serve with sauce made by combining remaining ingredients. Makes 4 servings.

Phyllis Silverman, Lake County Region

SALMON MOUSSE II

- 1 envelope (1 tablespoon) plain gelatin
- ¼ cup water
- ¾ cup boiling water
- 2 tablespoons sugar
- 1 tablespoon lemon juice
- 1 tablespoon vinegar
- 2 tablespoons grated onion
- ½ teaspoon salt
- 1 16-oz. can salmon, drained and flaked
- ½ cup chopped black olives
- ½ cup chopped celery
- ½ cup Miracle Whip
- 2 hard-cooked eggs, chopped

Avocado Sauce:

- 1 large avocado
- ½ cup dairy sour cream
- ¼ teaspoon salt
- 1 cucumber, pared, seeded and chopped
- Dill weed

Soften gelatin in cold water; add boiling water and stir until dissolved. Add sugar, lemon juice, vinegar, onion and salt; chill until partially set. Add flaked salmon and remaining ingredients. Turn into a fish shape mold; chill until firm. Unmold and serve with sauce made by combining ingredients (do not mix ahead). Makes 4 servings.

Diane Segal, Lake County Region

CREAMY SHRIMP SALAD MOLD

- 1 3-oz. package lemon flavored gelatin
- 1 cup boiling water
- ½ cup heavy cream, whipped
- ½ cup mayonnaise
- 1 4½-oz. can shrimps, drained
- 3 hard-cooked eggs, chopped
- 3 cups diced celery
- 1 teaspoon diced green pepper
- 1 teaspoon grated onion
- ½ cup grated Cheddar cheese
- 1 cup chopped nuts
- ½ teaspoon salt

Dissolve gelatin in boiling water; chill until mixture begins to thicken. Add whipped cream and mayonnaise. Blend remaining ingredients and add to gelatin mixture. Turn into mold; chill until firm. Unmold and serve on salad greens. Makes about 4 to 6 servings.

Carole Butwinick, Twin Cities Region

APRICOT-ORANGE GELATIN

2 16-oz. can apricot halves
2 3-oz. packages orange gelatin
Dash of salt
1 6-oz. can frozen orange juice
3 tablespoons lemon juice
1 7-oz. bottle lemon-lime beverage

Drain apricots, reserving 1½ cups syrup. Puree apricots. Combine reserved syrup, gelatin and salt; heat to boiling to dissolve gelatin. Remove from heat; add puree, orange juice and lemon juice. Gradually add lemon-lime beverage. Pour into mold; chill until firm. Makes 10 to 12 servings.

Sharon Sak, Indianapolis Chapter-at-Large

APRICOT MOLD

2 3-oz. packages apricot gelatin
2 cups boiling water
1 16-oz. can pitted peeled apricots
¼ cup mayonnaise
1 package whipped topping mix

Dissolve gelatin in boiling water; add liquid drained from apricots. Chill until partially thickened. Whip mayonnaise into gelatin; prepare whipped topping according to directions and fold into mixture. Add cut-up apricots. Turn into an oiled 8-cup ring mold. Chill until firm. Makes 10 to 12 servings.

Dorothy K. Moss, Lake County Region

APRICOT GELATIN

2 large 6-oz. packages apricot gelatin
3 cups boiling water
1 9-oz. container Cool Whip
2 cups cold water
1 13¼-oz. can pineapple tidbits, drained
½ cup chopped pecans
2 bananas

Dissolve gelatin in boiling water. Add cool whip and let dissolve. Mix well. Add cold water. Blend in pineapple tidbits, nuts and sliced bananas. Turn into a large mold or bundt pan. Chill overnight. Makes 16 to 20 servings.

Francie Rosen, South Bend Chapter-at-Large

BLUEBERRY CHEESE MOLD

2 3-oz. packages lemon gelatin
Boiling water
1 8-oz. package cream cheese
3 tablespoons confectioners' sugar
½ teaspoon vanilla
1 cup heavy cream, whipped
1 15-oz. can blueberries

Dissolve 1 package gelatin in 1 cup boiling water; cool. Blend cream cheese, sugar and vanilla. Add chilled gelatin; mix until blended. Fold in whipped cream; turn into mold and chill until firm. For second layer, dissolve remaining gelatin in 2 cups boiling water. Add blueberries plus liquid. Pour over cheese layer; chill until firm. Makes 10 to 12 servings.

Margot Moos, Lake County Region

CHEESE-TOPPED PINEAPPLE MOLD

2 3-oz. packages lemon gelatin
1 20-oz. can sliced pineapple
2 bananas, sliced

Topping:
½ cup sugar
2 tablespoons flour
1 cup pineapple juice plus water
2 eggs, beaten
⅛ teaspoon salt
1 envelope (1 tablespoon) plain gelatin
1 cup cold water
1 cup heavy cream, whipped
1 cup grated sharp Cheddar cheese

Prepare lemon gelatin according to package directions; chill until partially thickened. Drain liquid from pineapple and reserve. Cut pineapple into small pieces and fold into gelatin with banana. Turn into a 9 x 13-inch pan. Chill until firm. For sauce: Mix sugar, flour and pineapple juice plus water into a saucepan. Stir in eggs and salt; cook over low heat, stirring, until thickened. Soften gelatin in cold water; add to hot mixture, stirring to dissolve. Chill until partially thickened. Fold in whipped cream. Pile lightly onto firm gelatin. Sprinkle with cheese. Chill for several hours. Cut into squares and serve on crisp greens. Makes 12 to 16 servings.

Madlyn Spark, Lake County Region

STRAWBERRY BANANA MOLD

- 2 packages strawberry-banana flavored gelatin
- 2 cups boiling water
- 1 cup cold water
- 2 10-oz. packages frozen strawberries
- 3 ripe bananas
- 1 pint dairy sour cream
- 1 pint fresh strawberries

Dissolve gelatin in boiling water; add cold water and 1 package strawberries. Chill in refrigerator until partially set. Cut 2 bananas; add to gelatin and turn into a ring mold. Chill until firm. Mash remaining banana, blend with remaining strawberries and sour cream. Chill. To serve, unmold salad, top with sour cream sauce and fill center with fresh berries. Makes 8 to 10 servings.

Carolyn Lieder, Chicago Region

MOLDED CRANBERRY SALAD

- 1 envelope (1 tablespoon) plain gelatin
- 1/4 cup sugar
- 1 3/4 cups cranberry juice cocktail
- 2 tablespoons lemon juice
- 1 cup chopped unpared apple
- 1/2 cup diced celery
- 1 3-oz. package cream cheese
- 1/2 cup finely chopped pecans

Apple Dressing:

- 1/2 cup applesauce
- 1/2 cup dairy sour cream
- 1/2 cup salad dressing
- 1 teaspoon celery seed

Mix gelatin and sugar in saucepan; stir in 3/4 cup cranberry juice. Cook and stir over low heat until gelatin is dissolved. Remove from heat; stir in remaining cranberry juice and lemon juice. Chill until partially thickened. Fold in apple, celery and cream cheese balls rolled in nuts. To prepare balls, cut cheese into 1/2-inch cubes; roll in nuts. Turn into an oiled 3-cup mold; chill until firm. Serve with chilled apple dressing prepared by blending remaining ingredients. Makes 4 to 6 servings.

Ceil Berger, Northern Illinois Region

TART LEMON SNOW

- 1 envelope (1 tablespoon) plain gelatin
- ½ cup cold water
- ½ cup boiling water
- ½ cup sugar
- 1 6-oz. can lemonade, thawed
- 2 cups Cool Whip, thawed
- Fresh strawberry garnish

Soften gelatin in cold water; add boiling water and stir until dissolved. Add sugar and lemonade. Chill until slightly thickened. Beat with electric mixer until fluffy and thick. Blend in Cool Whip. Pour into 6-cup mold; chill overnight. Unmold and garnish with strawberries. Makes 6 to 8 servings.

Judy Hirsh, Northern Illinois Region

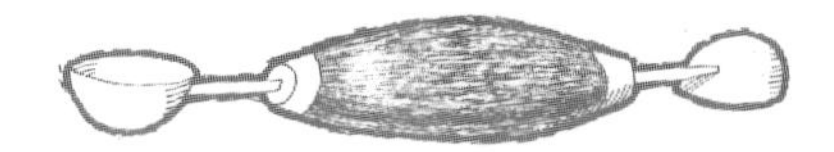

FROSTED LEMON GELATIN

- 1 3-oz. package lemon gelatin
- 1 3-oz. package orange gelatin
- 2 cups hot water
- Juice of 1 lemon
- 1 13¼-oz. can crushed pineapple
- 2 bananas, diced
- 100 small marshmallows

Topping:

- 2 tablespoons flour
- ½ cup sugar
- 2 tablespoons butter
- 1 cup heavy cream

Dissolve gelatin in hot water; add juice of 1 lemon plus water to make 2 cups. Chill until partly thickened. Thoroughly drain pineapple; reserve juice for topping. Fold pineapple, bananas and marshmallows into gelatin; turn into a 9 x 13-inch pan; chill until firm. To prepare topping: In saucepan, mix flour and sugar. Blend in pineapple juice and butter. Cook until thick, stirring constantly. Cool; fold in whipped cream. Spread on firm gelatin. Makes 12 to 16 servings.

Sandi Martin, Omaha Chapter-at-Large

CHERRY NUT SALAD

- **2 3-oz. packages cherry gelatin**
- **1 cup boiling water**
- **1 20-oz. can crushed pineapple, drained**
- **3 medium bananas, mashed**
- **1 cup coarsely chopped walnuts**
- **1 30-oz. can pitted dark sweet cherries, halved**
- **1 pint dairy sour cream**

Dissolve gelatin in boiling water. Immediately add pineapple, bananas, nuts and cherries plus liquid. Pour half of gelatin mixture into a bundt pan or a 12 x 8 x 2-inch pan. Refrigerate until almost set. Spread sour cream evenly over gelatin. Gently spoon remaining gelatin mixture over cream. Chill until firm. Makes 12 servings.

Linda Kline, Des Moines Chapter-at-Large

STRAWBERRIES 'N' CREAM MOLD

- **3 3-oz. packages strawberry gelatin**
- **3 cups boiling water**
- **2 cups cold water**
- **1 9-oz. container Cool Whip**
- **2 3-oz. packages frozen strawberries, thawed and drained**

Dissolve gelatin in boiling water. Add cold water; chill until partially thickened. Whip gelatin in electric mixer; add Cool Whip and beat until blended. Fold in well drained strawberries. Turn into a large ring mold; chill until firm. Unmold and garnish, if you wish, with fresh berries. Makes 12 to 16 servings.

Enid Schultz, Lake County Region

RASPBERRY FLUFFY MOLD

- **2 3-oz. packages lemon gelatin**
- **2 3-oz. packages raspberry gelatin**
- **2 cups boiling water**
- **2 pints dairy sour cream**
- **2 20-oz. cans crushed pineapple**

Dissolve gelatin in boiling water; add sour cream and pineapple plus liquid. Blend well. Turn into a 12-cup gelatin mold. Chill until firm. Makes 12 servings.

Mrs. Stanley Gore, Lake County Region

RASPBERRY SHERBET MOLD

- 1 large 6-oz. package raspberry gelatin
- 2 cups boiling water
- 1 pint raspberry sherbet
- 2 10-oz. package frozen raspberries
- 1 1 lb. 13-oz. can pear halves, drained

Dissolve gelatin in boiling water; add sherbet and stir until dissolved. Add raspberry juice plus water to make 1 cup. Chill until partially set. Whip gelatin. Add raspberry and pears. Turn into a 6 to 8-cup ring mold; chill until firm. Makes 10 to 12 servings.

Mrs. Hal Levin, Des Moines Chapter-at-Large

SALAD SUPREME

- 1 3-oz. package raspberry gelatin
- 2 cups boiling water
- 1 21-oz. can cherry pie filling
- 1 3-oz. package lemon gelatin
- 1 3-oz. package cream cheese, softened
- 1/3 cup mayonnaise
- 1 8½-oz. can crushed pineapple
- 1 cup miniature marshmallows
- ½ cup heavy cream, whipped
- 2 tablespoons chopped pecans

Dissolve raspberry gelatin in 1 cup boiling water; stir in pie filling. Turn into an oiled 9-inch square pan. Chill until firm. Dissolve lemon gelatin in 1 cup boiling water; cool. Beat cream cheese with mayonnaise until blended and smooth; gradually add gelatin. Stir in pineapple plus liquid and marshmallows. Chill until partly set. Fold in whipped cream. Spoon over cherry layer; top with pecans. Chill until firm. Cut into squares to serve. For blueberry variation, substitute grape for raspberry gelatin and use 1 can blueberry pie filling. Makes 12 servings.

Ellen Kogen, Lake County Region

LAYERED ICE CREAM MOLD

- 1 3-oz. package cherry gelatin
- 1 cup boiling water
- 1 pint cherry ice cream
- 2 small ice cubes
- 1 3-oz. package lime gelatin
- 1 cup boiling water
- 1 pint vanilla ice cream

Dissolve cherry gelatin in water; add cherry ice cream and 1 ice cube; mix until ice cream is melted. Turn into a mold and chill for 1 hour. Dissolve lime gelatin in boiling water; add ice cream and ice cube. Pour over first layer. Chill until firm. Makes 8 to 12 servings.

Gloria Geiger, West Suburban Region

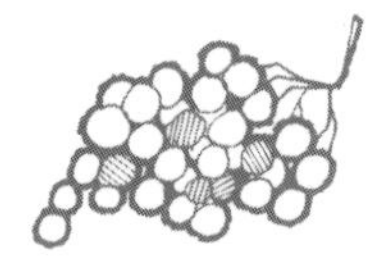

PINK CLOUD MOLD

- 2 3-oz. packages strawberry gelatin
- 3 cups boiling water
- ½ cup cold Milnot
- 1 cup mashed banana
- 1 cup drained crushed pineapple
- 2 tablespoon lemon juice
- 1 cup chopped walnuts

Dissolve gelatin in boiling water. Chill until partially thickened. Whip Milnot. Add gelatin and whip until light and fluffy. Add remaining ingredients and beat well. Pour into an 8-cup ring mold; chill until firm. Makes 16 servings.

Fay Nicholas, Northern Illinois Region

BRANDIED FRUIT

- Apothecary jar (clear)
- Sugar
- 1 cup drained diced peaches
- 1 cup drained diced pineapple tidbits
- 1 cup drained halved marachino cherries

In apothecary jar, or container with loose-fitting lid, combine 1 cup sugar and 1 cup drained canned peaches; store at room temperature. In two weeks, add 1 cup sugar and 1 cup diced pineapple tidbits; two weeks later add an additional cup of sugar and 1 cup halved maraschino cherries. Every two weeks add a cup of sugar and 1 cup of drained canned fruit in the order given. The fruit will ferment and become brandied, creating a delectable dessert sauce. Whenever you have over 3 cups of fermented fruit you can divide mixture into 2 portions. The mixture should be divided before you are ready to add ingredients. Do not refrigerate mixture. Stir occasionally so that the sugar can dissolve.

Rena Berman, Lake County Region

WINTER RUMTOPF

- 3 medium pears, cored and chopped
- 3 medium oranges, peeled and chopped
- 1 cup cranberries
- 1 cup sugar
- 1 cup rum

In a crock, combine fruit, sugar and rum; stir to blend. Loosely cover crock with cheesecloth. Refrigerate for 2 weeks before serving. For each cup of fruit you remove, add 1 cup fruit, 1/4 cup sugar and 1/4 cup rum. Delicious over ice cream or cake.

Betty Grossman, Northern Illinois Region

FRUITED RUM POT

- 2 cups well drained fruit (fresh, canned or frozen)
- 2 cups sugar
- Rum

Combine 2 cups fruit and 2 cups sugar in a 2-quart container. Add rum to cover fruit. Place a top on the container, not tightly. Store at room temperature for at least one month before using. A clear apothecary jar makes an ideal container. As you use fruit, add 1 cup canned peaches and 1 cup sugar to original starter. In 2 weeks, add 1 cup pineapple tidbits and 1 cup sugar. Two weeks later, add 1 cup maraschino cherries and 1 cup sugar. Share a cup of starter with a friend, telling her your fruit addition schedule. Great over vanilla ice cream and pound cake.

Eileen Kiess, Des Moines Chapter-at-Large

FRUIT WITH WHITE WINE AND CURRY

- 1 29-oz. can peach halves, drained
- 1 19-oz. can pear halves, halved and drained
- 1 20-oz. can pineapple spears, drained
- 2 11-oz. cans mandarin oranges, drained
- 1 8-oz. jar marachino cherries, drained
- 2 bananas, diagonally sliced
- ½ cup melted butter
- ½ cup brown sugar
- 1 to 2 teaspoons curry
- 1½ cups dry white wine
- 1 tablespoon cornstarch

Place all fruits except bananas in a shallow 3-quart baking dish. In saucepan, combine melted butter, sugar, curry and ½ cup wine. Cook until sugar is dissolved. Pour sauce over fruit and bake at 350° for 25 minutes. Add bananas the last 10 minutes. Drain sauce into a saucepan; blend cornstarch with a few tablespoons of remaining wine; add to sauce with wine and cook, stirring, until thickened and clear. Pour over fruit. Serve hot or cold. If served cold, add bananas about an hour before serving. Makes 12 servings.

Lee Bateman, Lake County Region

BAKED FRUIT WITH SOUR CREAM

1 16-oz. can pear halves
1 8¾-oz. can apricot halves
1 8¾-oz. can royal anne cherries
1 16-oz. can pineapple chunks
Juice of 1 lemon
¼ cup brown sugar
¼ teaspoon nutmeg
¼ teaspoon cinnamon
⅛ teaspoon ground cloves
¾ cup syrup from fruits
2 tablespoons butter
Sour Cream

Drain fruits, reserving syrup. Combine to make ¾ cup. Arrange fruits in a 2-quart casserole. Sprinkle with lemon juice. Combine sugar, spices and fruit syrup. Pour over fruit. Dot with butter. Bake at 350° for 20 minutes. Serve warm with sour cream sprinkled with nutmeg. Makes 6 servings.

Linda Kline, Des Moines Chapter-at-Large

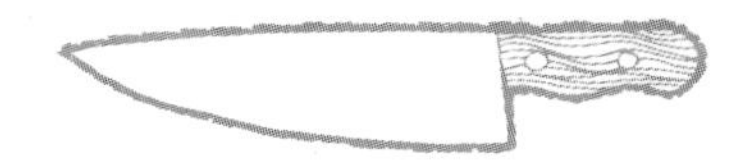

CURRIED FRUIT BAKE

⅓ cup butter
¾ cup firmly packed brown sugar
4 teaspoons curry powder
1 1-lb. can pear halves
1 1-lb. can cling peach or apricot halves
1 1-lb. 4-oz. can pineapple slices
Maraschino cherries with stems, drained

In saucepan melt butter; stir in sugar and curry powder. Drain pears, peaches and pineapple and dry well on paper towels. Layer fruit in a 1½-qt. shallow casserole, having peach or apricot halves on top. Pour in butter mixture; place a cherry in center of each peach or apricot half. Bake uncovered, at 325° for 1 hour. Can be made a day ahead, refrigerated and reheated at 350° for 30 minutes. Delicious with turkey, chicken or lamb. Makes 8 servings.

Florence Purnell, Des Moines Chapter-at-Large

FRUIT COMPOTE

- 2 pounds dried mixed fruit
- 1 20-oz. can pineapple chunks
- ½ cup sweet sheri nova
- 1 1 lb. 4-oz. can cherry pie filling

Wash and drain dried fruit. Place in a large casserole. Drain pineapple; measure ½ cup juice. Add pineapple chunks, sheri nova and pineapple juice; mix well. Cover mixed fruits with cherry pie filling, sealing to sides of casserole. Bake at 325° for 1½ hours. Makes 12 servings.

Blanche Wax, Chicago Region

FABULOUS FRUIT COMPOTE

- 1 1 lb. 1 oz. can pitted dark, sweet cherries
- 1 1 lb. can drained, sliced peaches
- 1 12-oz. package dried apricots
- 1 tablespoon grated orange peel
- 1 tablespoon grated lemon peel
- ½ cup orange juice
- ¼ cup lemon juice
- ¾ cup firmly packed light brown sugar
- Sour cream or sweetened whipped cream

Turn cherries and their liquid into a 2-quart casserole. Add peaches, apricots, orange and lemon peels and juices. Sprinkle with brown sugar. Cover dish and bake at 350° for 1½ hours. Let cool slightly; then refrigerate, covered, several hours or overnight to chill thoroughly. Serve with sour cream or sweetened whipped cream. Makes 6 to 8 servings.

June Minkus, Lake County Region

QUICK FRUIT COMPOTE

- 1 1-lb. can peach halves
- 1 1-lb. can pear halves
- 1 1-lb. can apricot halves
- 1 1-lb. can pineapple tidbits
- 1 small can mandarin oranges
- 1 1-lb. 4-oz. can cherry pie filling

Drain first five fruits well. Arrange evenly in square pan or large pie plate. Cover with canned cherry pie filling. Bake at 425° for 30 minutes. Makes 10 servings.

Faye Globerson, Lake County Region

HOT FRUIT COMPOTE

- 12 crumbled dried macaroons
- 4 cups canned fruits, drained
- ¼ cup brown sugar
- ½ cup sherry
- ½ cup toasted almonds, slivered
- ¼ cup melted butter

Butter 2½-qt. casserole. Cover bottom with macaroon crumbs, then alternate fruit and crumbs. Sprinkle with sugar, sherry and almonds. Bake at 350° for 30 minutes. Add melted butter. Serve hot or warm. Can be made ahead and reheated. Makes 8 servings.

Erika Brodsky, Lake County Region

BAKED CRANBERRY SAUCE

- 1 pound fresh cranberries
- 2 cups sugar
- 2 apples, pared and sliced thin
- ¼ cup crushed pineapple

Wash and pick over cranberries; drain. Place in heavy baking dish with cover; add sugar and apples. Bake at 350° for 50 minutes, or until cranberries pop. Add crushed pineapple, mixing well. Chill before serving. Makes 6 servings.

Debbie Wilner, Northern Illinois Region

CRANBERRY CHUTNEY

- 1 pound fresh cranberries
- 1 cup sugar
- 1 1 lb. 13-oz. can sliced cling peaches
- ½ cup chopped onion
- 2 tablespoons lemon juice
- 1 teaspoon salt
- Dash of cayenne
- 1 teaspoon powdered ginger
- 1 cup seedless raisins

Wash and pick over cranberries. Place in a large saucepan with sugar. Drain peaches; reserve syrup and add to cranberries with remaining ingredients. Cook, uncovered, over medium heat for 15 minutes, stirring occasionally. Add peaches and cook 5 minutes longer. Cool; refrigerate at least 2 to 3 days before serving. Makes about 1 quart.

Faye Press, Chicago Region

CRANBERRY-CUMBERLAND SAUCE

- 1 cup ruby Port wine
- 3 tablespoons grated orange rind
- 1/3 cup orange juice
- 1 tablespoon lemon juice
- 1/2 cup red currant jelly
- 1 8-oz. can whole cranberry sauce
- Dash of cayenne pepper

In medium saucepan, combine wine and orange rind. Cook over medium heat for about 10 minutes, until liquid is reduced to 2/3 cup. Add remaining ingredients and heat to boiling. Lower heat and simmer, uncovered, until jelly and cranberry sauce are melted, about 10 minutes. Cool. Refrigerate until ready to serve with turkey, chicken or other poultry. Makes about 1 pint.

Ruth Weissman, Lake County Region

SPICED APPLES AND CRANBERRIES

- 1 cup water
- 1 cup sugar
- 2 cups fresh cranberries
- 2 cups water
- 1 1/4 cups sugar
- 2 sticks cinnamon
- 8 large cooking apples, peeled and sliced

Combine 1 cup water and 1 cup sugar in saucepan; boil for 5 minutes. Add cranberries; simmer about 5 minutes, or until all skins pop open; cool. Combine remaining water and sugar in another saucepan with cinnamon. Cook for 10 minutes. Add apples and simmer until tender, about 5 minutes. Combine apples and cranberries; refrigerate until ready to serve. Makes 2 quarts.

Ronna Brown, Northern Illinois Region

EGGPLANT RELISH I

- 1 eggplant, about 1 1/2 pounds
- 1 small green pepper
- 1 small onion
- 6 hard-cooked eggs
- 1 hard roll
- Vinegar
- Sugar
- Salt and pepper, to taste

Bake eggplant at 350° for 30 minutes, or until tender. Peel eggplant; chop with green pepper and onion. Add eggs; chop until very fine. Soak a hard roll in vinegar; add sugar. Add to eggplant; season to taste and serve.

Mrs. Morris Zfaney, Chicago Region

BEET PRESERVES

- 4 cups beets—2 16-oz. cans sliced beets
- 3 cups sugar
- 1 cup honey
- 2 teaspoons ground ginger
- ¾ cup water
- 1 lemon, peeled and sliced thin
- 1 cup nuts, coarsely broken

Rinse beets well in cold water; cut into julienne strips. In a large saucepan, combine sugar, honey, ginger and water. Stir gently over low heat until sugar is dissolved. Heat to boiling; add lemon and beets. Cook gently until the beets begin to have a crystalline texture, about 1 to 1½ hours. Add nuts, mixing lightly. Increase heat, if necessary, to reduce syrup to a rich thickness. Fill sterilized jelly glasses and cover. If plain beets are used, cook until tender; peel and cut julienne style. Continue as directed. Makes about 10 8-oz. glasses.

Hilda Hirsh, Milwaukee Region

EGGPLANT RELISH II

- 1 large eggplant
- 2 tablespoons salad oil
- 2 tablespoons sugar
- ½ teaspoon salt
- Dash of pepper
- Dash of garlic powder

Place eggplant on open flame and let it actually burn on all sides until soft or bake at 350° for 1 hour until soft. Peel eggplant; cool and chop. Add oil and stir. Add remaining ingredients.

Rose Kaufman, Milwaukee Region

BLUEBERRY CAKE

- ½ cup butter (1 stick)
- 1 cup sugar
- 2 egg yolks
- 1 teaspoon vanilla
- 1½ cups flour
- 1 teaspoon baking powder
- ¼ teaspoon salt
- ⅓ cup milk
- 2 egg whites, beaten
- 1½ cups blueberries

Cream butter and sugar. Add egg yolks. Add vanilla. Alternately add sifted dry ingredients and milk. Fold in beaten egg whites. Spread half of batter in greased 9-inch square pan. Sprinkle berries on top. Cover berries with remaining batter. Bake at 350° for 35 minutes. Makes 9 servings.

R. Landsman, Chicago Region

CARAMEL CAKE

- 1 cup sugar
- 1 cup flour
- ¼ teaspoon salt
- 1 teapsoon baking soda
- 1 11-oz. can drained Mandarin oranges
- 2 tablespoons orange juice
- 1 egg

Topping:

- 1 cup firmly packed brown sugar
- ¼ cup butter (½ stick)
- ½ cup milk
- ½ cup chopped nuts
- ½ cup coconut

Blend cake ingredients together until moistened. Spread in a greased 9-inch square pan. Bake at 350° for 25 to 30 minutes. While cake is baking, boil together for 2 minutes brown sugar, butter and milk. Stir in nuts and coconut. Spread over cake as it comes out of oven. This cake is moist and keeps well. It is better made a day ahead. Freezes well. Makes 9 servings.

Bunny Cohen, Milwaukee Chapter

BLACK WALNUT CAKE

½ cup butter (1 stick)
1 cup sugar
2 eggs
1 cup dariy sour cream
1 teaspoon vanilla
1 teaspoon almond extract
2 cups flour
1 teaspoon baking soda
1 teaspoon baking powder
½ cup black walnuts, chopped

Topping:
⅓ cup brown sugar
¾ teaspoon cinnamon

Cream together butter and sugar. Add eggs, sour cream, vanilla and almond extract. Add flour, soda and baking powder. Blend well. Stir in walnuts. Pour half of batter into greased 9-inch square pan. Combine brown sugar and cinnamon and sprinkle two-thirds of mixture over batter in pan. Cover with remaining batter. Sprinkle remaining brown sugar-cinnamon mixture on top. Swirl into batter with spatula. Bake at 375° for 45 to 55 minutes. Makes 9 servings.

Carol Linch, Lake County Region

APPLESAUCE CAKE

1 cup oil
3 cups sugar
3 eggs
2 tablespoons vanilla
1 1-lb. can applesauce
1 1-lb. 4-oz. can crushed pineapple
6 cups flour
2 tablespoons baking soda
2 tablespoons cinnamon
1 teaspoon salt
1 applesauce can of water
½ box raisins (8 ounces)

Blend oil and sugar. Beat in eggs. Add vanilla, applesauce and pineapple. Sift together flour, soda, cinnamon and salt. Add dry ingredients alternately with water. Stir in raisins. Pour into two greased 13x9-inch pans. (One 13x9-inch pan and two 8-inch square pans may also be used.) Bake at 325° for 50 minutes to 1 hour; reduce time if using smaller pans. Makes 40 servings.

Sara Myers, St. Louis Region

SPICE CAKE

1 cup raisins
1 cup warm water
1 cup sugar
1 teaspoon cinnamon
½ teaspoon ground cloves
½ teaspoon salt
¼ cup butter
2 cups flour
1 teaspoon baking powder
1 teaspoon baking soda

Combine raisins, water, sugar, spices, salt and butter in a saucepan and boil for 1 minute. Remove from heat and set aside to cool. When liquid is cool, combine with sifted flour, baking powder and soda. Pour into greased 9-inch square pan. Bake at 350° for 1 hour. This cake freezes well. Makes 9 servings.

Bette Blair, Chicago Region

CHOCOLATE RIBBON CAKE

Ribbon Mixture:
2 tablespoons butter
1 8-oz. package cream cheese
¼ cup sugar
1 tablespoon cornstarch
1 egg
2 tablespoons milk
½ teaspoon vanilla

Cake:
2 cups sifted flour
2 cups sugar
1 teaspoon salt
1 teaspoon baking powder
½ teaspoon baking soda
½ cup butter (1 stick)
1⅓ cups milk
2 eggs
4 envelopes, premelted, unsweetened chocolate
1 teaspoon vanilla

Frosting:
½ cup milk
¼ cup butter (½ stick)
1 6-oz. package semi-sweet chocolate pieces
1 teaspoon vanilla
2½ cups sifted confectioners' sugar

To make ribbon mixture, cream butter with cream cheese, sugar and cornstarch. Add egg, milk and vanilla. Beat at high speed of mixer until smooth and creamy. To make cake batter, combine flour, sugar, salt, baking powder and soda in large mixing bowl. Add butter and 1 cup milk. Blend well at lowest mixer speed. Beat 1½ minutes at low speed. Add remaining ⅓ cup milk, eggs, chocolate and vanilla, beating 1½ minutes at low speed. Spread half of batter in greased and floured 13x9-inch pan. Spoon ribbon mixture over batter, spreading carefully to cover. Top with remaining cake batter. Bake at

350° for 50 to 60 minutes, until cake springs back when touched lightly in center. Cool and frost.

To make frosting, combine milk and butter in saucepan. Heat to boiling. Remove from heat. Blend in chocolate. Then add vanilla and confectioners' sugar. Beat until of spreading consistency. Frost cake. Freezes well. Makes 15 servings.

Arleen Dobkin, St. Louis Region

FRUIT COCKTAIL CAKE

- 1½ cups sugar
- 2 cups flour
- ¼ teaspoon salt
- 2 teaspoons baking soda
- 2 eggs
- 1 teaspoon vanilla
- 1 1-lb., 1-oz. can fruit cocktail, not drained
- ½ cup chopped nuts
- ½ cup brown sugar

Topping:

- ½ cup butter (1 stick)
- ½ cup sugar
- 1 teaspoon vanilla
- ⅔ cup milk

Combine sugar, flour, salt, soda, eggs and vanilla and mix until smooth. Fold in fruit cocktail, which has not been drained, and chopped nuts. Pour batter into greased 13x9-inch pan. Sprinkle brown sugar over batter. Bake at 350° for 45 to 50 minutes. After cake is baked, but still hot, combine topping ingredients in a saucepan. Boil a few minutes, then pour directly on top of warm cake. Wait at least 1 hour before serving. Makes 12 servings.

Sybil Kaplan, Lake County Region

EGGLESS RAISIN CAKE

- ½ cup vegetable oil
- 1 cup raisins
- 2 cups water
- 1½ cups sugar
- 2½ teaspoons cinnamon
- 1 teaspoon vanilla
- 2½ cups flour
- 1 teaspoon baking powder
- 1 teaspoon baking soda
- Pinch salt

Combine oil, raisins, water, sugar and cinnamon in saucepan. Boil 5 minutes. Let cool and add vanilla. Sift together flour, baking powder, soda and salt. Add flour mixture to raisin mixture and beat well. Pour into a greased and floured 13x9-inch pan. Bake at 350° for 40 minutes. This is an unfrosted cake which freezes well. Makes 12 to 15 servings.

Julie Smith, South Bend Chapter-at-Large

CHOCOLATE SOUR CREAM CAKE

3 1-oz. squares unsweetened chocolate
½ cup margarine (1 stick)
1 cup water
2 cups sifted cake flour
1¼ teaspoons baking soda
1 teaspoon salt
2 eggs
1 cup dairy sour cream
2 cups sugar
1½ teaspoons vanilla

Combine chocolate, margarine and water in top of double boiler and heat until melted. Cool. Sift flour, soda and salt into a large bowl. Beat eggs with sour cream until blended in a separate bowl; beat in sugar and vanilla; stir in cooled chocolate mixture. Stir egg mixture into flour mixture, blending until smooth. Batter will be thin. Pour into two greased and floured 4x8-inch loaf pans. Bake at 350° for 40 minutes. Freezes well. Makes 2 cakes, 6 servings each.

Helen N. Cohen, West Suburban Region

BANANA RIPPLE CAKE

½ cup semi-sweet chocolate pieces
¼ cup water
½ cup butter (1 stick)
1½ cups sugar
2 eggs, separated
2 cups sifted flour
¾ teaspoon baking soda
½ teaspoon salt
¼ teaspoon baking powder
1 cup mashed ripe bananas
⅓ cup dairy sour cream
1 teaspoon vanilla
⅓ cup chopped maraschino cherries, drained

Melt chocolate pieces with water in top of double boiler; cool. Cream butter and 1¼ cups sugar until light and fluffy. Add egg yolks; beat thoroughly. Sift flour with soda, salt and baking powder. Mix bananas with sour cream and vanilla. Add to creamed mixture alternately with dry ingredients, beating until smooth after each addition. Stir in cherries. Beat egg whites until soft peaks form; gradually beat in remaining ¼ cup sugar, continue beating until stiff but not dry. Gently fold into batter. Place one-third of batter in a greased nad floured 10-inch tube pan. Drizzle half of chocolate over batter. Repeat with one-third of batter and remaining chocolate. Top with remaining batter. Bake at 350° for 1 hour. Makes 12 to 16 servings.

Lee Bateman, Lake County Region

CHOCOLATE PECAN ANGEL FOOD CAKE

Cake:

1½ cups egg whites
2 teaspoons cream of tartar
2 tablespoons water
1 teaspoon vanilla
1 teaspoon almond extract
1⅞ cups sugar
1 cup cake flour
¼ teaspoon salt
½ cup cocoa
1 cup broken pecans

Chocolate Frosting:

½ cup butter (1 stick)
¾ cup sifted confectioners' sugar
2 egg yolks
2½ 1-oz. squares unsweetened chocolate, melted and cooled
2 stiffly beaten egg whites
Toasted, salted pecan halves

To make cake, beat egg whites until forthy. Sprinkle cream of tartar over top and continue beating until whites are stiff enough to form peaks, but not dry. Gradually add water and flavorings. Beat in half of sugar, sifting it 2 tablespoons at a time over surface. Sift cake flour before measuring, then sift with salt, cocoa and remaining sugar. Carefully fold sifted dry ingredients into first mixture, about ¼ cup at a time. Fold in pecans. Turn into an ungreased 10-inch tube pan. Bake at 400° for 35 minutes. Invert pan until cake is cool, about 1 hour. To make Chocolate Frosting, cream butter and sugar. Add egg yolks and chocolate, blending well. Fold in egg whites. Frost cake and garnish with pecans. Chill before serving. Makes 12 to 16 servings.

Ruth Ostreicher, Chicago Region

CHOCOLATE RING-O-ROUND

1 6-oz. package semi-sweet chocolate pieces
1 cup dairy sour cream
1 teaspoon baking soda
½ cup butter (1 stick)
¾ cup sugar
2 eggs
1 teaspoon vanilla
1½ cups sifted flour

Melt chocolate. Add soda to sour cream; set aside. Cream butter and sugar. Add eggs and vanilla; blend well. Add sour cream and soda mixture alternately with sifted flour. Beat until well blended. Blend in melted chocolate. Pour into greased and floured 10-inch tube pan. Bake at 350° for 45 minutes. This cake freezes well. Makes 16 servings.

Mrs. Milton Silverstein, Lake County Region

CHOCOLATE-NUT SPONGE CAKE

- 7 jumbo eggs, spearated
- 1 teaspoon cream of tartar
- 1½ cups sugar
- 2 tablespoons 2 teaspoons orange juice
- 1 teaspoon vanilla
- 1 cup flour
- Pinch of salt
- 1 1-oz. square unsweetened chocolate, grated
- ½ cup chopped nuts
- Confectioners' sugar

Use eggs at room temperature. Beat egg whites until foamy. Add cream of tartar and continue beating. While beating whites, gradually beat in 1 cup sugar, by adding 2 tablespoons at a time, until whites are stiff and stand up in peaks. Beat yolks until lemon yellow (about 5 minutes); then add alternately ½ cup sugar and the orange juice and vanilla. Add egg yolk mixture slowly to whites. Sift flour and salt together; use a wire whip to fold flour into eggs. Fold in chocolate and nuts. Pour into an ungreased 10-inch tube pan and bake at 325° for 30 minutes; increase oven heat to 350° and bake an additional 30 minutes. Cool upside down. To serve, decorate with confectioners' sugar. Freezes well. Makes 12 to 14 servings.

Eleanor Gibian, Lake County Region

FAMOUS LEMON POUND CAKE

- ¾ cup butter (1½ sticks)
- 1¼ cups sugar
- 8 egg yolks
- 2½ cups cake flour
- 1 tablespoon baking powder
- ¼ teaspoon salt
- ¾ cup milk
- 1 teaspoon vanilla
- 1 teapsoon lemon juice
- 1 teaspoon grated lemon rind
- Confectioners' sugar

Cream butter and sugar until light and fluffy. Beat egg yolks until light and lemon-colored; blend into creamed mixture. Sift together flour, baking powder and salt; resift three times. Add dry ingredients alternately with milk, beating after each addition. Add vanilla, lemon juice and rind and beat 2 minutes longer. Bake in greased 12-cup Bundt pan at 325° for 1 hour. When golden, remove from oven, cool 10 minutes on cake rack, then remove cake from pan and continue to cool. Dust with confectioners' sugar, if desired.

Lylus Brash, Chicago Region

CINNAMON POUND CAKE

1 cup butter (2 sticks)
2 cups sugar
4 eggs
3 cups flour
1 tablespoon baking powder
1 cup milk

Cinnamon sugar:
½ cup sugar
½ teaspoon cinnamon

Cream butter with sugar. Add eggs, one at a time, beating well after each addition. Sift together flour and baking powder. Add to creamed mixture alternately with milk. Grease a 10-inch tube pan. Pour half of batter into pan. Cover batter with cinnamon-sugar mixture. Cover with remaining batter. Bake at 350° for 1 hour. Do not invert to cool. Makes 12 to 14 servings.

Carolyn Kahn, Lake County Region

MARBLE CAKE

3½ cups sifted cake flour
1 tablespoon baking powder
¾ teaspoon salt
1 cup butter (2 sticks)
1 teaspoon almond extract
2 cups sugar
4 eggs
1 cup milk
¼ cup dry cocoa
1 teaspoon rum extract
2 tablespoons water

Glaze:
¼ cup dry cocoa
1 cup confectioners' sugar
¼ cup butter (½ stick)
2 tablespoons water

Sift flour, baking powder and salt. Cream butter with almond extract and 1½ cups sugar. Add eggs one at a time, beating well after each addition. Add flour mixture alternately with milk, beating well. Divide batter into two parts. Blend ½ cup sugar, cocoa, rum extract and water and stir into half of batter. Layer batters alternately in a greased 10-inch tube pan. Cut through batter to marble, but do not blend. Bake at 350° for 1 hour, or until done. Cool in pan 15 minutes, then remove cake from pan and glaze. To make glaze, combine cocoa and sugar. Heat butter and water in small pan. Add to sugar mixture. Blend well. Spread over cake. (Note: 1 envelope pre-melted unsweetened chocolate may be substituted for ¼ cup cocoa.) Makes 12 to 14 servings.

Dale Madansky, Northern Illinois Region

LEMON GOLD CAKE

- 2¼ cups sifted cake flour
- 1½ cups sugar
- 1 tablespoon baking powder
- 1 teaspoon salt
- ½ cup oil
- 6 eggs, separated
- ¾ cup cold water
- 2 teaspoons lemon juice
- 1 teaspoon grated lemon rind
- ½ teaspoon cream of tartar

Lemon Fluff Frosting:

- ½ cup margarine (1 stick)
- Dash of salt
- 4 cups sifted confectioners' sugar
- 3 tablespoons lemon juice
- 2 teaspoons grated lemon rind

Sift flour, sugar, baking powder and salt together in a bowl. Make a well and add in order the oil, egg yolks, water, lemon juice and rind. Beat with spoon until smooth. Add cream of tartar to egg whites; beat until very stiff. Pour egg yolk mixture gradually oven beaten whites, carefully folding with rubber scrapper just until blended. Do not stir. Pour into ungreased 10-inch tube pan. Bake at 325° for 1 hour, 10 minutes or until top springs back when touched. Invert cake to cool. When cold, loosen sides with spatula; remove cake from pan. To make Lemon Fluff Frosting, cream margarine. Add salt and part of sugar. Cream well. Add remaining sugar alternately with lemon juice, creaming until light and fluffy. Add lemon rind; mix until blended. Frost top and sides of cake. Makes 12 to 16 servings.

Susan Kaplan, Northern Illinois Region

MILK CHOCOLATE POUND CAKE

- 3 cups sugar
- 1 cup butter (2 sticks)
- ½ cup vegetable shortening
- 5 eggs
- 1 teaspoon vanilla
- 3 cups cake flour
- ½ teaspoon baking powder
- ½ teaspoon salt
- 4 heaping tablespoons cocoa
- 1 cup milk

Cream sugar, butter and shortening. Add eggs, one at a time, beating well after each addition. Add vanilla. Sift together flour, baking powder, salt and cocoa. Alternately add milk and flour. Mix until well blended. Pour into a greased 10-inch tube pan and bake at 350° for 1½ hours. Makes 12 to 16 servings.

Phyllis Silverman, Lake County Region

RHUBARB CAKE

- 1½ cups sugar
- ½ cup butter (1 stick)
- 1 teaspoon vanilla
- ½ teaspoon salt
- 1 egg
- 1 cup sour milk
- 2 cups flour
- 1 teaspoon baking soda
- 2 cups cut-up rhubarb

Topping:

- ½ cup brown sugar
- 1 teaspoon cinnamon
- ½ cup nuts

Cream together sugar, butter, vanilla and salt. Add egg, sour milk, flour and soda and mix well. Stir in rhubarb. Pour into a greased and floured 13x9-inch pan. Blend together topping ingredients and sprinkle evenly over batter before baking. Bake at 325° for 1 hour. Can be frozen. Makes 20 servings.

Eileen Kiess, Des Moines Chapter-at-Large

BANANA CAKE (Pareve)

- 2¼ cups sifted flour
- 1½ cups sugar
- 2½ teaspoons baking powder
- ½ teaspoon baking soda
- ½ teaspoon salt
- ½ cup soft shortening
- 1½ cups mashed bananas
- 2 eggs
- 1 teaspoon vanilla

Sift together flour, sugar, baking powder, soda and salt. Add shortening, ½ cup bananas and eggs. Beat two minutes at slow to medium speed with electric mixer. Add remaining bananas and vanilla. Beat 1 minute longer. Turn into two greased and flour 9-inch round pans. Bake at 350° for 30 to 35 minutes, or until cake tests done. Makes two 9-inch layers.

Enid Shultz, Lake County Region

BERRY TORTE

- 1 8-oz. package cream cheese
- 1 cup confectioners' sugar
- 2 envelopes Dream Whip
- Graham cracker crust ingredients
- 2 20-oz. cans blueberry, cherry or other pie filling

Cream together cream cheese and sugar. Blend with Dream Whip made according to package directions. Press graham cracker crust ingredients into a 13x9-inch pan. Top with cream cheese mixture. Cover with pie filling and chill. Makes 15 to 20 servings.

Mrs. Arthur Teplinsky, Milwaukee Region

CHOCOLATE SOUFFLE CAKE

- 1 cup sugar
- 1/4 cup margarine
- 4 eggs
- 1 16-oz. can chocolate syrup
- 1 cup sifted flour
- 2 1/2 teaspoons baking powder
- 1/4 teaspoon salt
- 1 teaspoon vanilla

Topping:

- 1 cup heavy cream, whipped
- 2 tablespoons confectioners' sugar
- 1 tablespoon instant coffee

Cream together sugar and margarine. Add eggs, one at a time, beating well after each addition. Blend in syrup, flour, baking powder, salt and vanilla. Beat well. Spread batter in a greased 9-inch springform and bake at 350° for 50 minutes or until cake tests done. Fold confectioners' sugar and instant coffee into whipped cream and serve over cake. Makes 12 servings.

Mildred Weinstock, Chicago Region

FEATHERY FUDGE CAKE

- 2/3 cup soft butter
- 1 3/4 cups sugar
- 2 eggs
- 1 teaspoon vanilla
- 2 1/2 1-oz. squares unsweetened chocolate, melted
- 2 1/2 cups sifted cake flour
- 1 1/4 teaspoons baking soda
- 1/2 teaspoon salt
- 1 1/4 cups ice water

Cream butter, sugar, eggs and vanilla until fluffy, beating for 5 minutes. Blend in chocolate. Sift flour, soda and salt and add to creamed mixture alternately with ice water. Pour into two greased 9-inch round pans and bake at 350° for 30 to 35 minutes (or use one greased 13x9-inch pan and bake for 45 to 50 minutes). Frost, if desired, when cool with creamy fudge frosting. Makes 12 to 15 servings.

Audrey Rosenberg, Des Moines Chapter-at-Large

PAREVE FUDGE CAKE

- 3 cups sifted cake flour
- 1½ teaspoons baking soda
- ½ teaspoon salt
- ¾ cup vegetable shortening
- 2¼ cups sugar
- 3 eggs
- 3 1-oz. squares unsweetened chocolate, melted
- 1½ teaspoons vanilla
- 1½ cups ice water

Measure flour and sift. Measure again and sift flour with soda and salt. Cream shortening and sugar until light and fluffy. Add eggs, one at a time, beating well after each addition. Blend in chocolate and vanilla. Add dry ingredients, in fourths, alternately with ice water beating well after each addition. Pour into greased, waxed paper-lined pans: 3 layer pans or one large oblong. Bake large pan at 350° for 40 to 45 minutes. Bake layers for 30 to 35 minutes. Frost with favorite frosting. Makes 12 to 15 servings.

Gertrude Lederman, Lake County Region

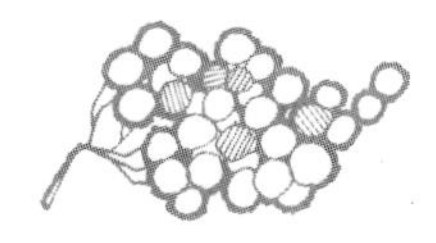

EASY NUT TORTE

- 4 eggs, separated
- ¾ cup sugar
- ¾ cup cracker meal
- 1 teaspoon baking powder
- 1 cup ground pecans
- 1 teaspoon vanilla

Filling & frosting:

- 1 cup heavy cream
- 1 teaspoon vanilla
- 2 tablespoons confectioners' sugar

Beat egg yolks with sugar. Combine cracker meal, baking powder and pecans. Mix with egg yolks. Add vanilla. Beat egg whites until stiff and gently fold into nut mixture. Spoon into two lightly-greased 9-inch round pans. Bake at 350° for 20 minutes. Allow to cool. Whip cream until nearly stiff; blend in vanilla and sugar to taste. Continue beating until stiff. Use as a filling between torte layers and spread on top and sides. Makes 8 servings.

Hannah Meyer, Chicago Region

POUND CAKE

- 2½ cups cake flour
- 1½ teaspoons baking powder
- 1 cup butter (2 sticks)
- 1½ cups sugar
- 4 eggs
- 1 teaspoon vanilla
- ½ cup milk
- Ground nuts

Sift flour. Add baking powder. In bowl, cream butter with sugar until lemon-colored. Add eggs and beat until light and fluffy. Add vanilla. Add flour mixture alternately with milk. Cover bottom of greased 9-inch square or 10-inch tube pan with ground nuts. Pour batter in pan. Bake at 375° for 15 minutes, then 325° for 45 minutes. When cake is inverted from pan, nuts will be on top. Makes 12 servings.

Frances Keno, Chicago Region

1-2-3 "CUP" CAKE

- 1 cup butter (2 sticks)
- 2 cups sugar
- 4 eggs, separated
- 3 cups flour
- 1 tablespoon baking powder
- ½ teaspoon salt
- 1 cup milk
- 2 teaspoons vanilla

Cream butter and sugar thoroughly. Add egg yolks, one at a time, beating until thoroughly mixed. Sift flour with baking powder and salt and fold into butter mixture alternately with milk. Beat egg whites until stiff, but not dry, and gently fold into batter. Add vanilla. Pour batter into a greased 12x8x2-inch pan and bake at 350° for 1 hour. (To make a Pound Cake, follow above recipe but instead of separating eggs, add the whole eggs to the butter and sugar. Bake in a greased 10-inch tube pan.) Freezes well. Makes 12 servings.

Mildred Karpf, West Suburban Region

RAISIN CAKE

- 1 cup white raisins
- 2 cups water
- 2 teaspoons baking soda
- 1½ cups sugar
- ¾ cup vegetable oil
- 4 eggs
- 3 cups flour
- 1 cup chopped walnuts, if desired

Bring raisins and water to boil in small saucepan. Remove from heat, stir in soda, let cool. In large mixing bowl, mix sugar and oil. Add eggs, one at a time. Alternately add flour and cooled raisin mixture. Blend in chopped walnuts, if desired. Pour into oiled 10-inch tube pan. Bake at 350° for 1¼ hours. Freezes well. Makes 18 servings.

Jean Best, Chicago Region

CREAMY FUDGE FROSTING

- ½ cup water
- ¼ cup butter (½ stick)
- 1 teaspoon vanilla
- 4 1-oz. squares unsweetened chocolate, melted
- 4 cups sifted confectioners' sugar

Heat water and butter; add vanilla and chocolate. Add confectioners' sugar and beat until of spreading consistency. Will frost tops and sides of two 9-inch layers or one large loaf cake.

Audrey Rosenberg, Des Moines Chapter-at-Large

SUNSHINE CAKE

- 10 eggs, separated
- 1½ cups sugar
- ½ cup orange juice
- Grated rind of 1 orange
- 1 cup sifted cake flour
- 1 teaspoon cream of tartar

Beat yolks with 1 cup sugar until light in color. Add juice and rind. Fold in cake flour. Beat egg whites with cream of tartar until softly peaked. Add ½ cup sugar gradually and continue beating. Fold yolk mixture into stiffly-beaten egg whites; turn into an ungreased 10-inch tube pan. Bake at 325° for 1 hour. Makes 12 servings.

Mrs. Marvin Topper, Milwaukee Region

BUNDT KUCHEN

- 1 cup margarine or vegetable shortening
- 2 cups sugar
- 1½ teaspoons vanilla
- 4 eggs, separated
- 3½ cups sifted cake flour
- 2½ teaspoons baking powder
- ¾ teaspoon salt
- 1 cup milk

Cream margarine, sugar and vanilla. Blend in egg yolks, one at a time. Sift together flour, baking powder and salt; add alternately with milk, mixing well after each addition. Fold in stiffly beaten egg whites. Pour into greased and floured 12 cup Bundt pan or 10-inch tube pan. Bake at 350° for 1 hour. Cool 10 minutes; turn out of pan. Makes 16 servings.

Inez Kurzin, Chicago Region

CHOCOLATE CHIP YELLOW CAKE

- 1 package yellow cake mix
- 1 package instant vanilla pudding
- 4 eggs
- ¾ cup water
- ¾ cup oil
- 1 4-oz. bar German sweet chocolate, grated
- 1 6-oz. package semi-sweet chocolate pieces

Combine cake mix, pudding, eggs and water and mix according to cake mix directions. Add oil. Mix thoroughly. Fold in grated chocolate; then semi-sweet chocolate pieces. Pour into a well-greased 12 cup Bundt pan or 10-inch tube pan. Bake at 350° for 50 minutes. Makes 12 to 16 servings.

Bess Brooks, Chicago Region

HARVEY WALLBANGER CAKE

1 package orange supreme cake mix
1 package instant vanilla pudding mix
½ cup oil
½ cup orange juice
4 eggs
6 tablespoons (3-oz.) vodka
6 tablespoons (3-oz.) Galiano

Frosting:
1 cup confectioners' sugar
1½ tablespoons orange juice
1½ tablespoons vodka
1½ tablespoons Galiano

Combine ingredients and put in greased and floured 10-inch tube or Bundt pan. Bake at 350° for 45 to 55 minutes. (¾ cup orange juice and ¼ cup each of vodka and Galiano may also be used.) If frosting is desired, combine ingredients and drizzle over warm cake. Makes 12 to 15 servings.

Sybil Kaplan, Lake County Region

ORANGE SURPRISE CAKE

1 package orange layer cake mix
2 tablespoons butter
⅓ cup firmly packed brown sugar
½ cup finely chopped nuts
3 eggs
1½ cups dairy sour cream
Confectioners' sugar

Measure ¼ cup dry cake mix into small bowl. Cut in butter and stir in brown sugar and nuts. Set aside. Blend together remaining cake mix, eggs and sour cream in large bowl, using mixer at low speed and scraping bowl frequently. Batter will be thick and slightly lumpy. Pour half of batter into greased and floured 10-inch tube pan. Sprinkle nut mixture over batter. Gently spoon remaining batter over filling and spread carefully. Bake at 350° for 60-65 minutes or until top springs back when lightly touched. Cool 10 minutes in pan, then turn out on wire rack and cool completely. Sprinkle confectioners' sugar over top of cake. Makes 16 to 20 servings.

Miriam Witt, Chicago Region

LEMON APRICOT CAKE

1 package yellow cake mix
1 3-oz. package lemon gelatin
4 eggs, separated
2 teaspoons lemon extract
3/4 cup apricot nectar
3/4 cup corn oil

Glaze:
1/2 cup apricot nectar
1 cup confectioners' sugar
Dash salt

Combine all cake ingredients except egg whites. Mix well. Fold in beaten whites. Bake in greased and floured 10-inch tube pan at 350° for 1 hour. Combine glaze ingredients and pour over hot cake. Leave in pan until completely cool. Freezes well. Makes 12 to 16 servings.

Mrs. Arthur Teplinsky, Milwaukee Region

POPPYSEED WINE CAKE

1 package yellow cake mix
1 package instant French vanilla pudding
4 eggs
1 cup dairy sour cream
1/2 cup buttery flavor oil
1/2 cup cream sherry
1/3 cup poppyseeds

Combine all ingredients, stir to blend, beat at medium speed 5 minutes. Scrape sides often. Pour into greased 12-cup Bundt pan. Bake at 350° for 1 hour. Cool in pan on rack for 15 minutes. Freezes well. Makes 12 to 16 servings.

Erika Brodsky, Lake County Region

APRICOT-BANANA SQUARES

1/2 cup butter (1 stick)
1 cup firmly packed brown sugar
1 10-oz. jar apricot preserves
2 beaten eggs
1 teaspoon vanilla
1 3/4 cups flour
1/2 teaspoon baking powder
1/2 teaspoon baking soda
1/4 teaspoon salt
1 cup mashed ripe banana
1/2 cup chopped pecans

Lemon Glaze:
1 1/2 cups sifted confectioners' sugar
1 tablespoon water
1 tablespoon lemon juice

Cream butter and brown sugar. Blend in preserves, eggs and vanilla. Sift together flour, baking powder, soda and salt. Add dry ingredients alternately with mashed banana, mixing well after each addition. Stir in nuts. Pour into a greased and floured 13x9-inch pan. Bake at 350° for 35 to 40 minutes. Cool. Prepare Lemon Glaze by combining ingredients thoroughly. Drizzle on top and down sides of cake. Makes 12 servings.

Fay Nicholas, Northern Illinois Region

RUM CAKE

1 package yellow cake mix
1 package vanilla pudding mix
¼ cup oil
¼ cup soft butter (½ stick)
½ cup rum
½ cup chopped nuts
4 eggs, beaten

Glaze:
¼ cup butter (½ stick)
¼ cup water
1 cup sugar
¼ cup rum

Combine cake and pudding mixes in a large bowl. Stir in oil, butter, rum, nuts and beaten eggs. Beat well. Pour into a greased and floured 10-inch tube pan. Bake at 350° for 50 to 60 minutes. To make glaze, melt butter in saucepan. Add water and sugar. Boil 1 minute. Remove from heat; stir in rum. Spoon over hot cake. Leave in pan until cool. Makes 10 servings.

Gail Ginsburg, Omaha Chapter-at-Large

CHOCOLATE CAKE 'N FROSTING

2 8-oz. packages cream cheese
½ cup butter (1 stick)
1 teaspoon vanilla
6 cups confectioners' sugar
½ cup hot water
4 1-oz. squares unsweetened chocolate, melted
¼ cup butter (½ stick)
3 eggs
2¼ cups flour
2½ teaspoons baking soda
1 teaspoon salt
¾ cup milk

Blend cream cheese, butter and vanilla. Add confectioners' sugar and water alternately. Add melted chocolate. Divide batter in half. Place half aside to be used later for frosting. Combine ¼ cup butter and remaining chocolate mixture. Blend in eggs. Sift together flour, soda and salt and add alternately with milk. Spoon batter into a greased and floured 8x10-inch oblong pan. Bake at 350° for 30 to 35 minutes. Cool and frost with reserved batter. Makes 12 servings.

Mrs. Paul Friend, Lake County Region

7 UP CAKE

- 1½ cups margarine (3 sticks)
- 3 cups sugar
- 5 eggs
- 3 cups flour
- 2 tablespoons lemon extract
- ¾ cup (6-oz.) 7 Up

Cream together margarine and sugar until very light and fluffy. Add eggs one at a time. Blend in flour and lemon extract. Fold in 7 Up. Pour into a well-greased 12-cup Bundt pan. Bake at 325° for 1 to 1¼ hours. Freezes well. Makes 16 servings.

Janet Hoffman, South Bend Chapter-at-Large

HOT FUDGE PUDDING CAKE

- 1 cup sifted flour
- ¾ cup sugar
- 2 tablespoons cocoa
- 2 teaspoons baking powder
- ¼ teaspoon salt
- ½ cup milk
- 2 tablespoons melted butter
- ½ cup chopped nuts
- 1 cup firmly packed brown sugar
- ¼ cup cocoa
- 1¾ cup hot water
- Vanilla ice cream

Sift dry ingredients together into a bowl. Stir in milk and butter. Mix until smooth. Add nuts. Turn into greased and floured 9-inch square pan. Combine brown sugar, cocoa and hot water. Pour over batter. Bake at 350° for 40 minutes. Serve warm over vanilla ice cream. Makes 8 servings.

Meryl Liner, Northern Illinois Region

LUSCIOUS LEMON CAKE 'N CUSTARD

- ⅔ cup sugar
- 3 tablespoons flour
- ¼ teaspoon salt
- 3 tablespoons melted butter
- 3 eggs, separated
- 1¼ cups milk
- 1 6-fl.-oz. can frozen concentrated lemonade

Combine sugar, flour, salt, melted butter and egg yolks. Beat until smooth. Add milk gradually, then frozen lemonade. Beat egg whites until stiff. Fold into batter. Pour into a lightly greased 10x6-inch baking dish or custard cups. Set baking dish in pan containing an inch of hot water and bake at 325° about 45 minutes. After baking, sponge cake is on top and lemon custard sauce on bottom. Serve with sauce on top. Can also be baked in a partially baked pastry shell. Makes 6 servings.

Natalie Sklansky, Chicago Region

CHERRY CHEESECAKE

2 cups graham cracker crumbs
1/3 cup sugar
1/2 cup melted butter (1 stick)

Filling:
2 8-oz. packages softened cream cheese
1/3 cup sugar
2 eggs
1 teaspoon vanilla

Topping:
1 21-oz. can cherry pie filling
2 drops red food coloring

Combine crumbs, sugar and butter in a 10-inch glass pie pan. Press firmly and evenly against bottom and sides of pan. For filling, beat cream cheese with electric mixer. Gradually add sugar while beating continues. Add eggs and vanilla; continue beating until thoroughly blended. Pour into crumbed pan. Bake at 350° for 25 minutes. Chill. Combine pie filling with food coloring. Spread on chilled cake. Return to refrigerator until thoroughly chilled. Makes 8 servings.

Barbara Rubenstein, Northern Illinois Region

MARBLE CHEESECAKE

1 cup graham cracker crumbs
3 tablespoons melted margarine
1 tablespoon sugar

Filling:
3 8-oz. packages cream cheese
3/4 cup sugar
1 teaspoon vanilla
3 eggs
1 1-oz. square unsweetened chocolate, melted

Topping:
1 cup dairy sour cream
1 tablespoon sugar
1/2 teaspoon vanilla

Combine crust ingredients. Press into a 9-inch springform. Bake at 350° for 10 minutes. For filling, combine cheese, sugar and vanilla. Mix well. Add eggs, one at a time, beating well after each addition. To 1 cup of filling, add chocolate and mix thoroughly. Spoon plain and chocolate filling alternately into crust. Cut through batter with a knife several times to marble. Bake at 350° for 40 minutes. Cool. Mix together topping ingredients; spread overall and bake at 350° an additional 10 minutes. Makes 8 to 10 servings.

Lynn Forrest, Northern Illinois Region

CHERRY CHEESE TARTLETS

Crust:
1¼ cups graham cracker crumbs
⅔ stick butter, melted
1½ tablespoons sugar

Filling:
1 8-oz. package soft cream cheese
¼ cup sugar
1 egg
1 teaspoon vanilla
1 21-oz. can cherry pie filling

Arrange 24 cupcake papers in muffins pans. Combine crust ingredients, mix together thoroughly, and spoon 1 tablespoon into each cupcake paper. Press down. Beat together filling ingredients until smooth. Spoon 1 scant tablespoon of filling over crumbs. Bake at 375° for 10 minutes. When cool, spoon cherry pie filling over each tart, allowing 3 cherries for each. Makes 24.

Renee Drehl, West Suburban Region

CHOCOLATE CUPCAKE SURPRISE

1½ cups flour
1 cup sugar
¼ cup cocoa
1 teaspoon baking soda
½ teaspoon salt
1 cup water
⅓ cup oil
1 tablespoon vinegar
1 teaspoon vanilla

Filling:
1 8-oz. package cream cheese
½ cup sugar
⅛ teaspoon salt
1 6-oz. package semi-sweet chocolate pieces
Maraschino cherry halves, if desired

Sift together flour, sugar, cocoa, soda and salt. Add water, oil, vinegar and vanilla. Beat well. In a separate bowl, beat cream cheese, sugar and salt. Fold in chocolate. Fill cupcake pans three-fourths full, then drop one teaspoon of cheese mixture on top and garnish with maraschino cherry half, if desired. Bake at 350° for 25 minutes. (May also be baked in a greased 9-inch square pan for 50 to 60 minutes.) Makes 3 dozen small cupcakes.

Pinkey Auster, Lake County Region

MILWAUKEE CHEESECAKE

Crust & topping:

- 2½ cups graham cracker crumbs
- ⅓ cup sugar
- ⅔ cup butter, melted

Filling:

- 1 pound marshmallows
- ¾ cup milk
- 2 8-oz. packages cream cheese
- 2 cups heavy cream, whipped

Combine crust ingredients. Press three-fourths of mixture into bottom of 13x9-inch pan. Save remainder for topping. Prepare filling by heating marshmallows and milk in top of double boiler until melted. Pour into mixer bowl. Add cheese and beat until smooth. Cool. Fold whipped cream into mixture and pour into crust. Top with reserved crumbs. Chill at least 8 hours. Makes 16 servings.

Mrs. Maynard J. Seidmon, Northern Illinois Region

MOCHA LOG

- 4 eggs
- ¾ cup sugar
- ½ teaspoon vanilla
- ¼ cup sifted flour
- ¼ cup dry cocoa
- ¼ teaspoon baking powder
- ¼ teaspoon salt

Coffee Cream:

- 2 cups heavy cream
- ¼ cup confectioners' sugar
- 4 teaspoons instant coffee powder
- 1 teaspoon vanilla
- Chocolate curls

Beat eggs in medium-size bowl; beat in sugar gradually until mixture is thick. Stir in vanilla. Sift dry ingredients together and fold in. Pour into a greased, waxed paper-lined 15x10x1-inch jelly roll pan. Bake at 350° for 25 minutes, or until top springs back when lightly pressed. Turn cake out onto a clean towel sprinkled with confectioners' sugar; peel off paper. Roll up cake in towel and cool. Prepare Coffee Cream. Whip cream with confectioners' sugar, instant coffee and vanilla until stiff in a large bowl. Unroll cake carefully; spread evenly with half of Coffee Cream. Reroll. Frost with remaining Coffee Cream; springle with chocolate curls. (To make chocolate curls, shave thin slices from a square of unsweetened chocolate with a vegetable parer.) Chill roll 1 hour, or until serving time. Slice crosswise into 1-inch servings. Makes 15 servings.

Millicent Pine, Northern Illinois Region

LINZER TORTE

½ lb. butter
½ cup sugar
2 egg yolks
2 cups flour
½ teapsoon salt
½ teaspoon baking powder
½ teaspoon vanilla
8-oz. jar jelly

Cream butter and sugar. Add egg yolks and vanilla. Sift dry ingredients and add to sugar mixture. Reserve ¼ dough for lattice strips on top. Spread dough in 9x9-inch pan. Spread jelly over dough. Roll reserved dough into strips and lay in lattice design over top. Bake at 350 for 30 minutes, then lower oven to 325° and bake additional 30 minutes.

Jackie Brown, Lake County Region

FRENCH CHOCOLATE CUPCAKES

½ cup butter (1 stick)
2 1-oz. squares unsweetened chocolate
1 cup granulated sugar
1 egg
Milk
1 cup flour
1 teaspoon baking powder
Pinch of salt

Frosting:
2 1-oz. squares unsweetened chocolate
¼ cup butter (½ stick)
1½ cups sifted confectioners' sugar
Pinch of salt
2 tablespoons warm milk

Using a heavy-bottomed pan, melt together butter and chocolate over low heat. Remove from heat. Stir in sugar. Allow to cool. Break egg into a 1 cup glass measure. Pour milk in over egg to measure 1 cup. Add to chocolate mixture and mix well. Sift together flour, baking powder and salt. Blend into chocolate mixture. Divide into 12 paper-lined cupcake pans and bake at 350° for 15 to 18 minutes. Cool cupcakes before frosting. To prepare frosting, melt chocolate and butter in top of double boiler. Blend in sugar and salt. Add milk and beat well. Should be of medium consistency. If frosting is too stiff, add more milk. When frosting barely holds shape, frost cakes and allow to dry. Makes 12.

Emma Osterreicher, Chicago Region

PASTRY

- 2 cups flour
- 1½ teaspoons salt
- ½ cup oil
- ¼ cup milk

Combine all ingredients. Blend well and refrigerate briefly. Roll out on a floured surface. Makes two 9-inch crusts.

Ronna Brown, Northern Illinois Region

ALL-PURPOSE PASTRY
(for quiches, pot pies, etc.)

- 3⅓ cups flour
- 1 tablespoon sugar
- 1 teaspoon salt
- 1½ cups butter (3 sticks), cut in pieces
- ½ cup ice water

Place first four ingredients in electric mixer; cover with clean dish towel to prevent splattering. Beat at medium speed about 4 minutes or until the dough is "yellow" and well blended. Add water and beat for 10 seconds. Roll into a ball, wrap securely and refrigerate 1 hour, longer, if necessary. Recipe makes two generous crusts. One can be rolled and used immediately; the remainder can be frozen in a plastic bag, either as a ball or rolled onto a pie plate. If recipe calls for a baked pie crust, bake at 400° for 25 minutes with enough rice on brown or waxed paper on top of the shell so it does not puff up. When done, remove rice and paper, and bake an additional 5 minutes. Fits up to a 10-inch pie plate. Makes 2 crusts.

Ruth Weissman, Lake County Region

RICH, DELICATE PASTRY

- ½ cup butter (1 stick)
- 1 egg
- 3 tablespoons sugar
- 1½ cups sifted flour

Cream butter. Add egg, sugar and flour. Blend with spoon initially; then use hands. Add additional flour, if necessary, to keep dough from sticking. Dough will be quite soft. Roll out on a floured pastry cloth. Line 9 or 10-inch pie plate, prick with fork and bake at 350° for 10 to 12 minutes, until lightly browned. Makes one 9 or 10-inch crust.

Lily Frandzel, Chicago Region

PEACH GLAZE PIE

Crust:

- 16 graham crackers, finely crushed
- 5 tablespoons melted butter
- 2 tablespoons sugar
- Dash salt
- ¼ teaspoon cinnamon

Cream filling:

- 2 3-oz. packages cream cheese
- ¼ cup undiluted evaporated milk
- ¼ cup sugar
- Dash salt
- 1 egg
- ¼ teaspoon grated lemon rind

Glaze topping:

- 1 teaspoon lemon juice
- 1 teaspoon unflavored gelatin
- ½ cup drained peach juice
- ¼ teaspoon grated lemon rind
- 2 teaspoons sugar
- ¼ teaspoon orange rind
- 1 29-oz. can cling peaches, drained

Blend together crust ingredients. Press into a 9-inch pie pan and bake at 350° for 10 minutes. Put cream filling ingredients into mixer bowl and beat until very creamy. Spoon mixture into crust and bake at 350° for 20 minutes. Cool. To make glaze, mix lemon juice and gelatin. Set aside. In saucepan, combine peach juice, lemon rind, sugar and orange rind. Heat; then blend in gelatin until dissolved. Drain peaches well and arrange on top of filling. When glaze is tepid, spoon over peaches and refrigerate 6 hours. Makes 6 to 8 servings.

Irene Silverman, Lake County Region

BLUEBERRY TARTS AU COINTREAU

- 1 3½-oz. package instant vanilla pudding
- 1 cup milk
- 1 cup heavy cream
- ⅛ teaspoon salt
- 1 tablespoon cointreau
- 12 baked tart shells
- 3 cups blueberries
- Confectioners' sugar
- Whipped cream topping

Follow package directions to prepare instant pudding, using milk and heavy cream for liquid. Add salt and cointreau and blend in. Fill tart shells with pudding mixture. Dust blueberries with confectioners' sugar. Heap blueberries on top of pudding in tart shells. Sprinkle overall with confectioners' sugar. Top with whipped cream. Makes 12 tarts.

Mildred Rubenstein, Chicago Region

SLIVERED ALMOND CHERRY CREAM PIE

Cookie crust:

- ½ cup margarine (1 stick)
- 2 tablespoons sugar
- 1¼ cups flour
- ½ cup slivered, finely-sliced almonds

Filling:

- 1 can Eagle brand condensed milk
- ⅓ cup lemon juice
- 1 teaspoon vanilla
- ¼ teaspoon almond extract
- 1 cup heavy cream

Topping:

- 1 1-lb. 4-oz. can pitted tart red cherries, drained
- ⅔ cup cherry juice
- 1 tablespoon cornstarch
- Few drops red food coloring

Combine crust ingredients and press into a 10-inch pie pan. Bake at 350° for 20 minutes. Cool. To prepare filling, mix together milk, lemon juice, vanilla and almond extract. Mixture will thicken; do not cook. Whip heavy cream and fold into filling. Turn into cookie crust. Blend cornstarch with cherry juice. Add cherries. Cook over low heat until thick and clear. Stir in food coloring. Spread over pie filling. Refrigerate 2 to 3 hours. Makes 10 servings.

Meryl Liner, Northern Illinois Region

PINEAPPLE-APRICOT PIE

- 1 1-lb. 4-oz. can pineapple chunks
- 1 package instant French vanilla pudding mix
- 1 cup whipping or sour cream
- 1 8-inch baked graham cracker pie shell
- 1 cup cooled, melted apricot preserves

Drain can of pineapple chunks. Reserve ½ cup syrup. Combine vanilla pudding mix with whipping (or sour) cream. Beat until thick. Beat in pineapple syrup. Pour into pie shell. Spoon drained pineapple chunks over pudding. Glaze with melted apricot preserves. Chill ½ hour. Makes 8 servings.

Doris Charak, Lake County Region

CHOCOLATE ALMOND PIE

- 6 9/16-oz. milk chocolate-almond candy bars
- 15 large marshmallows
- ½ cup milk
- 1 cup heavy cream, whipped
- 1 9-inch prepared graham cracker crust

In top of double boiler, combine chocolate bars, marshmallows and milk. Cook over simmering water, stirring constantly, until melted and smooth. Cool completely. Gently fold in whipped cream and pour into prepared crust. Chill 3 hours., Makes 6 servings.

Sheila Schwartz, West Suburban Region

CHOCOLATE SILK CHIFFON PIE

- ½ cup butter (1 stick)
- ¾ cup sugar
- 1 1-oz. square semi-sweet chocolate, melted and cooled
- ½ teaspoon vanilla
- 2 eggs
- 1 8 or 9-inch baked graham cracker crust

Cream butter and sugar. Blend in chocolate. Add vanilla and 1 egg and beat at medium speed for 2 minutes. Add second egg and beat 2 or 3 additional minutes. Pour into crust and chill several hours. Makes 6 servings.

Mrs. Stan Zeldin, Kansas City Chapter-at-Large

CHOCOLATE RUM PIE

- ½ cup sugar
- 1 envelope unflavored gelatin
- Dash salt
- 1 cup milk
- 2 beaten egg yolks
- 1 6-oz. package semi-sweet chocolate pieces
- ⅓ cup rum
- 2 egg whites
- ¼ cup sugar
- 1 cup heavy cream
- 1 teaspoon vanilla
- 1 baked 9-inch pie shell
- Shaved chocolate garnish

In heavy saucepan, combine ½ cup sugar, gelatin and salt. Stir in milk and egg yolks. Cook and stir over low heat until slightly thickened. Remove from heat, add chocolate pieces and stir until melted. Add rum. Chill until partially set. Beat egg whites till soft peaks form. Gradually add ¼ cup sugar, beating until stiff peaks form. Fold into chocolate mixture. Whip cream with vanilla. Fold into chocolate-egg white mixture. Pour into pie shell. Decorate with shaved chocolate. Chill. Makes 8 servings.

Florence Purnell, Des Moines Chapter-at-Large

PUMPKIN CHIFFON PIE

- 1 envelope unflavored gelatin
- ½ cup sugar
- ½ teaspoon salt
- ½ teaspoon nutmeg
- ½ teaspoon ginger
- 1 teaspoon cinnamon
- ⅛ teaspoon ground cloves
- ⅔ cup evaporated milk
- 3 egg yolks
- 1¼ cups pumpkin
- 3 egg whites
- ¼ cup sugar
- 1 9-inch baked pie shell
- Whipped cream topping

Combine gelatin, ½ cup sugar, salt and spices in saucepan. Stri in evaporated milk and egg yolks and blend well. Cook slowly, stirring constantly, until gelatin softens and dissolves and mixture thickens slightly. Remove from heat and stir in pumpkin. Chill in refrigerator, stirring occasionally, until mixture starts to set. Beat egg whites until softly peaked; then gradually add ¼ cup sugar. Beat whites until very stiff. Fold into pumpkin mixture; then turn into baked pie shell and chill until firm. Top with whipped cream. Makes 6 to 8 servings.

Phyllis Silver, Northern Illinois Region

LIME CHIFFON PIE

1 envelope unflavored gelatin
¼ cup cold water
¾ cup sugar
½ cup lime juice
1 teaspoon grated lime rind
½ teaspoon salt
4 eggs, separated
Green food coloring
1 9-inch baked pie shell or cooky crust
Sliced fresh lime garnish

Soften gelatin in cold water. Combine ½ cup sugar, lime juice, rind and salt. Beat yolks and blend into lime mixture. Cook over hot water, stirring constantly, until thickened and mixture coats spoon. Remove from heat, add gelatin, and stir until gelatin dissolves. Cool until slightly thickened. Beat egg whites until stiff, but not dry, adding remaining ¼ cup sugar gradually while beating. Fold lime mixture into egg whites. Add green coloring and pile into shell. Chill. Garnish with fresh lime slices before serving. Makes 8 servings.

Eenie Frost, Lake County Region

FRESH PEACH CHIFFON PIE

2 cups fresh diced peaches
¾ cup sugar
1 tablespoon lemon juice
1 envelope unflavored gelatin
¼ cup cold water
½ cup hot water
Dash salt
Few drops yellow food coloring
½ cup heavy cream, whipped
1 9-inch baked pie shell

Combine peaches, sugar and lemon juice in bowl. Refrigerate ½ hour. Soften gelatin in ¼ cup cold water; then dissolve in ½ cup hot water. Add peaches and salt. Chill until partially set. Fold in whipped cream. Pour into pie shell. Chill 4 hours or more. Makes 6 to 8 servings.

Dorothy Novick, West Suburban Region

GERMAN CHOCOLATE ANGEL PIE

Crust:
2 egg whites
1/8 teaspoon salt
1/8 teaspoon cream of tartar
1/2 cup sugar
1/2 cup chopped nuts
1/2 teaspoon vanilla

Filling:
1 4-oz. bar German sweet chocolate
3 tablespoons water
1 teaspoon vanilla
1 cup heavy cream, whipped
Whipped cream and shaved chocolate garnish

Beat egg whites until foamy. Add salt and cream of tartar. Continue beating, adding sugar gradually. Beat until egg whites are stiff. Fold in nuts and 1/2 teaspoon vanilla. Fill a 10-inch pie plate, building crust up at sides. Bake at 300° for 50 to 55 minutes. Cool. To prepare filling, melt chocolate bar in water. Blend in vanilla. Fold chocolate mixture gently into whipped cream. Fill meringue shell. Garnish with additional whipped cream and chocolate shavings. Makes 8 to 10 servings.

Ellen Friend, Lake County Region

HEAVENLY PIE

1 1/2 cups sugar
1/4 teaspoon cream of tartar
4 eggs, separated
3 tablespoons lemon juice
1 tablespoon lemon rind, finely grated
1/8 teaspoon salt
1 pint heavy cream, whipped
Shaved chocolate garnish

Sift together 1 cup sugar and cream of tartar. Beat egg whites until stiff, but not dry. Gradually add sugar mixture and beat until thoroughly blended. Use this meringue to line bottom and sides of well greased 9 or 10-inch pie plate, hollowing out most of the center, and being careful not to spread the meringue too close to rim. Bake at 275° for 1 hour. Cool. Beat egg yolks slightly. Add remaining 1/2 cup sugar, lemon juice, rind and salt. Cook in top of double boiler, over boiling water, until very thick, 8 to 10 minutes. Cool. Whip cream and combine half or three-fourths of cream with lemon egg mixture. Fill meringue shell. Decorate with remaining whipped cream. Shave chocolate on top. Chill in refrigerator about 24 hours before serving. Makes 6 to 8 servings.

Sadye Anhalt, Milwaukee Region

LEMON CHEESECAKE PIE

- 3 3-oz. packages or 1 8-oz. package cream cheese
- 2 tablespoons butter
- ½ cup sugar
- 1 egg
- 2 tablespoons flour
- ⅔ cup milk
- ¼ cup fresh lemon juice
- 2 tablespoons grated lemon rind
- 1 8 or 9-inch unbaked graham cracker crust
- Reserved graham cracker crumbs for topping
- Dairy sour cream

Cream cheese with butter. Add sugar and egg. Beat well. Add flour; then milk. Stir in lemon juice and rind. Pour into crust. Sprinkle with crumbs. Bake at 350° for 35 minutes. Chill; serve topped with sour cream. Makes 6 to 8 servings.

Natalie Sklansky, Chicago Region

SUPER CHEESE PIE

Crust:

- 1½ cups graham cracker crumbs
- ⅓ cup brown sugar
- ½ teaspoon cinnamon
- ⅓ cup melted butter

Filling:

- 1½ 8-oz. packages softened cream cheese
- 2 eggs
- ½ cup sugar
- ½ teaspoon vanilla
- 1 cup dairy sour cream
- Sliced strawberries or peaches, if desired

To make crust, combine crumbs, brown sugar, cinnamon and butter. Mix thoroughly. With back of spoon, press crumbs to bottom and up sides of well-greased 9-inch pie plate. Do not spread on rim. Refrigerate. Using mixer or egg beater, beat cream cheese, eggs, sugar and vanilla until smooth and creamy. Turn cheese mixture into chilled pie shell. Bake at 350° for 35 minutes. Spread sour cream on top. Refrigerate. At serving time, if desired, top pie with fresh or drained, frozen sliced strawberries or fresh or frozen peach slices. Also delicious plain. May be made ahead and frozen. Makes 8 to 10 servings.

Rosalie Hersh, Northern Illinois Region

RASPBERRY ICE CREAM PIE

- 1 3-oz. package raspberry gelatin
- 1 cup boiling water
- 1 pint vanilla ice cream
- 1 10-oz. package frozen raspberries
- 1 8-inch prepared graham cracker crust

Dissolve raspberry gelatin in boiling water. Stir in ice cream and frozen raspberries and keep stirring until gelatin thickens. Spoon into crust. Chill until firm. Can be prepared 24 hours in advance, but must be refrigerated. Makes 6 to 8 servings.

Mrs. S. J. Hiller, Milwaukee Region

CHEDDAR CHEESECAKE PIE

- 1¼ cups graham cracker crumbs
- 3 tablespoons melted butter
- 2 8-oz. packages cream cheese
- ½ cup shredded sharp Cheddar cheese
- ¾ cup sugar
- 3 eggs
- ½ teaspoon grated orange rind
- ¼ teaspoon grated lemon rind
- 2 tablespoons flour
- ¾ cup heavy cream

Mix crumbs with butter; press loosely into 9-inch pie pan. Bake at 350° for 5 minutes. Combine cheeses and sugar; beat until fluffy. Beat in eggs one at a time. Blend in rinds, flour and heavy cream. Pour into crust. Bake at 350° for 40 to 45 minutes, until center is set. Makes 6 to 8 servings.

Maxine Weindruch, Lake County Region

MILE-HIGH FROZEN STRAWBERRY PIE

2 egg whites, stiffly beaten
1 10-oz. package partially thawed frozen strawberries
1 cup sugar
½ tablespoon lemon juice
½ teaspoon salt
1 cup heavy cream
1 teaspoon vanilla
1 9-inch graham cracker pie shell

Beat egg whites until stiff. Add strawberries, sugar, lemon juice and salt. Beat mixture at high speed in electric mixer for 20 minutes. Whip cream and vanilla. Gently fold whipped cream into egg white mixture. Mound into pie shell and freeze. Makes 8 to 10 servings.

Jean Emer, Lake County Region

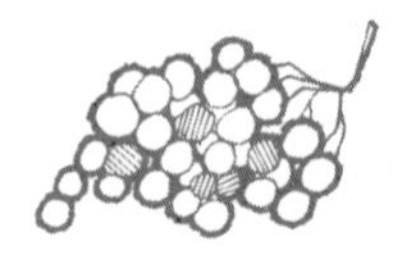

CANDY CRUST MINT PIE

Crust:
1 6-oz. package semi-sweet chocolate pieces
3 tablespoons butter
2 cups crisp rice cereal
1 1-oz. square unsweetened chocolate, shaved
Chocolate-flavored whipped cream

Filling:
1 quart green mint ice cream

To make crust, melt chocolate and butter over hot water, stirring until smooth. Mix in cereal. Press into 9-inch pie plate. Chill until firm. Let crust stand at room temperature 5 minutes. Fill with alternate layers of ice cream and shave chocolate. Frost with whipped cream. Garnish with shaved chocolate. Serve at once. Or freeze filled pie, let stand at room temperature 10 to 15 minutes; serve. Makes 8 servings.

Beverly Braun, Northern Illinois Region

FROZEN LEMON FLUFF PIE

3 eggs, separated
½ cup sugar
2 tablespoons water
⅓ cup fresh lemon juice
1 tablespoon grated lemon rind
¼ teaspoon cream of tartar
3 tablespoons sugar
1 9-inch graham cracker pie shell
Shaved chocolate or whipped cream topping

Mix egg yolks, ½ cup sugar, water, lemon juice and rind in saucepan. Cook over low heat, stirring constantly, until thick. Remove from heat. Beat egg whites and cream of tartar until foamy. Gradually add sugar, continuing to beat until whites are stiff. Fold into cooked filling. Pour into graham cracker crust. Cool and freeze until ready to serve. Sprinkle shaved chocolate over top just before serving or cover with whipped cream. Makes 8 to 10 servings.

Gert Kaufman, Northern Illinois Region

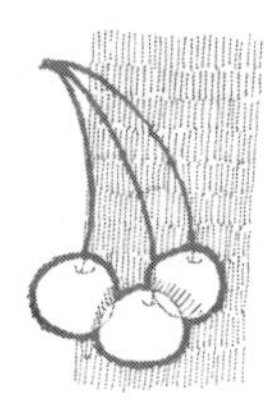

FRANGO MINT PIE

1 cup butter (2 sticks)
2 cups confectioners' sugar
4 eggs
4 1-oz. squares unsweetened chocolate, melted and cooled
1 teaspoon peppermint flavoring
2 teaspoons vanilla
1 9-inch graham cracker pie shell
Whipped cream topping
Maraschino cherry garnish

Cream together butter and sugar. Add eggs and beat well. Blend in chocolate, peppermint and vanilla. Place chocolate mixture in graham cracker crust and freeze. Whipped cream topping can be placed on top before freezing or just before pie is served. Remove from freezer 5 minutes before serving. Garnish with a maraschino cherry in the center. Makes 8 to 10 servings.

Phyllis Silverman, Lake County Region

FROZEN CREME DE MENTHE PIE

Crust:
- 24 cream-filled chocolate cookies, finely crushed
- ¼ cup melted butter (½ stick)

Filling:
- ¼ cup green creme de menthe
- 1 7-oz. jar marshmallow creme
- 2 cups heavy cream, whipped

Mix cookie crumbs with butter. Reserve ½ cup for topping. Press remaining crumb mixture onto bottom of 9-inch springform. To prepare filling, gradually blend creme de menthe into marshmallow creme. Fold whipped cream into marshmallow mixture. Pour into crumb-lined pan. Sprinkle reserved crumbs around edge and in center of pie. Freeze several hours until firm. Makes 8 to 10 servings.

Rochelle Kroot, Indianapolis Chapter-at-Large

FUDGE SUNDAE PIE

- 1 cup evaporated milk
- 1 6-oz. package semi-sweet chocolate pieces
- 1 cup miniature marshmallows
- ¼ teaspoon salt
- Vanilla wafers
- 1 quart vanilla ice cream

Combine evaporated milk, chocolate, marshmallows and salt in a 1-quart saucepan. Stir over medium heat until chocolate and marshmallows melt and mixture thickens. Cool to room temperature. Line bottom and sides of a 9-inch pie plate with whole vanilla wafers. Spoon half of ice cream over wafers. Cover with half of chocolate mixture. Layer ice cream and chocolate once again. Freeze firmly for 3 to 5 hours. Makes 8 to 10 servings.

Florence Edelson, Lake County Region

NEW ORLEANS PECAN PIE

- ½ cup brown sugar
- 3 eggs, slightly beaten
- 1 tablespoon melted butter
- 1 cup light corn syrup
- 1 teaspoon vanilla
- 1 cup pecan halves
- Unbaked 9-inch pie shell

Combine sugar, eggs, melted butter, syrup and vanilla. Pour into unbaked pie shell. Place nuts on top. Bake at 350° for 45 minutes. Makes 8 servings.

Beatrice Rapkin, Milwaukee Region

LEMON-PINEAPPLE BAVARIAN CREAM

- Juice and rind from ½ lemon
- ½ cup pineapple juice or other fruit juice
- ⅓ cup sugar
- 2 eggs
- 1 teaspoon plain gelatin
- 1 tablespoon cold water
- Ladyfingers or individual spongecake molds
- Fruit and whipped cream garnish

Mix lemon juice and rind, fruit juice, sugar and egg yolks. Cook over hot water until thick and smooth, stirring constantly. Mix gelatin with cold water and dissolve in heated egg mixture. Beat egg whites until stiff and fold into egg yolk mixture. Set in a pan of ice water and beat with egg beater until thick enough to hold its shape. Turn into a mold lined with ladyfingers or into individual spongecake molds. Refrigerate. Garnish with fruit and whipped cream before serving. Makes 4 to 6 servings.

Beatrice Rapkin, Milwaukee Region

APPLE CRISP

- 4 cups sliced peeled apples
- ¼ cup water
- ¾ cup flour
- 1 cup sugar
- 1 teaspoon cinnamon
- ¼ teaspoon salt
- ⅓ cup margarine

Place apples and water in a 10x6-inch baking pan. Sift flour, sugar, cinnamon and salt into bowl. Cut in margarine until mixture resembles coarse crumbs. Sprinkle over apples. Bake at 350° for 40 minutes or until apples are tender. Makes 6 servings.

Joyce Kossy, Northern Illinois Region

BANANAS FOSTER

½ cup firmly packed brown sugar
¼ cup butter (½ stick)
4 ripe bananas, peeled and quartered
Dash of cinnamon
1 tablespoon lemon juice
½ cup light rum
¼ cup banana liqueur
Vanilla Ice Cream

Melt brown sugar and butter in chafing dish or skillet, stirring often. Add bananas and saute until soft, but don't overcook. Sprinkle cinnamon and lemon juice over bananas. Heat rum and banana liqueur in small saucepan. Pour over bananas, **but do not stir in sauce.** Carefully light liquor and keep spooning sauce over bananas until flame dies. Scoop ice cream in four large dessert dishes. Spoon bananas and sauce over and serve immediately. Makes 4 servings.

Sheila Schwartz, West Suburban Region

CHOCOLATE DELIGHT

1 6-oz. package semi-sweet chocolate pieces
4 eggs, well-beaten
1 cup heavy cream, whipped
1 teaspoon vanilla
¾ cup chopped nuts
1 angel food loaf or ½ 10-inch tube cake

Melt chocolate and cool. Mix with eggs, fold in whipped cream, vanilla and half of nuts. Tear angel food cake into small pieces and line 13x9-inch pan with half of cake pieces. Pour over half of chocolate mixture. Cover with remaining cake and filling. Sprinkle with nuts. Chill and cut in squares. Makes 15 servings.

Ronna Locketz, Twin Cities Region

CHILLED APRICOTS 'N CIDER

Dried apricots
Apple cider
Butter
Sugar
Slivered almonds

Soak apricots in cider overnight. Then simmer gently until tender. Add butter and sugar to taste. Chill. Spoon into sherbet glasses and sprinkle with slivered almonds.

Norma L. Platt, Chicago Region

DESSERT PANCAKE

- 2 eggs
- 1/4 cup sugar
- 1/4 cup flour
- 1/4 teaspoon baking powder
- 1/4 teaspoon salt
- 1/2 cup sour half 'n half or cream
- 3/4 cup milk
- 1 15-oz. jar chunky-style applesauce with strawberries
- 1 cup sliced, sugared strawberries
- Confectioners' sugar

Beat eggs and sugar together until light and fluffy. Add flour, baking powder and salt. Mix sour half 'n half and milk together and then combine with pancake ingredients. Pour into heavily buttered 10-inch deep dish pie plate or decorative skillet. Swirl in applesauce and sprinkle berry slices on top. Bake at 400° for 45 minutes. Sprinkle with confectioners' sugar and serve at once. Makes 6 servings.

Ruth Weissman, Lake County Region

STRUDEL

- 1 cup butter (2 sticks)
- 1 cup dairy sour half 'n half
- 1 teaspoon sugar
- 2 cups flour

Filling:

- Preserves
- Bread crumbs
- Coconut
- White raisins, cut up

Blend butter and sour half 'n half lightly with knife. Add sugar and flour and blend until mixture forms a ball. Refrigerate 2 hours. Cut in 4 pieces. On a floured board, roll each into as large a rectangle as you can. Spread with preserves, then sprinkle on crumbs, coconut and raisins. Roll up dough, using a long knife to help. Place 2 strips each on ungreased cooky sheet. Cut three-fourths of the way through about every 2 inches. Bake at 350° for 50 minutes. When baked, immediately cut rest of way through. Cool; sprinkle with confectioners' sugar. Makes 4 dozen pieces.

Mrs. Howard Adler, Northern Illinois Region

LEMON FLUFF REFRIGERATOR DESSERT

- ¾ lb. vanilla wafers or graham crackers
- ⅓ cup melted butter
- 2 envelopes plain gelatin
- ⅓ cup cold water
- 7 eggs, separated
- 2 cups sugar
- 4 lemons, juice and rind
- ¼ teaspoon salt

Crush wafers or crackers; add butter. Line sides and bottom of a shallow 9-inch springform with mixture, reserving ½ cup. Soak gelatin in cold water. Beat egg yolks with 1 cup sugar until light. Add lemon juice, rind and gelatin. Cook in double boiler until thick. Cool. Add salt to egg whites; beat stiff, gradually adding 1 cup sugar while beating. Fold in cooled lemon mixture. Pour into springform. Top with remaining crushed crumbs and refrigerate several hours or overnight. Makes 12 servings.

Mrs. Gerald Steinfeld, Indianapolis Chapter-at-Large

STRAWBERRIES ROMANOFF

- 1 qt. fresh strawberries, cleaned and hulled
- ¼ cup orange juice
- ¼ cup Curacao
- 1 cup heavy cream
- 2 tablespoons confectioners' sugar
- ½ teaspoon vanilla

Marinate strawberries in mixture of orange juice and Curacao for several hours, stirring occasionally. Place strawberries in stemmed sherbet glasses. Whip cream; fold in sugar and vanilla. Spoon cream over strawberries or pipe over berries using pastry bag with fluted tip. Makes 6 to 8 servings.

Myra Weis, Chicago Region

CHOCOLATE MINT MOUSSE

- 2 packages ladyfingers
- 1 12-oz. package chocolate mint pieces
- 2 8-oz. packages cream cheese
- 1½ cups light brown sugar
- ¼ teaspoon salt
- 1 teaspoon vanilla
- 4 eggs, separated
- 1 cup heavy cream, whipped
- Whipped cream garnish

Arrange ladyfingers around sides and bottom of 9 or 10-inch spring form pan. Melt chocolate pieces and cool. Blend cream cheese with sugar, salt and vanilla. Beat in yolks, one at a time, then chocolate. Beat egg whites until stiff and fold into cream cheese-chocolate mixture. Whip cream and fold into mixture. Turn into ladyfinger-lined pan and chill several hours or overnight. To serve, remove sides of pan and garnish with whipped cream. Makes 12 servings.

Mrs. Stanley Gore, Lake County Region

INDIVIDUAL COFFEE WALNUT SOUFFLES

- 2 envelopes plain gelatin
- ½ cup sugar
- ¼ cup instant coffee powder
- ¼ teaspoon salt
- 4 eggs, separated
- 2½ cups milk
- 1 teaspoon vanilla
- ½ cup sugar
- 2 cups heavy cream, whipped
- ½ cup finely chopped walnuts
- Chopped walnuts for garnish

Combine gelatin, ½ cup sugar, instant coffee and salt in a 2½-qt. saucepan. Beat egg yolks with milk. Add to gelatin mixture. Stir over low heat until gelatin dissolves and mixture thickens slightly, about 10 to 12 minutes. Remove from heat and add vanilla. Chill, stirring occasionally until mixture mounds slightly when dropped from a spoon. Prepare collars on 12 (4-oz.) or 8 (6-oz.) dessert glasses by binding a double strip of aluminum foil firmly around the top of each glass with the strip extending 1 inch above the top of each glass. Beat egg whites until stiff but not dry, gradually adding ½ cup sugar during beating process. Beat until stiff. Fold into gelatin mixture. Whip cream and fold in with walnuts. Spoon into prepared dessert glasses. Chill until firm. Remove collars and garnish with additional chopped walnuts. Makes 8 or 12 servings.

Florence Kaplan, Chicago Region

WALNUT RUM MOUSSE

- 1 cup walnuts
- 2 tablespoons (2 envelopes) plain gelatin
- ½ cup cold water
- 5 eggs, separated
- ½ cup firmly packed brown sugar
- 2 teaspoons instant coffee powder
- ¼ teaspoon salt
- 1 cup milk, scalded
- ¼ to ½ cup dark rum
- 18 ladyfingers, split
- 1 teaspoon vanilla
- ¾ cup sugar
- 1 cup heavy cream, whipped

Drop walnuts into boiling water and boil 3 minutes. Drain. Spread nuts in shallow pan and bake at 350°, stirring several times, for 15 to 20 minutes, until crisp. Chop medium fine. Soften gelatin in water. Beat yolks (in top of double boiler); add brown sugar, coffee and salt. Gradually blend in milk. Cook over boiling water, stirring constantly, 5 minutes or until thickened. Remove from heat, add gelatin and stir until dissolved. Blend in rum. Chill until thick, but not set. Line sides and bottom of 9-inch springform with ladyfingers. Beat egg whites until fluffy, add vanilla, then beat in sugar a tablespoon at a time, to make a stiff meringue. Fold ⅔ cup walnuts, custard and cream into meringue. Pour into pan, decorate with remaining walnuts. Chill several hours or overnight. To serve, remove pan rim. Makes 12 servings.

Lee Bateman, Lake County Region

APPLE SUPREME DESSERT

- 8 or 9 baking apples
- 1 20-oz. can crushed pineapple
- Juice of ½ lemon
- Cinnamon
- Nutmeg
- 1 cup walnuts

Topping:

- ½ cup firmly packed brown sugar
- 6 tablespoons flour
- 6 tablespoons melted butter

Combine apples, pineapple, lemon juice, spices and nuts, using enough cinnamon and nutmeg to please your taste. Pour into well-buttered 13x9-inch pan. Sprinkle blended topping ingredients over fruit. Bake at 375° for 40 minutes. Serve with whipped cream or vanilla ice cream. Makes 6 servings.

Harriet Rosen, Chicago Region

CREPES WITH ORANGE SAUCE

1 cup sifted flour
1 teaspoon salt
2 tablespoons sugar
3 eggs, well beaten
2 cups milk
1 tablespoon melted butter

Orange Sauce:
1 jar orange marmalade
Orange juice

Add sifted dry ingredients to eggs and milk. Beat together well and add butter. Drop by spoonfuls of batter onto hot well-buttered 4-inch skillet until bottom is thinly covered. Bake until bubbly and brown on under side. Turn and brown. To prepare Orange Sauce, heat marmalade in saucepan. Thin slightly with orange juice. Pour over crepes. If pancakes must wait, brush with butter, stack and wrap them in foil and keep warm in low oven. Makes 6 servings.

Barbara Rubenstein, Northern Illinois Region

MARSHMALLOW FUDGE ICE CREAM CAKE

1 13-oz. can evaporated milk
1 10½-oz. package miniature marshmallows
1 6-oz. package semi-sweet chocolate pieces

Crust:
½ cup melted margarine (1 stick)
Nuts
2 cups graham cracker crumbs

½ gallon vanilla ice cream

Heat milk, marshmallows and chocolate in top of double boiler until completely melted. Set aside to cool. Combine melted margarine, nuts and crumbs and mix thoroughly. Pat ¾ of crumb mixture into bottom of 13 x 9-inch pan. Cut ice cream into slices and place ½ onto crust. Pour half of sauce over ice cream. Repeat ice cream and sauce layers. Top with remaining crumb mixture. Cover with foil and freeze. Makes 12 servings.

Sheryl Reinstein, Chicago Region

CHOCOLATE TOFFEE ANGEL DESSERT

- 1 package angel food cake mix
- 1/8 teaspoon nutmeg
- 2 cups heavy cream
- 2/3 cup fudge sauce
- 1/2 lb. crushed English toffee

Make 10-inch angel food cake, adding nutmeg to batter. When cool, cut cake crosswise into two even layers. Whip cream until stiff and fold in fudge sauce. Frost lower layer of cake with cream mixture and sprinkle with crushed toffee. Repeat above for top layer and sides. Refrigerate at least 12 hours. Makes 12 servings.

Mrs. Paul Friend, Lake County Region

ORANGE CRANBERRY FREEZE

- 1 pint orange sherbet
- 1 1 lb. can whole cranberry sauce

Soften sherbet. Put in blender with cranberries. Blend and pour into small mold. Freeze until hard. Remove from freezer 1/2 hour before serving so it will cut easily. Makes 6 servings.

Barbara Korman, Lake County Region

STRAWBERRY DELIGHT

6 egg yolks
¼ cup sugar
⅓ cup Curacao
½ cup heavy cream, whipped
2 pints cleaned, hulled strawberries
1 tablespoon sugar
1 teaspoon Curacao

In top of double boiler, beat egg yolks. Add sugar and continue beating until fluffy and pale yellow. Place double boiler over simmering water, but be sure pan bottom does not touch water. Slowly add Curacao and continue beating until thick, about 8 to 10 minutes. Remove pan and place in ice water. Continue beating a few minutes and add the whipped cream. Refrigerate. One hour before serving, add sugar and Curacao to strawberries. Return berries to refrigerator and allow to marinate 1 hour. To serve, spoon sauce on top of berries. Makes 4 to 6 servings.

Mrs. Fred Blumenthal, Northern Illinois Region

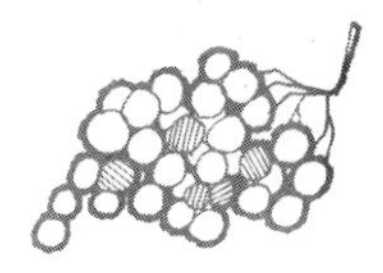

CHOCOLATE FONDUE

½ cup heavy cream
¼ cup half and half
1 12-oz. package semi-sweet chocolate pieces
2 tablespoons Cointreau or brandy

In heavy saucepan, combine whipping cream, half and half and chocolate; heat over low heat, stirring until chocolate melts and mixture is smooth. Remove from heat; stir in Cointreau. Pour into fondue pot to keep warm. To serve, spear any of the following onto fondue forks, then twirl in chocolate mixture: apple wedges, banana slices, melon balls, pineapple chunks, pear or peach wedges, orange or mandarin orange segments, fresh strawberries, seedless grapes, maraschino cherries. Can be frozen, then re-heated to serve. Makes 8 servings.

Michele Gutter, South Bend Chapter

CHERRIES JUBILEE

1 10-oz. jar currant jelly
1 tablespoon orange marmalade
1½ cups (1-lb. can) drained, pitted Bing cherries
Brandy, if desired
Vanilla ice cream

Melt jelly and marmalade over low heat. Add cherries; heat to simmering. If desired, add brandy and flame. Spoon over vanilla ice cream. Makes 8 servings.

Barbara Ackerman, St. Louis Region

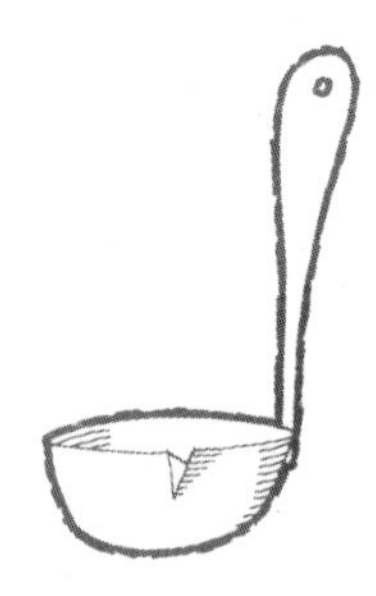

STRAWBERRIES DIVINE

4 pints strawberries, washed and hulled
¼ cup, plus 2 tablespoons confectioners' sugar
1 pint heavy cream
1 quart French vanilla ice cream
½ cup Grand Marnier or orange-flavored cordial or brandy
¼ cup Cognac or brandy
¼ cup creme de cacao

Slice all berries in half, crushing the 12 softest ones. Sprinkle ¼ cup confectioners' sugar on the sliced berries, the remaining sugar on the crushed berries; set aside. Whip cream until firm. Fold whipped cream gently into softened ice cream. Add brandies and crushed berries. Fold in sliced berries. Spoon into a shallow 3-quart glass casserole or similar dish. Cover dish with foil shaped like a tent. Chill at least 4 hours. The cream will form a light crust on top, the mixture will be "soupy" underneath and must be served in small bowls. Makes 12 servings.

Ruth Weissman, Lake County Region

RUM CHOCOLATE MOUSSE

2 3¾-oz. packages chocolate pudding mix
3 cups milk
1 egg yolk, slightly beaten
3 tablespoons rum
3 egg whites
⅓ cup sugar

Empty pudding mix into saucepan. Slowly add milk, stirring to keep mixture smooth. Stir in slightly beaten egg yolk. Cook over medium high heat, stirring steadily, until pudding just starts to boil. Blend in rum. Pour into a bowl. Place waxed paper or plastic wrap directly on pudding. Chill. Beat egg whites till foamy. Gradually beat in sugar. Continue beating until stiff peaks form. Stir pudding to soften. Fold in meringue. Spoon into dessert dishes. Refrigerate 1 hour. Makes 6 to 8 servings.

Myra Weis, Chicago Region

BROWN SUGAR SAUCE

1 cup firmly packed brown sugar
3 tablespoons flour
½ cup cold water
½ cup dry white wine
3 tablespoons cream
1 tablespoon butter
½ teaspoon vanilla
Pinch of salt
⅓ cup blanched, coarsely chopped, toasted almonds

Blend brown sugar and flour. Add water and wine and stir to a smooth paste. Cook over medium heat until mixture is thick and clear, stirring frequently. Blend in remaining ingredients. Serve warm as a cake or dessert sauce.

Edythe Oleck, Northern Illinois Region

HOT FUDGE SAUCE

½ cup butter, melted (1 stick)
2¼ cups confectioners' sugar
1 6-oz. can evaporated milk
6 1-oz. squares unsweetened chocolate

Mix butter and sugar in top of double boiler. Add chocolate and milk. **Do not** stir while cooking over hot water 30 minutes. Remove from heat and beat till smooth.

Arleen Levy, Lake County Region

HOT LEMON SAUCE

- 3 tablespoons cornstarch
- ¼ cup cold water
- 1¼ cups boiling water
- ¾ cup sugar or less
- Juice from 1½ lemons
- Rind of 1 lemon

Mix cornstarch with cold water until smooth. Boil water and sugar together. Stir in cornstarch and cook until thickened. Blend in lemon juice and rind. Use as a dessert sauce or for carrot pudding.

Launa Annes, Lake County Region

CHOCOLATE SAUCE SUPREME

- 5 1-oz. squares unsweetened chocolate
- 1½ cups sugar
- 1½ cups water
- ½ teaspoon salt
- 1 15-oz. can sweetened condensed milk

Combine chocolate, sugar, water and salt in top of double boiler. Heat until chocolate melts and mixture is smooth, about 5 minutes. Add condensed milk. Continue cooking over hot water in double boiler until mixture coats a silver spoon. Can be made ahead and refrigerated; it thickens when stored, but liquifies when reheated. Especially good when used for fondues. Makes 3 cups.

Mrs. Martin Fishkin, Chicago Region

PEPPERMINT MOCHA ICE CREAM CAKE

- 2 boxes Nabisco chocolate wafers
- 1 cup melted butter (2 sticks)
- 1 quart coffee ice cream
- 1 quart chocolate ice cream
- 1 quart peppermint ice cream

Crush wafers to make crumbs. Mix with butter. Use 3 cups buttered crumbs to line bottom and sides of a greased 10-inch tube pan or springform; freeze 1 hour. Reserve remaining crumbs for topping. Layer coffee ice cream over crumbs in bottom of pan. Freeze. Layer chocolate ice cream next. Freeze again. Layer peppermint ice cream; freeze. Top with remaining crumbs and arrange crumbs on sides so ice cream is completely crumb-encased. Freeze. Remove from freezer 15 minutes before serving. Cut with a freezer knife or a hot knife. Makes 12 to 16 servings.

Arleen Levy, Lake County Region

RAINBOW ICE CREAM DESSERT

- 1 10-inch round angel food cake
- 1 3-oz. package each strawberry, lime and orange gelatin
- 1 10-oz. package frozen sliced strawberries, partially thawed
- ½ gallon vanilla ice cream, slightly softened
- 1 10-oz. package frozen blueberries, partially thawed
- 1 11-oz. can mandarin oranges, drained

Tear cake into small pieces. Divide into thirds; place in three medium-size bowls. Sprinkle strawberry gelatin over one bowl of cake, lime over the second and orange over the third. Toss each lightly with a fork until cake is well coated with gelatin. Place strawberry cake pieces in bottom of a 10-inch tube pan; sprinkle any excess gelatin over cake. Spoon strawberries over cake. Spread ⅓ of ice cream over strawberries. Repeat layers with lime cake pieces, blueberries, ice cream, orange cake pieces, oranges and ice cream. Freeze until firm. Unmold on a chilled dessert plate. Makes 16 to 20 servings.

Lee Bateman, Lake County Region

COOKIES

CALIFORNIA DREAM BARS

Crust:
½ cup brown sugar
½ cup melted butter (1 stick)
1 cup flour

Topping:
2 eggs
1 cup chopped pecans
2 tablespoons flour
¼ teaspoon salt
1 cup brown sugar
1 cup coconut
½ teaspoon baking powder

Mix crust ingredients well. Press firmly into a greased 7½x 11½-inch pan. Bake at 375° for 15 minutes. To make Topping, beat eggs until light. Add remaining ingredients and mix well. Spread over crust and return to 375° oven for 12 to 15 minutes. Cool and cut into bars. Makes 24.

Jean Goldrosen, Northern Illinois Region

CHOCOLATE HONEY CRISPS

½ cup honey
1 12-oz. package semi-sweet chocolate pieces
5 cups ready-to-eat crisp rice cereal

Melt chocolate pieces in honey over pan of hot water. Add rice cereal and mix until well blended. Spread in buttered 13x9-inch pan. When cool, cut in bars or squares. Makes 40 bars.

Florence M. Mayron, Chicago Region

CHEESECAKE COOKIES

Crust:
- 1/3 cup butter
- 1/3 cup brown sugar, firmly packed
- 1 cup flour
- 1/2 cup finely chopped walnuts

Filling:
- 1/4 cup sugar
- 1 8-oz. package cream cheese
- 1 egg
- 2 tablespoons milk
- 1 tablespoon lemon juice
- 1/2 teaspoon vanilla

Cream butter and brown sugar. Add flour and nuts to make crumb mixture. Save 1 cup for topping. Press rest of mixture in bottom of 8-inch square baking pan. Bake at 350° for 12 to 15 minutes. Cool. To make filling, blend sugar and cream cheese until smooth. Add egg, milk, lemon juice and vanilla. Beat well. Spread over baked crust. Sprinkle with reserved crumb mixture. Bake at 350° for 25 minutes. Cut in squares when cool. Makes 36.

Helen Leeds, Lake County Region

CHOCOLATE SYRUP BROWNIES

Brownies:
- 1 cup sugar
- 1 cup sifted flour
- 1/2 cup butter, melted (1 stick)
- 4 eggs
- 1 1-lb. can chocolate syrup
- 1/4 teaspoon salt
- Nuts, if desired

Frosting:
- 1 1/3 cups sugar
- 6 tablespoons butter
- 6 tablespoons milk
- 1/2 cup semi-sweet chocolate pieces

Mix all Brownie ingredients in large bowl until well blended. Pour into a 13x9-inch pan and bake at 350° for 30 minutes. To prepare Frosting, boil sugar, butter and milk together for 1 minute. Remove from heat and stir in chocolate pieces, continuing stirring until frosting is smooth and well blended. Cool slightly. Pour over baked brownies. Brownies will stay deliciously moist for over a week. Makes 2 1/2 dozen.

Carole Butwinick, Twin Cities Region

CONGO SQUARES

- ¾ cup butter (1½ sticks)
- 2¼ cups (1lb. box) brown sugar
- 3 eggs
- 2¾ cups flour
- 2½ teaspoons baking powder
- ½ teaspoon salt
- 1 6-oz. package semi-sweet chocolate pieces
- Confectioners' sugar

Melt butter. Stir in brown sugar and cool. Beat eggs into cooled brown sugar mixture, one at a time. Sift together flour, baking powder and salt and add to creamed mixture, blending well. Stir in chocolate pieces. Pour into greased 13x9-inch pan and bake at 350° for 25 to 30 minutes (it's better to underbake). Top with confectioners' sugar. Let cool and cut into squares. Makes 48.

Cynthia Glickman, West Suburban Region

CHOCOLATE CHIP MERINGUES

- 4 egg whites
- 1 teaspoon cream of tartar
- ½ cup sugar
- 1 12-oz. package semi-sweet chocolate pieces

Beat egg whites until thick. Add cream of tartar and continue beating. Add sugar gradually and beat until peaked. Blend in chocolate gently. Drop by teaspoonsful onto greased cooky sheet. Bake at 350° for 15 minutes until meringues are lightly browned. Makes 6 dozen.

Norine Freedman, Lake County Region

CHOCOLATE-NUT DROPS

- ½ cup softened butter (1 stick)
- 1 cup firmly packed light brown sugar
- 1 egg
- 1 teaspoon vanilla
- 2 cups sifted flour
- ½ teaspoon baking soda
- ¾ cup milk
- 2 1-oz. squares unsweetened chocolate, melted
- ½ cup chopped nuts

Cream together butter and sugar until light and fluffy; add egg and beat thoroughly. Add vanilla. Sift together flour and soda; add alternately with milk to creamed mixture, beginning and ending with dry ingredients. Blend in chocolate, then nuts. Drop by tablespoonsful onto greased cooky sheet. Bake at 350° for 10 to 12 minutes. Cool on wire rack. Frost with chocolate frosting when cool. Makes 5 dozen.

Enid Schultz, Lake County Region

CREAM CHEESE-FILLED BROWNIES

Filling:
1 8-oz. package cream cheese
⅓ cup sugar
1 egg
¼ teaspoon almond extract

Brownies:
2 1-oz. squares unsweetened chocolate
½ cup butter (1 stick)
2 eggs
1 cup sugar
¾ cup flour
½ teaspoon baking powder
½ teaspoon salt

To prepare filling, allow cream cheese to soften. Then combine with ⅓ cup sugar, egg and almond extract. Mix well and set aside. To make brownies, melt chocolate with butter. Let cool. Beat eggs, add 1 cup sugar, the cooled chocolate mixture and the dry ingredients. Pour half of the chocolate batter into a greased 8-inch square pan. Spread with the cream cheese mixture and pour remaining chocolate batter on top. Bake at 350° for 45 minutes. When cool, cut in bars. Makes 32.

Carole Baran, Northern Illinois Region

EASY-DO BUTTERLESS DATE-NUT BARS

3 eggs
Pinch of salt
1 cup sugar
1¼ cups sifted flour
1¼ teaspoons baking powder
1 cup cut-up dates
1 cup chopped walnuts
Confectioners' sugar

Beat eggs thoroughly, adding a pinch of salt. Add sugar to eggs gradually, and continue beating well. Sift together 1 cup flour and the baking powder and add to the egg mixture in 3 parts. Stir ¼ cup flour into the dates. Fold floured dates and nuts into batter. Pour into a greased 8-inch square baking pan and bake at 350° for 35 to 45 minutes. When cool, cut into squares. Dust with confectioners' sugar. Makes 16.

Rae Weintraub, Chicago Region

FRENCH NUT STICKS

- 3/4 cup butter (1 1/2 sticks)
- 2 cups sugar
- 2 eggs
- 3 cups sifted cake flour
- 1 teaspoon vanilla
- Apricot jam
- 2 egg whites
- Pinch of salt
- 1 tablespoon flour
- 1 cup chopped pecans

Cream together butter and 1 cup of the sugar until light and fluffy. Beat in eggs. Gradually add cake flour, beating until smooth. Stir in vanilla. Roll out 1/4-inch thick on greased cooky sheet. Spread with a thin layer of apricot jam. Bake at 350° for 6 minutes. Beat egg whites with salt until frothy, gradually beat in remaining sugar combined with 1 tablespoon flour. Fold in pecans. Spread over the cooky dough. Chill. Cut into sticks, 2 x 1/2 inches. Place on cooky sheet. Bake at 375° for about 15 minutes. Makes 3 dozen.

Myra Weis, Chicago Region

LUSCIOUS APRICOT BARS

- 2/3 cup dried apricots
- 1/2 cup soft butter (1 stick)
- 1 1/3 cups sifted flour
- 1/4 cup sugar
- 1/2 teaspoon baking powder
- 1/4 teaspoon salt
- 1 cup brown sugar, firmly packed
- 2 eggs
- 1/2 teaspoon vanilla
- 1/2 cup finely-chopped walnuts
- Confectioners' sugar

Rinse apricots. Cover with water in saucepan and simmer 10 minutes. Drain and cool. Chop fine and set aside. Grease and flour 8-inch square pan. Mix together butter, 1 cup flour and sugar until crumbly. Pack mixture into bottom of pan. Spread evenly and bake at 350° about 25 minutes or until lightly browned. Sift together remaining 1/3 cup flour, baking powder and salt. Beat brown sugar gradually into eggs. Add flour mixture, vanilla, walnuts and apricots and beat well. Spread evenly over baked layer in pan and bake at 350° for 25 minutes or until golden brown. Cool in pan. Cut into bars and dust with confectioners' sugar. Makes 32 bars.

Lylus Brash, Chicago Region

PECAN PIE BAR COOKIES

1 package yellow cake mix
½ cup melted butter (1 stick)
1 egg

Filling:
⅔ cup reserved cake mix
½ cup brown sugar, firmly packed
1½ cups dark corn syrup
1 teaspoon vanilla
3 eggs
1 cup chopped pecans

Grease bottom and sides of a 13x9-inch baking pan. Reserve ⅔ cup dry cake mix for filling. In a large bowl, combine remaining dry cake mix, butter and 1 egg. Mix until crumbly. Press into prepared pan. Bake at 350° for 15 minutes. Meanwhile prepare filling by combining remaining ingredients except pecans. Pour filling over partially baked crust. Sprinkle with pecans. Return to oven and bake for 30 minutes or until filling is set. Cut into bars. Makes 48.

Eileen Kiess, Des Moines Chapter-at-Large

SLOVAKIAN BARS

½ cup butter (1 stick)
½ cup sugar
2 egg yolks
1 tablespoon white vinegar
1½ cups flour

Filling:
8 egg whites
½ cup sugar
½ lb. (8 oz.) German sweet chocolate, melted
6 egg yolks
½ cup toasted ground walnuts

Cream butter and sugar. Add yolks and vinegar. Gradually mix in flour. Let dough rest. To make filling, beat egg whites until stiff, adding 2 tablespoons sugar at a time. Set aside. Add beaten yolks and walnuts to melted chocolate and fold into egg whites. Roll out dough between two sheets of waxed paper and pat into form in a 9x12x1-inch baking pan. Top with filling. Bake at 350° for 45 minutes. Cut while warm. Makes 32 bars.

Anne Kramer, Lake County Region

VANILLA BROWNIES

- ¾ cup butter (1½ sticks)
- ½ cup dark brown sugar
- ½ cup sugar
- 2 eggs
- 1 teaspoon vanilla
- 1 tablespoon water
- 2 cups sifted flour
- 1 teaspoon baking soda
- ¼ teaspoon salt
- 1 6-oz. package semi-sweet chocolate pieces
- 1 cup pecans
- 1 cup dark brown sugar

Cream butter and sugars until light and fluffy. Separate eggs and add yolks to creamed mixture. Reserve whites for topping. Add vanilla and water to creamed mixture; then sift in flour, soda and salt, blending well. Spoon mixture into a greased 13x9-inch pan and smooth out on top. Sprinkle chocolate pieces and pecans evenly over surface. Beat egg whites until stiff, then stir in brown sugar and spread overall. Bake at 350° for 25 minutes. Cut into squares or bars. Makes 40.

Carol Goodman, West Suburban Region

EASY CHEESY LEMON BARS

- 1 package lemon cake mix
- ½ cup butter, melted (1 stick)
- 1 egg, slightly beaten
- 1 package lemon frosting mix
- 1 8-oz. package cream cheese, softened
- 2 eggs

Combine cake mix, butter and 1 egg. Mix with fork until moist. Pat into 13x9-inch pan, greased on bottom only. Blend frosting mix into cream cheese, reserving ½ cup. Add 2 eggs to remaining frosting mixture. Beat 3 to 5 minutes. Spread over cake mixture. Bake at 350° for 35 to 40 minutes. Cool; spread with reserved frosting mixture. Makes 36.

Bunny Ellin, Lake County Region

CHOCOLATE MARBLE SQUARES

- 1 cup plus 1 tablespoon sifted flour
- ½ teaspoon baking soda
- ½ teaspoon salt
- ½ cup soft butter (1 stick)
- 6 tablespoons granulated sugar
- 6 tablespoons firmly packed brown sugar
- ½ teaspoon vanilla
- ¼ teaspoon water
- 1 egg
- ½ cup chopped nuts
- 1 6-oz. package semi-sweet chocolate pieces

Sift dry ingredients together and set aside. Combine butter, sugars, vanilla and water. Beat until creamy. Beat in egg. Add flour mixture; mix well. Stir in nuts. Spread in greased 13x9-inch pan. Sprinkle chocolate pieces on top and bake at 375° for 1 minute. Remove from oven, run knife through mixture to marble dough with chocolate pieces (some pieces melt; others do not). Return to oven and bake for 15 to 20 minutes. Cool. Cut into squares. Makes 24.

Judy Mazor, Northern Illinois Region

TOFFEE SQUARES

- 1 cup soft butter (2 sticks)
- 1 cup brown sugar
- 1 teaspoon vanilla
- 1 egg
- 2 cups flour
- ½ cup chopped nuts

Frosting:

- 2 1-oz. squares unsweetened chocolate, melted
- 1 teaspoon vanilla
- 1½ cups confectioners' sugar
- 1 teaspoon butter
- 1 tablespoon milk

Cream butter and brown sugar. Add vanilla, egg, flour and nuts and blend well. Spread in a greased 15x17-inch pan. Bake at 350° for 15 minutes. Blend together frosting ingredients and frost while warm. Cut in squares when cool. Makes 56.

Phyllis Silverman, Lake County Region

FUDGY BROWNIES

- 2 1-oz. squares unsweetened chocolate
- ½ cup semi-sweet chocolate pieces
- ½ cup butter (1 stick)
- 2 eggs
- 1 cup sugar
- 1 teaspoon vanilla
- ½ cup sifted flour
- ½ 7-oz. jar marshmallow fluff
- ½ cup broken nuts

Melt chocolate and butter over hot water in top of double boiler; remove from heat. Beat eggs until thick and lemon-colored. Blend into chocolate mixture in double boiler. Add sugar, vanilla, flour, marshmallow fluff and nuts. Mix well. Pour into greased and floured 9-inch square pan. Bake at 350° for 25 to 30 minutes. These stay moist several days. Makes 16.

Mrs. Jerry Harper, Kansas City Chapter

LEMON SQUARES

- ¼ cup sugar
- ½ cup soft butter (1 stick)
- 1 cup flour

Lemon Topping:

- 2 eggs, beaten
- 3½ tablespoons lemon juice
- Grated rind of 1 lemon
- 1 cup sugar
- Dash of salt
- 2 tablespoons flour

Cream butter and sugar until well blended; add flour and mix well. Press into a 9x9-inch square pan. Bake at 350° for 20 minutes. Beat eggs; add remaining topping ingredients and mix well. Pour over baked layer and return to oven at 325°. Bake for 20 to 25 minutes. Cool and sprinkle with confectioners' sugar. Cut into squares to serve.

Roddie Rosenthal, Lake County Region

CHOCOLATE PECAN PUFFS

- ½ cup butter (1 stick)
- ¾ cup sugar
- 1 egg
- 2 1-oz. squares unsweetened chocolate, melted
- 1¾ cups sifted flour
- ½ teaspoon baking soda
- ½ teaspoon salt
- ½ cup milk
- 1 teaspoon vanilla
- ½ cup chopped pecans

Cream butter and sugar. Blend in egg and melted chocolate. Sift dry ingredients. Add alternately to mixture with milk. Add vanilla and nuts. Drop rounded teaspoonsful about 2 inches apart on lightly greased cooky sheet. Bake at 350° for 8 minutes. Makes 24.

Meryl Liner, Northern Illinois Region

COCONUT DROP KISSES

- 1 15-oz. can sweetened condensed milk
- 3 cups coconut
- ½ teaspoon almond extract
- ¼ teaspoon salt

Combine all ingredients. Drop from a teaspoon onto a greased cooky sheet, 1-inch apart. Bake at 375° for 15 minutes. Remove from pans while warm. Makes 3½ dozen.

Ellen Kogen, Lake County Region

GRANNY'S COCONUT GROVE COOKIES

- ½ cup butter (1 stick)
- ½ cup sugar
- ½ teaspoon vanilla
- 1 egg
- 1 cup flour
- ½ teaspoon baking soda
- ½ teaspoon salt
- 4 coconut candy bars

In a large bowl, mix butter, sugar and vanilla. Add egg and blend well. Add flour, baking soda and salt, mixing thoroughly. Break candy into small pieces and mix into batter. Refrigerate for ½ hour. Drop by teaspoonsful onto ungreased cooky sheets. Bake at 350° for 10 to 15 minutes. Makes 36.

Francine Loutwait, Northern Illinois Region

MOLASSES OATMEAL COOKIES

½ cup soft shortening
1¼ cups sugar
2 eggs
6 tablespoons light molasses
1¾ cups sifted flour
1 teaspoon baking soda
1 teaspoon salt
1 teaspoon cinnamon
2 cups rolled oats
½ cup chopped walnuts
1 cup yellow raisins

Mix shortening, sugar, eggs and molasses together thoroughly. Sift flour, soda, salt and cinnamon together and add to shortening mixture. Blend oats, nuts and raisins in by hand. Batter will be quite stiff. Drop rounded teaspoonsful about 2 inches apart on lightly greased cooky sheet. Bake at 400° for 8 to 10 minutes, until cookies are lightly browned. Cookies will be soft when removed from oven. Do not overbake. Allow to cool slightly before removing from cooky sheet. Makes about 5 dozen 2½-inch cookies.

Janet Friedman, Northern Illinois Region

ANGEL WHISPERS

2 eggs
½ cup sugar
½ cup butter (1 stick)
¾ cup plus 2 tablespoons cake flour
¾ cup cornstarch
2 teaspoons baking powder
1 teaspoon almond extract
Confectioners' sugar

Lemon Butter Filling:
1 egg
Grated rind of 1 lemon
⅔ cup sugar
3 tablespoons lemon juice
1½ teaspoons soft butter

Beat eggs well. Add sugar and butter. Cream until fluffy. Sift dry ingredients together. Add to butter mixture. Add almond extract. Drop by half-teaspoonsful onto greased cooky sheets making each cookie slightly larger than a hazelnut. Bake at 350° for 10 minutes. Meanwhile, make Lemon Butter Filling. Beat egg lightly. Add lemon rind. Blend in remaining ingredients. Cook in top of double boiler, over simmering water, until thick. Cool. Use to fill cookies by putting flat sides of cookies together with lemon butter filling to form snowballs. Roll in confectioners' sugar while still warm. Makes 2 to 2½ dozen.

Sandi Schiller, Lake County Region

CHOCOLATE ACORNS

- 1 cup melted butter (2 sticks)
- ¾ cup brown sugar
- 1 teaspoon vanilla
- ½ cup chopped pecans
- 2½ cups sifted flour
- 1 teaspoon baking powder
- 1 large chocolate bar or 1 6-oz. package semi-sweet chocolate pieces
- ¾ cup finely chopped nuts

Stir sugar, vanilla and pecans into melted butter. Sift together flour and baking powder. Add to butter mixture. Form into 42 balls using 1 teaspoon for each. Flatten one end by pressing onto greased cooky sheet and pinch top to resemble acorn. Bake at 350° for 15 minutes. Cool. Melt chocolate over hot water. Dip flat end of cooky into chocolate; then into finely chopped nuts. Store in air-tight container. May also be frozen. Makes 3½ dozen.

Sandi Schiller, Lake County Region

NUT-FILLED CHOCOLATE SNOWBALLS

- 1¼ cups butter (2½ sticks)
- ⅔ cup sugar
- 1 teaspoon vanilla
- 2 cups flour
- ⅛ teaspoon salt
- ½ cup cocoa
- 2 cups chopped pecans
- 1½ cups semi-sweet chocolate pieces
- Confectioners' sugar

Cream butter with sugar. Add vanilla. Blend in flour, salt and cocoa. Stir in nuts and chocolate pieces. Refrigerate until dough is firm. Makes balls and place on ungreased cooky sheets. Bake at 350° for 15 to 20 minutes. When cool, roll in confectioners' sugar. Makes 4 dozen.

Betty Bornstein, Chicago Region

SWEETHEART DROP COOKIES

- 1 cup margarine (2 sticks)
- 1½ cups sugar
- 2 eggs
- 1 teaspoon vanilla
- 3 cups sifted flour
- 1 tablespoon baking powder
- ¼ cup milk

Melt margarine in large pan. Remove from heat and stir in sugar. Add eggs and vanilla and beat well. Sift flour with baking powder and add alternately with milk. Mix well. Refrigerate dough (covered) overnight. Drop dough by teaspoonsful onto ungreased cooky sheet. Bake at 350° for 10 to 12 minutes. Cool on rack. Bakes 3½ dozen.

Fay Nicholas, Northern Illinois Region

CHERRY BUTTONS

- 1 cup butter (2 sticks)
- ¾ cup sugar
- 1 teaspoon vanilla
- ½ teaspoon salt
- 2 egg yolks
- 2 cups sifted flour
- 2 egg whites, slightly beaten
- 1½ cups chopped walnuts
- 1 1-lb. 4-oz. can cherry pie filling

Thoroughly cream together butter, sugar, vanilla and salt. Add egg yolks and mix well. Blend in flour. Form dough into 1-inch balls; dip in slightly beaten egg whites, then roll in nuts. Place cookies about 1½ inches apart on lightly greased baking sheet. Press down centers. Bake at 350° about 15 minutes or until lightly browned. Remove from oven and again gently press down centers. Cool slightly before removing from baking pan. Spoon cherry pie filling into centers just before serving. Makes about 4 dozen.

Florence M. Mayron, Chicago Region

CHOCOLATE CANDY COOKIES

- 2 sticks pie crust mix, crumbled
- 1 3-oz. can chow mein noodles, crushed
- 1/3 cup brown sugar
- 1/4 cup peanut butter
- 1 egg, beaten
- 2 teaspoons water
- 1/2 teaspoon vanilla
- 1 11-oz. package chocolate covered peanut butter candy

Combine pie crust mix, noodles and brown sugar. Add peanut butter, egg, water and vanilla. Shape into 1-inch balls. Place on ungreased cooky sheet. Make a large depression in the center of each cooky. Bake at 375° for 8 minutes. Push candy into center of cooky and bake 3 additional minutes. Makes 40.

Eenie Frost, Lake County Region

CINNAMON SUGAR COOKIES

- 1 cup shortening (1/2 butter)
- 1 1/2 cups sugar
- 2 eggs
- 2 3/4 cups flour
- 2 teaspoons cream of tartar
- 1 teaspoon baking soda
- 1/4 teaspoon salt
- 2 tablespoons sugar
- 2 teaspoons cinnamon

Combine shortening, sugar and eggs. Add flour, cream of tartar, soda and salt. Mix thoroughly. Form mixture into balls the size of walnuts. Mix together sugar and cinnamon. Roll cooky balls in cinnamon-sugar mixture. Place on cooky sheet and bake at 400° for 8 to 10 minutes. Makes about 4 dozen.

Fran Shiffman, Indianapolis Chapter-at-Large

MELTAWAYS

- 1/2 cup butter (1 stick)
- 3 tablespoons confectioners' sugar
- 3/4 cup flour
- 1 teaspoon vanilla

Mix and knead all ingredients. Pinch off marble-sized pieces and chill. Place on ungreased cooky sheet and flatten with fork. Bake at 375° for 8 minutes. Cool 5 minutes and then remove from pan. Makes 3 dozen.

Shirley Ziv, Lake County Region

MOLASSES COOKIES

- 1 cup sugar
- ¼ cup molasses
- ½ cup butter (1 stick)
- ¼ cup shortening
- 1 egg
- 2 cups flour
- 2 teaspoons baking soda
- 1 teaspoon cinnamon
- ½ teaspoon ginger
- ½ teaspoon salt

Melt together sugar, molasses, butter and shortening. Add egg and remaining ingredients. Chill dough. Form into small balls and roll in granulated sugar. Bake at 375° for 8 to 10 minutes. Makes 3½ dozen.

Helga Schrimmer, Lake County Region

GRAHAM DELIGHTS

- ¾ cup butter (1½ sticks)
- 1 cup firmly packed brown sugar
- 1 cup chopped nuts
- 24 graham crackers

Melt butter. Add brown sugar and nuts. Place graham crackers on greased cookie sheet. Cover with butter, sugar and nut mixture. Bake at 350° for 10 minutes, watching carefully. Separate graham crackers on removing from oven and cut each in two. Makes 48.

Emma Osterreicher, Chicago Region

HASENBLUSEN

- 3 eggs
- Dash salt
- 2½ cups flour
- Confectioners' sugar

Beat eggs slightly, add salt, and then add flour to make a stiff dough. Knead until elastic. Roll into a very thin sheet. Cut into 4x1-inch strips. Twist each strip 2 or 3 times. Drop in deep hot fat and fry to a delicate brown. Dust with confectioners' sugar.

Shirley Morris, Chicago Region

TEATIME TASSIES

1 3-oz. package cream cheese
½ cup butter (1 stick)
1 cup sifted flour

Chocolate-Pecan Filling:
1 egg
¾ cup brown sugar
1 tablespoon soft butter
1 teaspoon vanilla
Dash salt
⅔ cup semi-sweet chocolate pieces
⅔ cup coarsely broken pecans

Blend softened cream cheese and butter. Stir in flour. Chill slightly, about 1 hour. Shape in 2 dozen 1-inch balls; place in tiny ungreased 1¾-inch muffin cups. Press dough on bottom and sides of cups. To make Chocolate-Pecan Filling, beat together egg, sugar, 1 tablespoon butter, vanilla and salt just until smooth. Add chocolate pieces. Divide half the pecans among pastry-lined cups; add egg mixture and top with remaining pecans. Bake at 325° for 25 minutes or until filling is set. Cool; remove from pans. These freeze beautifully for parties. To use this same recipe, to make Pecan Puffs, omit the chocolate pieces. Makes 24.

Lois Fingerman, Des Moines Chapter-at-Large

CHOCOLATE PUFFS

½ cup vegetable oil
4 squares unsweetened chocolate (4 oz. melted)
2 cups granulated sugar
4 eggs
2 teaspoons vanilla
2 cups sifted flour
2 teaspoons baking powder
½ teaspoon salt
1 cup confectioners sugar

Mix oil, chocolate and granulated sugar. Blend in 1 egg at a time until mixture is well blended. Add vanilla. Stir in flour, baking powder and salt. Chill several hours or overnight. Preheat oven to 350°. Drop by teaspoonfuls into confectioners' sugar. Roll, shape into balls and place 2 inches apart on greased cookie sheet. Bake 10 to 12 minutes. Do not overbake. Makes approximately 100 cookies.

Sylvia Levine, Northern Illinois Region

SPRITZ COOKIES

- 1 cup soft butter (2 sticks)
- ⅔ cup sugar
- 3 egg yolks
- 1 teaspoon vanilla
- 2½ cups flour

Blend all ingredients well. Put dough in cooky press. Press out cookies on ungreased cooky sheet. Decorate, if desired, before baking. Bake at 400° for 7 to 10 minutes. Makes about 80 cookies.

Sally Simon, Northern Illinois Region

POPPY SEED COOKIES

- 1 cup vegetable oil
- 1 cup sugar
- 3½ cups flour
- 4 eggs, slightly beaten
- 1 tablespoon baking soda
- ½ teaspoon salt
- Poppy seeds

Mix oil and sugar together. Stir in remaining ingredients. Roll dough on floured board. Cut into circles with cooky cutter. Arrange on cooky sheet. Bake at 350° for 20 minutes. Makes 2 to 3 dozen.

Arleen Cowan, Chicago Region

HAMANTASHEN

- ½ cup margarine (1 stick)
- 1 cup sugar
- 1 egg
- 2 tablespoons liquid (milk, water or juice)
- 1 teaspoon vanilla
- 2 cups sifted flour
- 2 teaspoons baking powder
- Canned fillings

Mix ingredients, add dry ingredients last. Roll out ¼-inch thick and cut with rim of glass. Use heaping teaspoons of canned fillings in each round and shape into 3-cornered Hamantashen. Bake at 350° for 15 minutes. Makes 24.

Eenie Frost, Lake County Region

OATMEAL CRISPS

- **3 cups quick oats**
- **1 cup flour**
- **¼ teaspoon salt**
- **1 cup brown sugar, firmly packed**
- **1 cup chopped nuts**
- **1 cup melted butter (2 sticks)**
- **¾ teaspoon baking soda**
- **¼ cup boiling water**

Combine dry ingredients. Mix with melted butter. Dissolve soda in boiling water and add to mixture. Blend well. Form into two or three firm cylinders, the diameter of a silver dollar. Wrap in waxed paper. Chill thoroughly or freeze. To bake, slice very thin. Place on greased cooky sheet and bake at 400° for 8 to 10 minutes, until golden. Remove from pan while warm. Frozen rolls keep well and slice better than thawed. Double or triple recipe and keep rolls in freezer until you need them; then just slice and bake. Makes 5 dozen.

Ellen Kogen, Lake County Region

PAGACH (Hungarian Sour Cream Cookies)

- **8 cups flour**
- **2 cups sugar**
- **1 teaspoon salt**
- **2 teaspoons baking powder**
- **2 cups butter (1 pound)**
- **4 egg yolks**
- **1 cup dairy sour cream**

Place flour in large bowl. Make a nest in the middle of it and put in the sugar, salt, baking powder and butter. Work with hands until it has a sandy texture. Make another nest and add egg yolks and sour cream. Work into a mass of dough. Divide into four sections. Roll each ¼-inch thick and cut into desired shapes with cooky cutters. Place on ungreased cooky sheet and bake at 350° 12 to 15 minutes, until lightly browned. Decorate cookies with sugar or chocolate sprinkles, if desired. Dough reworks beautifully and cookies freeze well. Makes about 6 dozen.

Joan Dicker, West Suburban Region

FAVORITE WALNUT CRISPS

- ½ cup butter (1 stick)
- ½ cup sugar
- 1 egg
- 1¾ cups sifted flour
- 2 teaspoons baking powder
- ½ teaspoon vanilla
- ⅓ cup chopped walnuts
- Cinnamon and sugar, mixed

Cream butter well, add sugar and continue beating until light and fluffy. Add egg and beat until light. Add flour and baking powder gradually, and when well mixed, add vanilla and then nuts. Form into 4 long rolls, about 1 inch high and 9 inches long, on cooky sheet. Sprinkle with cinnamon-sugar mixture. Bake at 350° for 15 to 18 minutes. Remove cooky sheet from oven and let cool 6 minutes. Carefully transfer each roll, one at a time, onto cutting board and with a thin, sharp knife, cut diagonally into ¼-inch thick slices. Return to a cooky sheet and when all are cut, toast in the oven, first on one side, then on the other, until lightly golden brown. Makes 10 dozen.

Rae Weintraub, Chicago Region

MANDELBRODT

- 1 cup sugar
- 1 cup vegetable oil
- 3 eggs, slightly beaten
- 1 teaspoon vanilla
- ¼ cup orange juice
- 2½ cups flour
- 2½ teaspoons baking powder
- Pinch of salt
- 1½ cups chopped nuts
- Cinnamon-sugar mixture

Beat sugar and oil together; add beaten eggs and vanilla. Add orange juice. Sift together flour, baking powder and salt, and add to sugar and egg mixture. Blend in nuts. Divide dough into three portions and form each into a loaf. Place on well-greased cooky sheet. Sprinkle with cinnamon-sugar. Bake at 350° for 35 minutes. Remove from oven and slice into thin slices. Toast in a slow oven. These keep in cooky jar for a month. Makes 6 dozen.

Mrs. B. Klein, St. Louis Chapter

CANDIES and CONFECTIONS

APRICOT-NUT BALLS

- ½ cup chopped pecans or walnuts
- 1½ cups dried apricots, chopped (12-oz. box)
- 2 cups shredded coconut
- ⅔ cup (½ can) sweetened condensed milk
- Confectioners' sugar

Combine nuts, apricots and coconut in mixing bowl. Blend in milk. Refrigerate for ½ hour until mixture is firm. Shape into 1-inch balls; roll in confectioners' sugar. Refrigerate. Makes 3 dozen.

Roddie Rosenthal, Lake County Region

CHANUKAH FRUIT BALLS

- 1 pound dates, cut up
- 1 pound candied red and green cherries, cut up
- 1 pound candied pineapple, cut up
- 1 pound chopped nuts
- ¼ pound shredded coconut
- 1 can sweetened condensed milk

Combine all ingredients in mixing bowl. Wet hands and shape mixture into 1-inch balls. Arrange on cookie sheet and bake at 350° for 15 to 20 minutes. Makes 6 dozen.

Roddie Rosenthal, Lake County Region

SUGAR PLUM BONBONS

- 1 cup softened butter (2 sticks)
- 1½ cups sifted confectioners sugar
- ¼ cup cocoa
- ¼ teaspoon almond, rum or vanilla extract
- ½ cup chopped almonds
- 2 cups quick uncooked oatmeal
- Flaked or shredded coconut

Beat butter and sugar until creamy. Blend in cocoa and extract. Stir in almonds and oats. Chill dough for 2 to 3 hours, or until stiff. Break off small pieces of dough and shape into 36 1-inch balls. Roll in coconut. Refrigerate until ready to serve; or freeze, if you wish. Makes 36.

Bina Levin, Northern Illinois Region

DATE BALLS

- ½ cup butter (1 stick)
- 1 cup chopped dates
- 1 egg, well beaten
- ¾ cup sugar
- ¾ cup chopped nuts
- 1 teaspoon vanilla
- 2½ cups crisp rice cereal
- Coconut or confectioners sugar

In saucepan, melt butter; add dates, egg and sugar. Cook, stirring, over low heat for 10 minutes. Remove from heat and add nuts, vanilla and cereal. Wet hands and shape mixture into balls; roll in coconut or sugar. Can be eaten immediately, but they are best in a day or two.

Gilda Lesser, Lake County Region

CREAMY MARSHMALLOW FUDGE

- 1/4 cup butter
- 16 marshmallows
- 2 1/2 cups sugar
- 1/4 teaspoon salt
- 1 cup evaporated milk
- 1 6-oz. package semi-sweet chocolate pieces
- 1/2 teaspoon vanilla
- 1 cup chopped pecans or walnuts

In large heavy saucepan, combine butter, marshmallows, sugar, salt and evaporated milk. Heat until butter and marshmallows are melted; bring to a rolling boil. Boil for 5 minutes, stirring constantly. Remove from heat and add chocolate; stir until melted. Add vanilla and nuts. Pour into an 8 or 9-inch square pan. Cool before cutting. This recipe can not be doubled.

Marcy Novit, Chicago Region

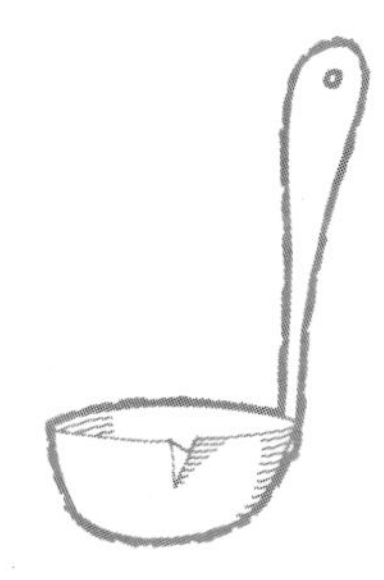

CHOCOLATE CANDY ROLL

- 1 12-oz. package semi-sweet chocolate pieces
- 1/2 cup butter (1 stick)
- 2 teaspoons vanilla
- 1 cup chopped nuts
- 1 package miniature marshmallows
- Shredded coconut (7-8 oz. package)

Melt chocolate pieces and butter in a double boiler and blend. Remove from heat, add nuts and marshmallows. On large sheet of wax paper, sprinkle 1/5 of coconut. Place about 1/5 of chocolate mixture and gently roll into a roll 15 inches long. Make five rolls, each about 1 inch in diameter. Place in refrigerator until ready to use. Slice into 1-inch pieces. Can be prepared in advance. Makes 70-75 pieces.

Abby Moline, Northern Illinois Region

FUDGE

- 4 cups sugar
- 5 to 6 heaping tablespoons cocoa
- 2 5⅓-oz. cans evaporated milk
- ¼ cup butter
- 1 12-oz. package semi-sweet chocolate pieces
- 1 cup chopped pecans (optional)

In saucepan, mix sugar and cocoa. Add milk; cook until mixture is thick. Add butter and boil until it melts; stir often. Remove from heat; add chocolate and nuts. Stir until chocolate melts. Pour immediately into a well greased jelly roll pan. Refrigerate for 30 to 45 minutes; cut fudge. Freeze until ready to serve. Makes 50 pieces.

Bonnie Friend, Lake County Region

MIXED NUT BRITTLE

- ⅓ cup each: walnut halves, blanched whole almonds, pecan halves, salted peanuts, brazil nuts and filberts
- 1½ cups sugar
- 1 teaspoon cream of tartar
- ½ cup cold water

Combine all nuts in a bowl. In a large saucepan, combine sugar, cream of tartar and water. Without stirring, cook over high heat, shaking pan occasionally, until mixture becomes a light golden syrup. Quickly stir nuts into syrup and immediately spread on a buttered cooky sheet. Cool; break into pieces.

Harriet Rosen, Chicago Region

APRICOT OR PEACH BRANDY

- 2 quarts vodka
- 2 pounds dried apricots or peaches
- 2 pounds granulated sugar

Mix all ingredients together in an air tight container. Set for 3 months in a cool, dry place, turning jar occasionally to re-mix contents. Put into clean bottles with tight lids or stoppers. Makes about 6 quarts.

Judith Fischer, West Suburan Region

BRANDIED ICE CREAM COOLER

- 1 2-oz. jigger brandy or Cognac
- 1 pint vanilla ice cream

Let ice cream soften in blender container. Add brandy. Just before serving, whip at high speed until creamy and thick enough to drink. Serve in goblets, accompanied with cookies. Makes 4 servings.

Judith Zwirn, West Suburban Region

CAFE NEW ORLEANS FLAMBE

- 1/4 cup brown sugar
- 2 whole allspice
- 1 cinnamon stick
- 1 teaspoon grated lemon rind
- 2 cups hot strong coffee
- 1/2 cup Cognac

In a chafing dish, combine sugar, spices, lemon rind and coffee. Heat to just below boiling, stirring constantly. In a warmed ladle, heat Cognac and ignite. Quickly pour over coffee mixture and stir. Ladle into demi-tasse cups. Makes 4 servings.

Myra Weis, Chicago Region

CAPPUCCINO COFFEE

- 4 to 6 cups strong brewed coffee
- 2 to 3 cups milk
- 2 jiggers brandy
- 1 jigger creme de cacao
- 1½ tablespoons cocoa
- 1½ tablespoons sugar
- 4 cinnamon sticks
- Whipped cream

In large saucepan, blend coffee, milk, brandy and liqueur. Mix cocoa and sugar and add to mixture. Heat just to boiling. Pour into individual cups. Add a cinnamon stick to each cup and top each with whipped cream. Makes 4 servings.

Bonnie Friend, Lake County Region

CHAMPAGNE SHERBET PUNCH

- 1 6-oz. can frozen orange juice
- 2 fifths sauterne wine, chilled
- 2 fifths Champagne, chilled
- 1 to 2 quarts orange sherbet
- Fresh mint, orange or lime slices for garnish

Put frozen orange juice in punch bowl. Blend in chilled wine. At serving time, pour in Champagne and add spoonfuls of sherbet. Serve in punch cups. Makes 40 servings.

Sally Simon, Northern Illinois Region

BRANDY ALEXANDER FRAPPES

- 1 quart vanilla ice cream
- ½ cup brandy
- ½ cup creme de cacao
- 1 square chocolate

Refrigerate 8 sherbet glasses for several hours to chill well. Place ice cream in refrigerator for about ½ hour, to soften. Just before serving, combine ice cream, brandy and liqueur in blender; blend at high speed until smooth. Pour into chilled sherbet glasses. Decorate each serving with a chocolate curl. To make curls, let square of chocolate warm to room temperature. With sharp paring knife, cut thin curls from back of square. Makes 8 servings.

Mildred Rubenstein, Chicago Region

CRANBERRY ICED TEA

2 cups cold water
4 tea bags
½ cup sugar
½ teaspoon ground allspice
3 to 4 whole cloves
2 cups cranberry juice
¼ cup lemon juice
1 14-oz. bottle club soda
Lime slices or mint leaves

Heat water to boiling in saucepan; remove from heat and add tea bags, sugar, allspice and cloves. Stir until sugar is dissolved. Cover and let steep for 4 minutes; strain into 2-quart pitcher and cool. Stir in cranberry and lemon juices. Chill mixture. Just before serving, add soda to tea and pour into wine glasses. Float a lime slice or mint leaf in each glass. Makes 6 servings.

Bobbie Katz, West Suburban Region

GLOGG

6 oranges
6 dozen whole cloves
1 fifth rum, heated (do not boil)
1 gallon apple cider, heated to boiling
3 sticks cinnamon

Stud each orange with 12 cloves. Place in baking pan in oven at 300° for 2 hours, or until juices start to run. Transfer to 2 gallon serving bowl or copper pan. Pour warm rum and hot apple cider over oranges; add cinnamon. Keep hot during serving time. Makes about 32 mug-size servings.

Sally Simon, Northern Illinois Region

GRAPE JUICE COCKTAIL

1 pint grape juice
1 pint sweet wine
3 tablespoons gin
1 quart softened vanilla ice cream

Blend all ingredients slowly in electric mixer. Serve in champagne glasses. Makes 16 4-oz. servings.

Sheila J. Seidmon, Northern Illinois Region

"KAHLUA"

2 cups water
½ cup instant coffee
3 cups sugar
1 pint Cognac
½ vanilla bean, split

Heat water to boiling; add coffee and sugar and stir until dissolved. Stir in Cognac and vanilla. Pour into a half-gallon glass container; let stand 45 days before serving.

Betty Grossman, Northern Illinois Region

PARTY FRUIT PUNCH

2 6-oz. cans frozen orange juice, thawed
1 6-oz. can frozen lemonade, thawed
1 20-oz. can crushed pineapple with juice
2 12-oz. packages frozen sliced strawberries, thawed
2 quarts ginger ale
1 fifth brandy (optional)
3 dozen ice cubes
Lemon or lime slices

Just before serving, combine orange juice, lemonade, pineapple, strawberries, ginger ale and brandy in punch bowl. Stir well and add ice cubes. Garnish with lemon or lime slices. Makes 50 to 60 servings.

Sue Colton, Milwaukee Region

RUSSIAN TEA

½ cup instant tea
1 cup orange flavored drink mix (Tang)
1 3-oz. package lemonade mix
1 cup sugar
½ teaspoon ground cloves
1 teaspoon ground cinnamon

Mix all ingredients; store in a jar with a tight-fitting lid. When ready to serve, blend 2 to 3 teaspoons with hot or cold water in cup or glass. Makes 12 to 15 servings.

Nancy Goldstein, Twin Cities Region

MENUS FOR SPECIAL OCCASIONS

APPETIZER BUFFET

California Rosé Wine
Hot Crabmeat Appetizer, *page 27* Bread Sticks
Chafing Dish Steak Bites, *page 23*
Crisp Vegetable Relishes Horseradish Dip, *page 16*
Shrimp Ball, *page 19* Assorted Crackers

* * *

LOW-CALORIE LUNCHEON

Minted Melon Cup
Low-Calorie Salmon Ring, *page 176*
Mixed Greens French Dressing II, *page 179*
Low-Calorie Sponge Cake, *page 180*
Beverage

* * *

FAR EASTERN DINNER

Chicken Wings Shanghai, *page 25*
Chinese Halibut with Pineapple, *page 123*
Wok Pepper Steak, *page 121* Hot Rice
Orange Sherbet with Mandarin Oranges
Almond Cookies
Tea

SPECIAL FAMILY OCCASION

Beef Fondue
Hot and Spicy Sauce, *page 63* Dilled Sour Cream
French Onion Pie, *page 31*
Tomatoes Vinaigrette, *page 206*
Vanilla Brownies, *page 286* Ice Cream
Beverage

* * *

ITALIAN DINNER

Antipasto I, *page 20*
Spaghetti with White Clam Sauce, *page 105*
Zucchini Halves with Cheese *page 197*
Italian Bread
Lemon Fluff Refrigerator Dessert, *page 270*
Beverage

* * *

ORT LUNCHEON

ORT Cheese Souffle, *page 130*
Savory Sauced Broccoli, *page 184*
Fruit Salad Favorite Dressing
Peppermint Mocha Ice Cream Cake, *page 279*
Beverage

SUMMER LUNCHEON

Watermelon Soup, *page 37*
Curried Shrimp Salad, *page 213*
Cottage Cheese Muffins, *page 40*
Rainbow Ice Cream Dessert, *page 279*
Beverage

* * *

CANDLELIGHT BUFFET

Beef Bordelaise, *page 51*
Mixed Vegetable Rice Mold, *page 198*
Tossed Salad Gourmet, *page 206*
Cherry Nut Salad, *page 222*
Harvey Wallbanger Cake, *page 247*
Coffee

* * *

MIDNIGHT SUPPER

Seafood Quiche, *page 31*
Overnight Vegetable Salad, *page 204*
New Orleans Pecan Pie, *page 266*
Cafe New Orleans Flambe, *page 303*

* * *

COMPANY DINNER

Artichoke Surprise, *page 23*
Florentine Sole, *page 104*
Wild Rice Tossed Greens with Croutons
Frozen Creme de Menthe Pie, *page 266*

* * *

COMPANY DINNER

Cherried Chicken, *page 81*
Onion Noodle Kugel, *page 169* Zesty Carrots, *page 188*
Watercress and Tomato Salad
Brandied Ice Cream Cooler, *page 303*

EASY COMPANY DINNER

Cherry Tomatoes and Stuffed Celery
Veal Scaloppine Marsala, *page 158*
Venetian Rice, *page 174*
Tossed Greens with Artichoke Hearts, Olives
Cherries Jubilee, *page 276*
Beverage

* * *

ROSH HOSHANAH

Sweet and Sour Trout, *page 139*
Chicken Soup with Easy Kreplach, *page 131*
Brisket of Beef, *page 62*
Baked Farfel, *page 113* Meatless Tzimmes, *page 135*
Sunshine Cake, *page 245*

* * *

CHANUKAH PARTY

Potato Pancakes, *page 135* Fruited Rum Pot, *page 226*
Caviar-Lox Mold, *page 14*
Gefilte Fish Mold, *page 133*
Sweet and Sour Meat Balls in Chafing Dish, *page 29*
Chanukah Fruit Balls, *page 299*
Cherry Buttons, *page 292* Chocolate Acorns, *page 291*
Poppy Seed Cookies, *page 296*

* * *

PASSOVER MENUS
DINNERS

Mock Gefilte Fish, *page 141*
Matzo Balls, *page 141*
Orange Roast Brisket, *page 146*
Carrot Mold, *page 187*
Hot Fruit Compote, *page 229* Wine Gelatin Mold, *page 142*
Chocolate Wine Cake, *page 150 or* Passover Sponge Cake, *page 151*

* * *

Beef Borsht Bisque, *page 140*
Pickled Fish, *page 139*
Glazed Chicken with Matzo Nut Stuffing, *page 147*
Fruited Matzo Pudding, *page 144*
Spinach Souffle, *page 144*
Passover Lemon Cream Puffs, *page 152*

INDEX

S
P